AF269972

The Germans and the Dieppe Raid

The Germans and the Dieppe Raid

How Hitler's Wehrmacht Crushed Operation Jubilee

James Shelley

Pen & Sword
MILITARY

First published in Great Britain in 2023 by
Pen & Sword Military
An imprint of Pen & Sword Books Limited
Yorkshire – Philadelphia

ISBN 978 1 39903 060 1

A CIP catalogue record for this book is
available from the British Library

Typeset by Mac Style
Printed in the UK by CPI Group (UK) Ltd, Croydon, CR0 4YY.

Pen & Sword Books Limited incorporates the imprints of After the
Battle, Atlas, Archaeology, Aviation, Discovery, Family History,
Fiction, History, Maritime, Military, Military Classics, Politics,
Select, Transport, True Crime, Air World, Frontline Publishing,
Leo Cooper, Remember When, Seaforth Publishing, The Praetorian
Press, Wharncliffe Local History, Wharncliffe Transport,
Wharncliffe True Crime and White Owl.

For a complete list of Pen & Sword titles please contact

PEN & SWORD BOOKS LIMITED
47 Church Street, Barnsley, South Yorkshire, S70 2AS, England
E-mail: enquiries@pen-and-sword.co.uk
Website: www.pen-and-sword.co.uk
or
PEN AND SWORD BOOKS
1950 Lawrence Rd, Havertown, PA 19083, USA
E-mail: Uspen-and-sword@casematepublishers.com
Website: www.penandswordbooks.com

Contents

Note on the Text

The Allied force that embarked on the Dieppe raid included servicemen from a multitude of different nations' armed forces. In order to maintain simplicity and for ease of comprehension, the term 'Allied' is used to describe the allegiance of the Jubilee land, sea and air components. Their 'German' opponents were to an extent multinational as well – there were many forcibly conscripted Poles (amongst others) at Dieppe – but I have referred to all the defenders as German, except when specifically referring to a non-German unit or individual. To ensure that German ranks are readily understood, their British equivalents are given in their place throughout – for example, the Wehrmacht rank of *Generaloberst*, literally 'Colonel General', is not translated as such but as (full four-star) 'General'. Officers holding the various general and admiral ranks are sometimes referred to simply as 'General' and 'Admiral' respectively in shorthand. The six-star rank of *Reichsmarschall* held solely by Hermann Göring does not have an English equivalent, and so is rendered in German. All translations from German-language sources have been made by the author. While the German air and naval services are referred to as the Luftwaffe and Kriegsmarine respectively, as these terms are known to an English-speaking audience, the term 'Heer' is not, so the German 'Army' is referred to as such throughout. During the battle narrative, German time is used – this was one hour ahead of British time.

Principal Commanders and Characters

German

Adolf Hitler – Führer, Supreme Commander of the Armed Forces (*Wehrmacht*) and Commander-in-Chief of the Army

Joseph Goebbels – Reichsminister for Public Enlightenment and Propaganda

Otto Dietrich – Reich Press Minister

Reichsmarschall Hermann Göring – Commander-in-Chief of the German Air Force (*Luftwaffe*)

Admiral of the Fleet Erich Raeder – Commander-in-Chief of the German Navy (*Kriegsmarine*)

Field Marshal Wilhelm Keitel – Chief of the Armed Forces High Command (OKW, *Oberkommando der Wehrmacht*)

Field Marshal Gerd von Rundstedt – Supreme Commander in the West (OB West, *Oberbefehlshaber West*)

Field Marshal Hugo Sperrle – Commanding Officer, Air Fleet 3 (*Luftflotte 3*)

Admiral Alfred Saalwächter – Commanding Officer, Naval Group West (*Marineoberkommando West*)

Brigadier (later Lieutenant General) Kurt Zeitzler – OB West Chief of Staff (until September)

General Curt Haase – Commanding Officer, Fifteenth Army

Lieutenant General Adolf-Friedrich Kuntzen – Commanding Officer, LXXXI (81st) Corps

Major General Konrad Haase – Commanding Officer, 302nd Infantry Division

French

Philippe Pétain – Head of State

Pierre Laval – Head of Government (President of the Council)

Allied

Winston Churchill – British Prime Minister

Vice Admiral Lord Louis Mountbatten – Chief of Combined Operations

Major General John Roberts – Jubilee Military (Land) Force Commander and Commanding Officer, 2nd Canadian Division

Captain John Hughes-Hallett – Jubilee Naval Force Commander

Air Marshal Trafford Leigh-Mallory – Jubilee Air Force Command

Maps

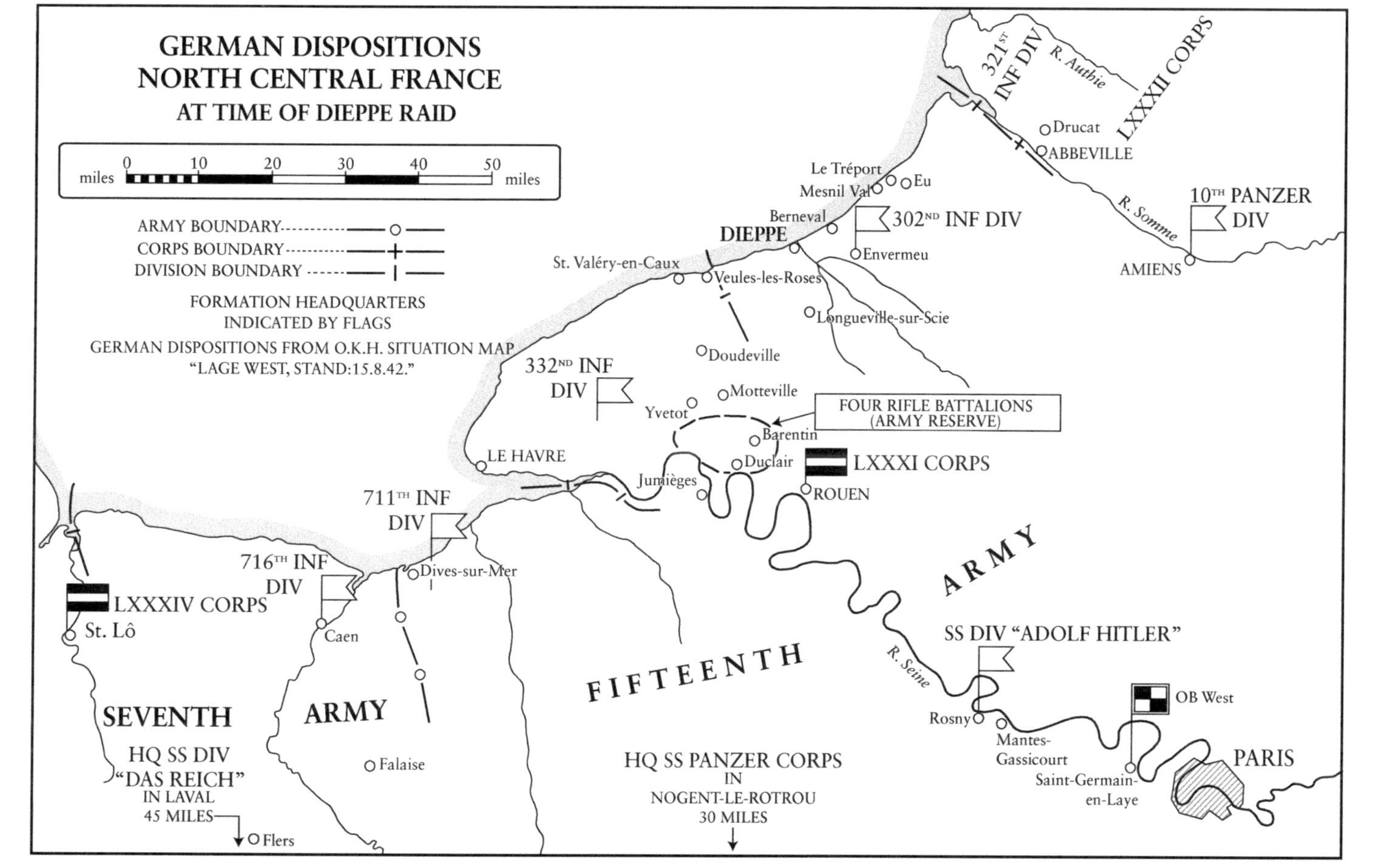

GERMAN DISPOSITIONS
NORTH CENTRAL FRANCE
AT TIME OF DIEPPE RAID
miles
0 10 20 30 40 50 miles
ARMY BOUNDARY
CORPS BOUNDARY
DIVISION BOUNDARY
FORMATION HEADQUARTERS
INDICATED BY FLAGS
GERMAN DISPOSITIONS FROM O.K.H. SITUATION MAP
"LAGE WEST, STAND:15.8.42."
321st INF DIV
R. Authie
LXXXII CORPS
Drucat
ABBEVILLE
R. Somme
10TH PANZER DIV
AMIENS
Le Tréport
Mesnil Val
Eu
Berneval
302ND INF DIV
DIEPPE
Envermeu
St. Valéry-en-Caux
Veules-les-Roses
Longueville-sur-Scie
Doudeville
332ND INF DIV
Motteville
Yvetot
Barentin
FOUR RIFLE BATTALIONS
(ARMY RESERVE)
LE HAVRE
Duclair
LXXXI CORPS
Jumièges
ROUEN
711TH INF DIV
716TH INF DIV
Dives-sur-Mer
LXXXIV CORPS
St. Lô
Caen
ARMY
SS DIV "ADOLF HITLER"
R. Seine
OB West
Rosny
FIFTEENTH
Mantes-Gassicourt
Saint-Germain-en-Laye
PARIS
SEVENTH
ARMY
HQ SS DIV "DAS REICH"
IN LAVAL
45 MILES
Falaise
HQ SS PANZER CORPS
IN NOGENT-LE-ROTROU
30 MILES
Flers

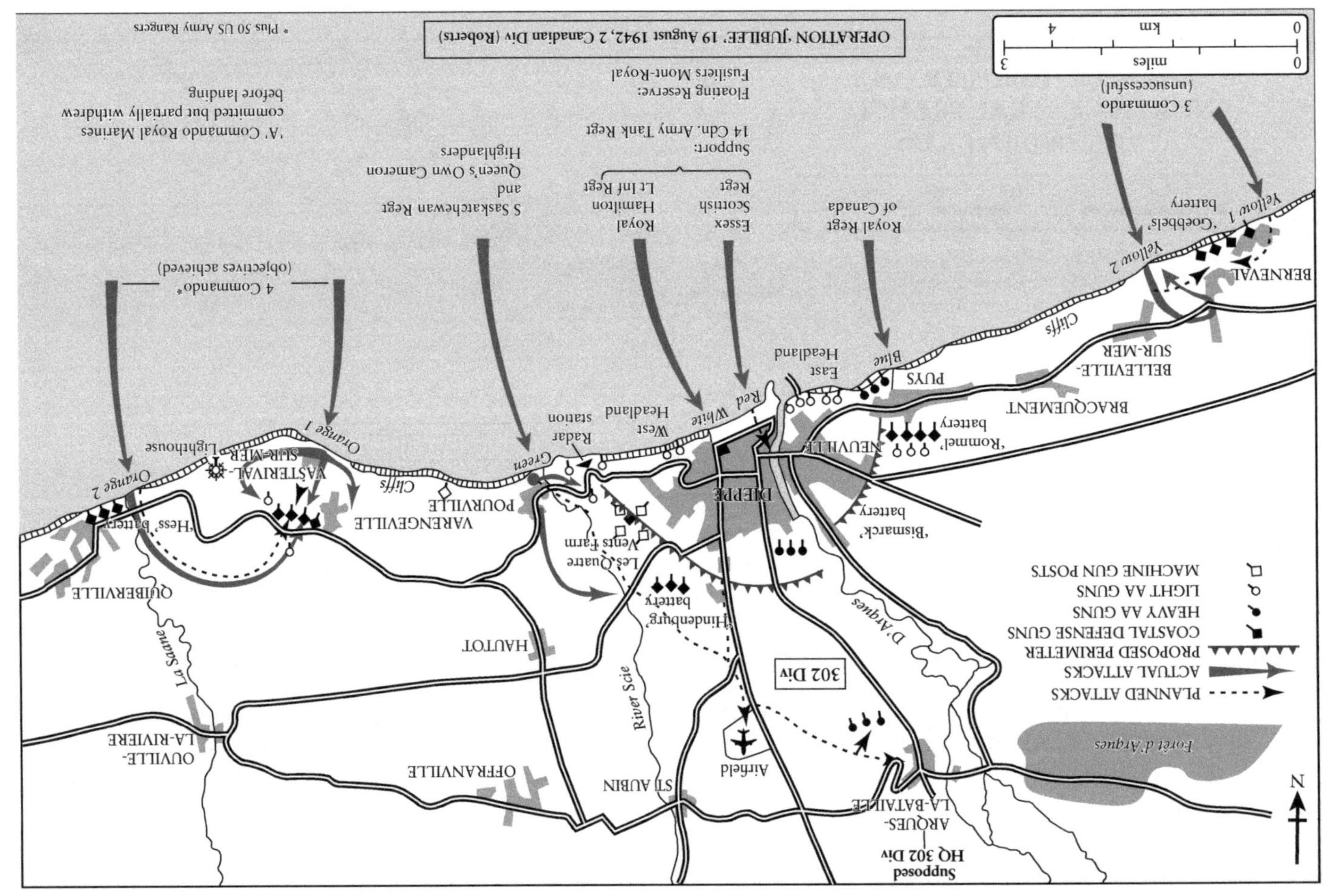

N
Supposed HQ 302 Div
ARQUES-LA-BATAILLE
Forêt d'Arques
OUVILLE-LA-RIVIERE
La Saane
QUIBERVILLE
OFFRANVILLE
HAUTOT
ST AUBIN
River Scie
Airfield
302 Div
D'Arques
'Hindenburg' battery
Les Quatre Vents Farm
'Bismarck' battery
'Rommel' battery
'Hess' battery
'Goebbels' battery
VASTERIVAL-SUR-MER
Lighthouse
VARENGEVILLE
POURVILLE
Cliffs
Green
Radar station
West Headland
Red White
DIEPPE
NEUVILLE
PUYS
East Headland
Blue
BRACQUEMENT
BELLEVILLE-SUR-MER
Cliffs
BERNEVAL
Yellow 1
Yellow 2
Orange 1
Orange 2
4 Commando*
(objectives achieved)
3 Commando
(unsuccessful)
S Saskatchewan Regt
and
Queen's Own Cameron
Highlanders
Royal
Hamilton
Lt Inf Regt
Essex
Scottish
Regt
Support:
14 Cdn. Army Tank Regt
Floating Reserve:
Fusiliers Mont-Royal
Royal Regt
of Canada
'A' Commando Royal Marines
commited but partially withdrew
before landing
* Plus 50 US Army Rangers
PLANNED ATTACKS
ACTUAL ATTACKS
PROPOSED PERIMETER
COASTAL DEFENSE GUNS
HEAVY AA GUNS
LIGHT AA GUNS
MACHINE GUN POSTS
OPERATION 'JUBILEE' 19 August 1942, 2 Canadian Div (Roberts)
miles
km
0
0
3
4

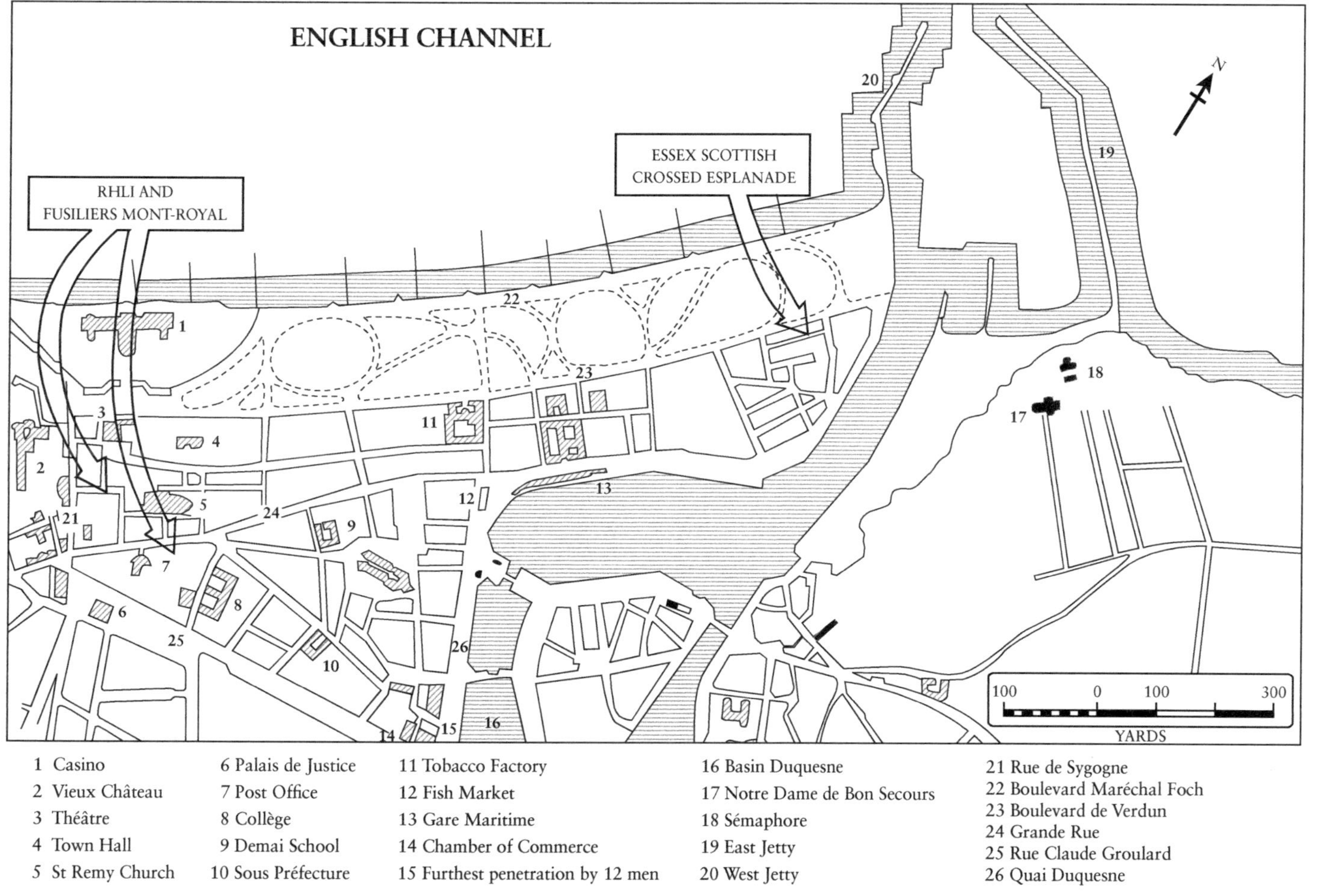

ENGLISH CHANNEL
ESSEX SCOTTISH CROSSED ESPLANADE
RHLI AND FUSILIERS MONT-ROYAL
N
100   0   100   300
YARDS

1 Casino
2 Vieux Château
3 Théâtre
4 Town Hall
5 St Remy Church
6 Palais de Justice
7 Post Office
8 Collège
9 Demai School
10 Sous Préfecture
11 Tobacco Factory
12 Fish Market
13 Gare Maritime
14 Chamber of Commerce
15 Furthest penetration by 12 men
16 Basin Duquesne
17 Notre Dame de Bon Secours
18 Sémaphore
19 East Jetty
20 West Jetty
21 Rue de Sygogne
22 Boulevard Maréchal Foch
23 Boulevard de Verdun
24 Grande Rue
25 Rue Claude Groulard
26 Quai Duquesne

Acknowledgements

There are many places where acknowledgement is warranted. First and foremost, I would like to express my deep gratitude to Dr David Ian Hall, formerly of the Joint Services Command and Staff College (JSCSC) in Shrivenham. David has been a constant source of advice and motivation in researching and writing this book, and through my historical work more generally. He kindly invited me to deliver a lecture at the JSCSC on some of the Dieppe research included here. Certainly, this book would not have been produced had I not received David's ever-generous support and motivation.

Research was conducted at various locations both in Germany and Britain, and the staff of those libraries and archives deserve recognition. Abroad, I would like to thank the staff of the Freiburg and Berlin sites of the German Bundesarchiv state archival network, who were able to facilitate (nearly!) frictionless archival visits. In Britain, great thanks are due to the librarians of the Hobson Library at the JSCSC, Singleton Campus library at Swansea University and British Library in London. The staff at The National Archives in Kew facilitated my research there wonderfully. Both at home and abroad, I have profited immensely from the willingness of others to provide material and answer various and wide-ranging queries.

Ruth Rose provided invaluable assistance with translating and checking French-language material, as well as assisting in communications with archives in France. I would also like to extend my heartfelt thanks to Jim Walker, whose comments and critiques significantly improved my prose, and made the information contained in this book easier to digest. In addition, I benefitted tremendously from discussing my research with Commander (Retd) Peter O'Brien, who brought his decades of military experience as a Commando-trained Royal Navy officer to the table.

George Chamier, as my editor, caught what would have been some rather embarrassing errors. Matt Jones, the production manager at Pen and Sword was rapid in putting together all the material in the book. Heartfelt thanks also go to Henry Wilson, who took a chance on a young and unpublished author.

Lastly, it would be remiss of me if I did not thank my mother and father. They have always offered the carrot, and not the stick!

Even after all of this support, any errors remaining in the final text are naturally my own.

Introduction

With the possible exception of Operation Market Garden, the 'magnificent disaster' of 'A Bridge Too Far' infamy, no unsuccessful military undertaking has received such intense attention in the English-speaking world as the Dieppe Raid. Primarily, 19 August 1942 was a Canadian tragedy, and has burned itself into that nation's collective conscience. To this day, each year the Canadian Prime Minister makes a statement on that day in honour of those who served and fell in what was codenamed Operation 'Jubilee'. From the main 5,000-strong Canadian land component, 3,367 became casualties, of whom 1,946 were made prisoners of war – more than were taken prisoner in Canada's entire 1944/45 campaign in North-West Europe. This figure does not include the heavy losses inflicted on the British Army and Royal Marine units. The Allied naval forces fared little better; the Germans accounted for one destroyer, and thirty-three landing craft of various types were destroyed. In the air, a staggering total of 106 Allied aircraft were lost. Dieppe remains the costliest single day in the Royal Air Force's history in terms of aircraft lost.

Such tragedy has inevitably created a great swathe of historical interest. Brian Loring Villa, an accomplished Canadian historian of the raid, put it well: 'Had Dieppe been a success, not one-thousandth of what has been written about it would ever have crossed the minds of the many historians who have tackled the subject.'[1] The Dieppe literature is monumental, and justifiably so. Why did the raid happen? How did it fail so spectacularly and who was to blame? Did the Allies learn anything useful from the experience? These are all important questions, not just to the military, which is required to learn from its mistakes, but also to the wider public whom the military serves, and they have all been argued at length. Yet one simple question remains unanswered: what did the raid look like from the German point of view? This fundamental question has never been asked in earnest. A brief look at the Dieppe raid's bibliography shows the distinct lack of attention to the German side of the story.

As historians have written about what happened at Dieppe, some critical debates have emerged. One of the most contentious has been over responsibility and authority. Operation Jubilee, as executed on 19 August, was in fact a carbon copy of Operation Rutter, a previous plan for an attack on Dieppe. The only difference of consequence was that Rutter envisaged using paratroops to secure the operation's flanks, while Jubilee employed sea-landed Commandos instead. Rutter was ultimately cancelled after a period of bad weather and a German air attack on the assembled landing craft in Yarmouth. Did Lord Mountbatten, who led Churchill's raids on occupied Europe, actually have authorization from the British Chiefs of Staff Committee to remount Rutter as Jubilee? The foremost figure arguing that he did not is Brian Loring Villa. In his outstanding revisionist work *Unauthorized Action*, Villa contended that Soviet demands for a 'Second Front' in Europe and Mountbatten's personal ambition, amongst other reasons, caused him to proceed without any authority at all. There is, he finds, no signed document to prove that he had obtained proper approval. Presenting the counter-argument most forcefully is Peter Henshaw. He submits that while the Chiefs of Staff Committee never specifically approved the raid, they had already given Mountbatten permission to revive cancelled raids (like Rutter) on his own authority. This debate culminated in a historical grudge match played out in the pages of the *Canadian Historical Review* which left no clear victor.

The idea of 'lessons learned' always plays a role in the study of military history. Learning from past mistakes is a prime driving force behind all historical study. The Dieppe raid is no exception, but regrettably we see a total focus from contemporaries and later military historians on the Allied lessons learned. Most controversially, post-war accounts have sought to argue that the high Canadian casualties on the Dieppe beaches were worth the 'lessons learned'. In his history of the Second World War, Winston Churchill printed Lord Louis Mountbatten's narrative essentially verbatim. Mountbatten was Chief of Combined Operations during 1942 and also the moving force behind Jubilee's execution, especially after the cancellation of its forerunner Rutter. Mountbatten's account as accepted by Churchill read in part:

Looking back, the casualties of the memorable action may seem out of proportion to the results. It would be wrong to judge the episode solely by such a standard. Dieppe occupies a place of its own in the story of the war, and the grim casualty figures must not class it as a failure.[2]

Mountbatten and Churchill argued that far from representing a great defeat, the casualties sustained at Dieppe represented a great 'learning experience' from which lessons could be drawn and improvements made – all in time for D-Day on 6 June 1944. This mantle was eagerly picked up by a wave of historians following in their wake. Quoting *Hamlet*, the RAF's official history declared that '"Enterprises of great pith and moment" like the invasion of Europe cannot be undertaken without a few realistic and even expensive rehearsals.'[3] Ken Ford claimed in his short book *Dieppe 1942: Prelude to D-Day* that 'the great German victory eventually contributed to their ultimate defeat. Although the losses had proved dreadful, much was in fact gained by the Allies, for the lessons learned at Dieppe helped pave the way for victory when the Allies returned to France in earnest.[4] Ronald Atkin signalled his agenda on the very first page of his contribution by quoting a 1943 article from the *New York Times*:

Someday there will be two spots on the French coast sacred to the British and the Allies. One will be Dunkirk, where Britain was saved because a beaten army would not surrender. The other will be Dieppe, where brave men died without hope for the sake of proving that there is a wrong way to invade. They will have their share of glory when the right way is tried.[5]

Books on Dieppe have long argued that the Allies learned the importance of shore bombardment, amphibious armour and the need to bring mobile ports with them (these would manifest themselves as the Mulberry harbours on 6 June). This debate has not been a one-way street, of course. Hugh Henry put the opposite case most strongly:

It is not true that important new strategic lessons were learned, since none were unknown beforehand. More appropriate is it to say that they were relearned … The experience necessary for the major invasion of the Continent could have been gained far more easily and with far less casualties from the amphibious landings on Sicily, the Italian mainland, North Africa and the Japanese-held Pacific islands.[6]

The study of Dieppe has at some points entered a truly conspiratorial space. In the 1960s David Irving, to whom the job title 'historian' is applied with great caution, proudly claimed that he had found evidence that the Germans knew that the Dieppe raid was coming. This foreknowledge, Irving suggested, was the sole reason for the Anglo-Canadian defeat on 19 August. In fact, Irving based his claim on wilful mistranslation and cherry-picked source material, and his argument was rightfully demolished by Captain Stephen Roskill, author of the Royal Navy's official history. At the same time, E. H. Cookridge, a writer on Allied intelligence during the war, claimed in the 1960s that an intelligence leak led to defeat on 19 August. On Canadian television he called for an investigation into the matter to 'relieve many families of those brave boys who were lost on the Dieppe beaches' of their pain.[7] German foreknowledge even formed the basis of military fiction when the prolific writer Charles Whiting published *Forced March*, a novel based on the notion that German spies in Britain revealed the Allies' plans a week in advance. To this day doubts remain about how much the Germans knew, if anything, about the planned raid before it happened. This issue was greatly complicated by the revelations contained in the second edition of Loring Villa's book, which showed that some elements of the cancelled Operation Rutter were purposefully leaked to the Germans as part of a deception effort.

Yet surely, as every child learns early on in history class at school, there must be two sides to every story? What of the Germans? Writing about Dieppe without the German perspective is, to use two military history analogies, akin to studying the Battle of Hastings without mentioning William the Conqueror, or the Spanish Armada without Sir Francis Drake. No historian can tell a story without examining all sides of the events in question. It is impossible to imagine a battle with only one army fighting. Thanks to the work of historians of Dieppe, we have a full and detailed picture of events from the Allied side of the Channel. Unfortunately for our collective historical knowledge, until now we only have scraps from the German side. The historical imbalance is striking. Strangely, the Germans have managed to completely avoid the ever-enquiring eye of historians. Ronald Atkin's *Dieppe 1942: The Jubilee Disaster*, undoubtedly the best treatment of the raid in its entirety, dedicates only a few pages to the German story, and even then only as an afterthought. In another popular book, Tim Saunders dismisses the German experience with one simple sentence: 'While the Allies critically studied the results of the Dieppe raid in detail, the German victor accepted his success far less critically.'[8] Even the official Canadian historian Colonel Charles Perry Stacey, who devoted two whole chapters to Dieppe, gives only a few pages to the German perspective. This unfortunate pattern repeats itself wherever we look, from the dry and insular world of academic theses to the flashy and exciting realm of popular magazines and television documentaries. Even in debating questions that have been pored over time and again, like German foreknowledge or Allied 'lessons learned', Anglo-American and Canadian historians have never truly engaged with German sources.

The question of why we have collectively failed to look at the German experience of Dieppe is most puzzling. All military events of Dieppe's scale and tragedy merit – and normally receive – full treatment, so it seems particularly odd that the entire German experience has been left untouched. One may naturally assume that there must be a lack of documentary evidence. True, many German documents were destroyed as the Allied and Soviet armies closed in on Germany in 1945. This is especially true for documents and papers originating from the Luftwaffe. Nevertheless, there remains a remarkable amount of source evidence out there, in Britain, America, Germany and even Russia. A key feature of this book is its reliance on German-language sources, both archival and those contained in published collections. Some of the former is made all the more accessible by the admirable work of national archives around the world to digitize their holdings for all to see. One conversation I had in 2019 illustrates this point well. I had the pleasure of discussing my research with a lecturer at Britain's Joint Services and Command and Staff College, near the Oxfordshire village of Shrivenham. A veteran archival adventurer of many years, one sadly accustomed to the mountains of bureaucracy, unreliable technology and less-than-helpful archivists all too common in days gone by, was astounded at the ease with which I had collected all my original archival material in Germany's Federal Archives. Merely by sending an email, signing a few forms and turning up on time (not an unimportant matter for Germans), I could have stacks of 70-year-old documents on a table ready to peruse and photograph at my leisure. Additionally, much primary source material and secondary literature is also freely available online. In the course of researching this book, many a visit to libraries far afield has been spared by a simple search online for digital copies of physical publications. For the historian, digitization is one of the greatest conveniences of working in the twenty-first century.

If source material like this is so readily accessible, there must be another explanation for the dearth of German material on Dieppe. It cannot be a question of any language barrier – German-language interviews, reports, letters and diaries have been used by multilingual historians (and those who have translators to hand) for decades. In all likelihood, then, it is simply an issue of focus. Canadians wish to know why their boys were sent on what was tantamount to a suicide mission, while British readers are drawn overwhelmingly to their national contribution to a world first in human warfare – an air-sea-land amphibious landing on a divisional scale. The involvement of Lord Louis Mountbatten, uncle of Prince Philip and second cousin once removed of Her Majesty Queen Elizabeth II herself, as the operation's grand architect has surely not reduced their interest.

Sadly, but also for perfectly understandable historical reasons, 'military history' as anyone in the English-speaking world would understand it hardly exists in Germany. With the dual issues of *Vergangenheitsbewältigung* (loosely 'coming to terms with the past') and *Kollektivschuld* (collective guilt) arising from the war, there is little popular interest in examining the military aspects of Germany's Second World War. For the same reason, the Wehrmacht's soldiers, sailors and airmen, unlike their victorious counterparts, did not write memoirs, or appear in television and radio programmes. Consequently, there has always been a restricted number of first-hand eyewitness accounts available to historians. Regrettably for the historical record, the vast majority of German veterans died before committing their thoughts to paper. In this study's case, the German division at Dieppe – 302nd Infantry – was surrounded and destroyed in 1944 in modern-day Moldova. Hence, there were relatively few survivors to tell their side of the confrontation in France. One German veteran, who later compiled the divisional history, lamented after the war that 'those who survived, they form a small circle; unfortunately, the better part of the division lies buried in Russia.'[9]

German aversion to military history extends beyond being disinclined to record individual wartime experiences. In a lecture on Dieppe at the Laurier Centre in Canada, the military historian David Ian Hall made an important point. He professed that if he were German and spoke about military affairs as something to be studied and learned from, he would be labelled an *NS-Historiker* (crudely 'Historian of National Socialism') and consigned to teaching at a few specialist military colleges, with little hope of an institutional position or funding outside of that reclusive arena. Much German military history comes out of the Military History Research Office based in Freiburg, part of the modern-day German Armed Forces, the *Bundeswehr*. Reinhard Stumpf, who lectured there for more than a decade, once lamented that in Germany, 'despite its thematic and numerical expansion, academic military history has remained a specialized subject to this day, with little grounding at universities ... Only a few working groups provide contacts amongst those interested in military history.'[10] With such cultural aversion to teaching military history, it is little wonder that very few Germans wish to engage with it. German-language contributions to Dieppe's historiography can be split into two groups: either hopelessly short article pieces that are so superficial that they bring nothing new to the table, or else simple regurgitations of literature that has already appeared in English. Even Germany's official Second World War history, whose authors enjoyed unrestricted access to the nation's military archives, dedicated less than a single page to the topic.

Whatever the real reason for their oversight, historians have done Second World War history a great disservice by ignoring the German perspective on Dieppe. If we continue to exclude the enemy's point of view – the 'other side of the hill' as Colonel Stacey put it in one his wartime reports – Dieppe will never truly receive the attention it deserves. This point is not just relevant to those who study military history in detail at military academies or staff colleges, but more broadly to the general reading public. The Dieppe raid contains the vital lesson that all contemporary viewpoints are valuable to historical study. Indeed, it may well be that since the Germans eventually lost the war, Dieppe seems in hindsight nothing more than a 'bump in the road' to inevitable total Allied victory in May 1945. This is not how we should view history, because that is not how contemporaries saw it. At Dieppe the Wehrmacht learned a great deal about coastal defence, but should we ignore this because Hitler's Atlantic Wall defences eventually failed? Clearly, the answer any reasonable historian or interested reader would give is 'no'. Contemporary views of past events are always historically valuable, whether or not they turn out to be wrong.

Before writing this contribution to Operation Jubilee's considerable literature, I had some simple questions in mind: did German commanders make preparations for a Dieppe-style operation? What did the raid look like from the German point of view and what did they learn? How did Goebbels and his propaganda machine use the Dieppe victory in their never-ending struggle to shape German public opinion? Having spent a couple of years buried in research, I can say that I have satisfied the curiosity that I felt years ago. All of my original questions and more besides have been answered in the book you are holding now. My curiosity has been more than satisfied by writing it.

The German experience makes a truly engrossing story. It is appropriate, then, that this book is presented in narrative form. It begins by 'setting the scene' in mid-1942, looking at how the Germans were preparing for an attack in the West. After all, history is only complete when seen in context. Next follows a battle narrative from the German viewpoint. Although many books on the raid contain snippets of information about the German conduct of the battle, this will be the first time that it is seen from the occupied side of the Channel. After this comes the aftermath and immediate German 'lessons learned' regarding the coastal defence of Europe. In a penultimate section, the book examines longer-term and more significant plans and ideas that the Germans devised to deal with further Dieppe-style operations. Notably, there is a distinction to be drawn between theoretical German plans and how far these were implemented in practical terms. Finally, a closing chapter draws together the book's conclusions and considers their wider significance.

The Dieppe story as told by the Germans provides us living in the twenty-first century with some lessons, too. It reminds us that in war both sides must do their utmost to win. The enemy is intelligent and will learn to fight better. What were the Germans doing before, during and after that day in August 1942? Nevertheless, to tell the full story, both sides are required. The Germans are just as important in the Dieppe story as the Canadians or the British. So many words have been put on paper about Dieppe. Invariably, they tell an overwhelmingly Allied tale. This book presents the other viewpoint – an essential account of the Dieppe raid from the other side of the hill.

Part I

The Raid in its German Context

Chapter 1

1942 – War in West and East

In 1942, the vast majority of Hitler's land forces found themselves committed in the unimaginably brutal struggle on the Eastern Front against the Red Army of Stalin, an equally reprehensible dictator, while Rommel's Afrika Korps found itself in North Africa's baking and featureless wasteland deserts. In the air, Germany and its occupied territories came under increasing Allied bombing attack. At sea, the commander-in-chief of the German Navy – the *Kriegsmarine* – Admiral of the Fleet Erich Raeder maintained a U-boat force which struggled to starve Britain out of hostilities in the Atlantic. In attacking the British Empire and the Soviets, and declaring war on the United States, Hitler had by his own choosing brought down upon his Third Reich a formidable coalition of military might.

It was imperative that the Germans protected their occupied territories in Norway, Denmark, France, Belgium and the Netherlands, for their British adversaries stood only a few miles away across the Channel. Almost as soon as Hitler's armies had invaded the Soviet Union on 22 June 1941, Stalin had pleaded with his awkward new bedfellow Winston Churchill to open a 'second front' against their common enemy, in order to draw German strength away from the east. One typical demand came in a cable from Stalin to Churchill on 3 September 1941, just a couple of months after the Soviets had joined the war: 'I think the only way is to open a Second Front this year somewhere in the Balkans or in France, one that would divert 30–40 German divisions from the Eastern Front.'[1] Yet Britain was certainly in no position to offer an undertaking on such a huge scale, and it is probable that there was a certain disingenuousness in Stalin's requests; by demanding the impossible, he forced Churchill to make compensation in the form of massive Anglo-American Lend-Lease supplies.

So, in the absence of a true 'second front', Churchill had to remain content with offering a series of raids against the coastlines of occupied

Europe. These small-scale operations were organized under the auspices of the British Combined Operations Headquarters, which had been set up in July 1940 under Admiral of the Fleet Roger Keyes. However, the largest-scale and most daring raids were launched in 1942 under the leadership of Lord Louis Mountbatten. Mountbatten had headed COHQ since October 1941 and had proved an ambitious and aggressive commander. Britain's lack of offensive activity in mid-1942 – and his own ego – persuaded Mountbatten of the need to strike hard and often at occupied Europe. Operation Biting, the successful capture of a German *Würzburg* coastal radar in late February 1942, was commanded by Major John Frost, later of Arnhem fame. Also known as the Bruneval raid, this intelligence 'pinch' went down in Parachute Regiment folklore and helped to cement the reputation of airborne forces. In May, so enthused was Churchill by the Commando concept and Mountbatten's stewardship of COHQ that he had this zealous officer made 'Chief of Combined Operations'. This shiny new title also came with a seat on the Chiefs of Staff Committee and a handy promotion all the way to vice admiral – a rank far above his middling experience and skills. Mountbatten's rise alienated many of Britain's most senior military officers, not least General Sir Alan Brooke, head of the Chiefs of Staff Committee, who later grumbled that 'there was no reason for [Mountbatten's] inclusion in the COS Committee, where he frequently wasted his own time and ours'.[2] No doubt encouraged by Churchill's favour, the ambitious new Admiral then launched the expansive Operation Chariot. This action was not a subtle one; HMS *Campbeltown*, an old American First World War destroyer, was converted into a sailing bomb in order to ram Saint-Nazaire's dock, the only one on the western French coast capable of holding vessels like the battleship *Tirpitz*. *Campbeltown* duly exploded, causing irreparable damage to the dock. Hitler was furious, and demanded that the most important naval bases – submarine bases being the most important of all – be rendered impervious to amphibious attack. This most audacious attack reminded the Germans in the West – if they needed any further warning at all – that the British would not sit still while Hitler's armies fought the Soviet Union in the East. The British alliance with Stalin was too important to allow his demands to go unfulfilled.

Britain's Combined Operations Headquarters, and the effects of its raiding programme, represented a major headache for Hitler in early

1942. One man who shared his concern was *Generalfeldmarschall* (Field Marshal) Gerd von Rundstedt. Having entered the Prussian Army in 1892, Rundstedt could look back on a lengthy military tradition in his family tree. One Hans von Rundstedt had served William of Orange in the 1500s, and in the 1700s a Joachim von Rundstedt fought the Jacobite uprisings in Britain in Hessian service. The family had always been wealthy and landed, so much so that Charles Messenger's biography dubbed Gerd 'The Last Prussian'. Rundstedt served the Kaiser in the First World War and was one of the select few officers kept on in the Weimar Republic's 100,000-man army, the *Reichsheer*.[3] By the time of his first retirement in 1938, Rundstedt had been promoted all the way to full general. Yet his career would reach new heights in Hitler's wartime armies.

Recalled to the colours in 1939, he commanded an Army Group in Poland, then again in the 1940 campaign in France. Throughout his career, Rundstedt had repeatedly shown himself to be a dedicated yet unassuming character. He was by no means as charismatic as some of his contemporaries like Patton or Montgomery, nor did he owe his success to a deep belief in Nazi ideology. The British historian Basil Liddell Hart, who interviewed many senior German generals after the war, thought Rundstedt closest to mirroring the 'iron Prussian' stereotype. 'He has a rather orthodox mind', he wrote of the elderly field marshal, 'but it is an able and sensitive mind, backed by a character that makes him outstanding. He is dignified without being arrogant, and essentially aristocratic in outlook – giving that term its best sense. He has an austere appearance that is offset by a pleasant smile and a nice gleam of humour.' Liddell Hart added that 'Rundstedt was a gentleman to his core.'[4] Rundstedt was a steadfast and admired character, well liked by his subordinates despite never having sought to consciously win favour or popularity. Of his generalship, Richard Brett-Smith made the most succinct assessment, judging that 'abilities, character and sagacity … placed him firmly among the outstandingly expert though not among the greatest German military commanders.'[5]

Rundstedt led Army Group South during the invasion of the Soviet Union until he was sacked in December 1941 after authorizing a withdrawal from the Soviet city of Rostov. Hitler, ever-intent on keeping complete control over his men in the field, had ordered that the city be held. Angered by this seemingly brazen affront to his absolute authority, the Führer summarily relieved Rundstedt of his post in December 1941. Subsequently, though, Hitler displayed rare regret for his rashness and assured his now unemployed field marshal that he would soon be called upon again. Even during his time in the East, Rundstedt had been concerned about German weakness in the West as the Wehrmacht advanced deep into the Soviet Union. His warnings were so persistent that they reportedly got on Hitler's nerves.[6]

When Field Marshal Erwin von Witzleben retired from the position of 'Supreme Commander West' or *Oberbefehlshaber West*, there seemed no better-qualified candidate amongst Hitler's field marshals to replace him than Rundstedt, inactive now for some months. His family's history and his own long personal service to Germany – in the various forms it had taken since he entered the armed forces in the late nineteenth century – had imbued him with a traditional sense of duty. If his country needed him, he would serve, whoever the commander-in-chief might be. Rundstedt was also well suited to the strategic-level demands of the role. The position of *Oberbefehlshaber West* (OB West for short) was not that of a tactical front-line general – he would be thinking and making decisions on a much higher strategic level, such as which of his generals' impassioned requests for scarce men and materiel he should grant, or how to best integrate air, land and sea forces into an effective and unified fighting force. Importantly, the term 'OB West' referred both to the person in command and to the unit he led. Brigadier Günther Blumentritt, Rundstedt's chief of staff for most of his time as OB West, remarked that the old Prussian had 'a pronounced strategic-operational sense and never troubled himself with military details', preferring to view his maps in large scale, at least 1:1,000,000.[7]

Rundstedt took up his new position in March 1942, just a fortnight before Operation Chariot. Other than his headquarters being situated in the luxurious and resplendent Hotel Pavillon Henri IV in Paris, his new command brought few benefits. It entailed authority over and responsibility for all operations in occupied Western Europe – this meant a coastline running from the Franco-Spanish border facing the Atlantic Ocean to the Dutch-German border facing the North Sea. Although it was geographically massive, OB West was hardly the pick of Wehrmacht's wartime commands, being covered by only twenty-five land divisions, many of them under-strength. Western Europe was a low-priority theatre with little in the way of action. Save the possibility of a small Commando raid here, and perhaps an anti-Resistance operation there, little action of note could be expected. This was wonderful for the individual soldier – more time to enjoy the occupation of France, for example – but for a field marshal it was not a prized position. Resources were scarce, so much so that training often had to be curtailed for lack of fuel. However, most of Rundstedt's men did not enjoy the benefits of motorized transport anyway – this was all allocated to vastly more important commands.

Rundstedt reached Paris in March 1942 with one hand effectively tied behind his back. Although his title may have been Supreme Commander West, his authority was anything but absolute. Neither the Luftwaffe nor the Kriegsmarine were part of his chain of command. Consequently, any and all 'orders' he gave to Kriegsmarine and Luftwaffe forces were purely advisory. Given the importance of cooperation along a coastline – where air, land and naval forces operated in close proximity – this was a highly significant weakness in the German command structure. Even more significantly, the 'Last Prussian' did not even hold command over all land forces in the West – the military governors of Paris and Brussels, for example, did not report to him directly. Such was the Wehrmacht's predisposition to maintain personal fiefdoms. Indeed, perhaps even using the word 'Wehrmacht' is inaccurate. Although it was the German term for 'the Armed Forces' in Hitler's Germany, it implies some kind of inherent unity. But no student at any modern staff college would receive many marks in their exams if they described Rundstedt's OB West as the truly tri-service integrated joint command it was supposed to be. One German general remarked after the war: 'The chain of command in the West was … no special handicap for the western command, but rather a burden to which the commanders-in-chief in all theatres of war had to resign themselves.'[8] Rundstedt's continual attempts to unify his control over France, Belgium and the Netherlands bore no fruit.

Inter-service tension and rivalry would rear its ugly head in a matter of crucial importance to the defence of any coastline, and further stymie Rundstedt's preparation to face an operation like Jubilee. Coastal artillery was a central part of German defensive plans, but because of the overprotective attitude of the Kriegsmarine and the Army towards their own assets, there was always tension regarding the simple question of control – who would enjoy operational command of artillery along the coast during a landing? There were two schools of thought. The Army argued that, since the prime objective of an amphibious invasion was achieving a foothold on land, the focus of fire support on the coast should be directed at the foot soldiers when they reached the beach. Since this was a land target, the Army should naturally have the final say as to which targets should be prioritized. The Kriegsmarine on the other hand advanced the completely opposite argument: surely, since the most vulnerable time for an amphibious force is while it is still huddled in its landing craft, it should be engaged at sea and not on land? By this logic, naval personnel should control any guns on a coastline. Both were reasonable arguments, but the nature of the Wehrmacht did not allow it to come down with confidence on either side, or even come up with a workable compromise.

Unfortunately for the Germans, Hitler had failed to bring about an acceptable solution for either side. Under Führer Directive 40, issued late in March 1942, Hitler divided command of coastal artillery between the Army and Kriegsmarine, depending on the target. Directive 40 dictated that batteries were controlled by the Kriegsmarine when attacking naval targets, and the Army when attacking land targets, with primacy conferred on the battle at sea – this meant that marine targets took priority over those on land. By all accounts, this was a confusing and inefficient non-solution. The order was one of Hitler's 'Führer Directives' which, by the mere fact of being issued over the Führer's signature, superseded any civil or military laws or orders. Directive 40 was entitled 'Competence of Commanders in Coastal Area', which carried more than a hint of irony, for it brought about a less-than-competent command arrangement. Its preamble warned that 'failure in other theatres of war, obligations to allies, and political considerations may persuade [the enemy] to take decisions which appear unlikely from a purely military point of view.'[9] Clearly, Hitler had one eye on Stalin's incessant demands for a second front and Churchill's desperation to appease and relieve his eastern ally. With this fact in mind, the Directive made some progress in appointing a single commander with responsibility for coastal defence. At the theatre command level, it meant that Rundstedt would finally have full planning authority. For instance, he was subsequently able to issue a series of orders which harmonized the terminology involved in planning coastal defence. Moreover, every local Army commander (at the divisional level) benefited. Each divisional commander, invariably a major general, gained full authority for coastal defence in his area of command – not just during a landing attempt as had been the case previously. This represented a success for the land forces. However, the problem remained – and indeed was exacerbated by Directive 40 – that operational command of air, land and sea units ultimately remained within their respective services. Consequently, any cross-service cooperation occurred entirely at the discretion of individual commanders.

The Kriegsmarine was not entirely comfortable with the awkward settlement of the command disputes reached under Directive 40, but recognized that it still represented a favourable outcome for maritime interests. Crucially, coastal batteries were subordinate to the Kriegsmarine and only transferred tactical control to the Army when engaging land targets. Exercising this control of target selection were the commanders of the Kriegsmarine's various 'Sea Defence Zones' covering Western Europe's coastlines. Almost invariably, these officers held the rank of captain. Naturally, these would, more often than not, be unwilling to give up control of their batteries to their Army counterparts. Directive 40 gave priority to the war at sea, based on the logic that it was better to destroy the enemy before he landed than afterwards – i.e. as far away from the coast as possible. Kriegsmarine commander-in-chief Admiral of the Fleet Erich Raeder was quick to stress that his men in naval uniform still retained significant control of coastal operations: 'Even if the fight for the coast extends to the coastal areas within reach of the … Army coastal artillery, command over the bombardment of targets at sea remains in the hands of the naval shore commanders.' The Kriegsmarine was given priority for new coastal defence guns, so much so that many Army weapons were converted field guns that had to be modified to be placed inside coastal defence bunkers. Moreover, because coastal guns were rarely replaced and upgraded, the Army in particular was saddled with a variety of old and captured weapons, which created a host of logistical and training problems.

As Raeder was also keen to point out, the only situation in which a German Army divisional commander could give the Kriegsmarine orders was when the defence of ground along a coastline was involved. He made this abundantly clear in a response to the directive penned just four days after it was released. The Kriegsmarine was swift to protect its interests when Directive 40's arrangements were challenged. In late May, Rundstedt attempted to go over the Kriegsmarine's head by demanding from Alfred Jodl's OKW Operations Staff that, in the event of a landing, he as Supreme Commander West should be 'authorized to take charge of whatever naval forces [could] be contacted'. In practice, this would mean that OB West could take operational control of naval forces without prior authorization or discussion with Raeder's naval staff. The Kriegsmarine staff at OKW naturally rejected this proposal out of hand. Jodl had no interest in becoming involved in mediating in a dispute and promptly dismissed Rundstedt's initiative.[10]

The split command of coastal artillery created some obvious and utterly avoidable problems. Firstly, it meant that there existed no single entity to provide training. Consequently, the batteries were trained by the Kriegsmarine for naval targeting and the Army for land targeting. Many batteries inland, those generally manned by Army personnel, did not have the star (illuminating) shells that the Kriegsmarine possesssed. Admiral Otto Schulze, a former U-boat ace of the First World War and in 1942 Commanding Admiral of France, complained personally to Raeder on this point. Alas, this was just the first on Schulze's long list of grievances; incorrect sights for naval targets was another.[11] Army personnel were equally dissatisfied.

With the ever-present danger of Allied raids against his coastline, Rundstedt had a serious task at hand in preparing for action what was a low-priority command. Soon after the new OB West had taken up his position, Hitler had sacked Rundstedt's chief of staff for supposed failures over the Saint-Nazaire raid. That embarrassment hung over Rundstedt like an omnipresent dark cloud. It was how he framed the early months of his new command – would he be able to defeat a similar operation in future? A mere fortnight after Operation Chariot, a conference took place at Hitler's *Wolfsschanze* (Wolf's Lair) HQ in East Prussia. Present alongside the Führer were, amongst others, Wilhelm Keitel and Alfred Jodl, head of Hitler's High Command and its Operations Staff respectively. At this meeting on 16 April 1942, Kriegsmarine commander-in-chief Raeder presented to Hitler an assessment of British intentions and capabilities. His warning was anything but modest: 'British operations against the Norwegian and French coasts show that the British, taking advantage of the fact that the German Army and Luftwaffe are heavily engaged in the East, are determined and able to attack the extensive German coast more frequently and on a larger scale than we have thus far expected.' In effect, Raeder's Kriegsmarine was arguing – with some justification – that a new era of coastal warfare in the West had begun. No longer could the Germans expect only small Commando raids. HMS *Campbeltown*'s audacious dash into Saint-Nazaire's docks had made that fact more than plain. Yet Raeder's staff concluded dimly that, in the face of widespread shortages, 'the available forces are completely inadequate everywhere'.[12]

All of the commitments that the German Wehrmacht faced on other fronts in mid-1942 meant that there was little help coming Rundstedt's way. In fact, experienced, battle-hardened German soldiers were being transferred away from France, Belgium and Holland to make up for shortfalls on the Eastern Front. So neglected was the French coastline in particular, that much of its coastal artillery was still in its offensive 1940 positions, ready to fire in support of a German invasion of Britain. Clearly, this was not a realistic possibility in 1942, but the resources were simply not available to relocate the guns to more suitable defensive positions. Furthermore, many artillery batteries were isolated, being located in positions that could not be mutually supported by the infantry. In his very first order, the new Supreme Commander greeted his men with an unequivocal message: 'The small number of Army, Navy and Air Force units available in the West, as well as these units' poor equipment, demands that every and all means will be used to increase their fighting capacity and readiness … Every gun, every heavy infantry weapon must be used before and during every landing attempt. We depend on every single barrel!'[13] True, there was a paucity of ammunition reserves in the West. Rundstedt estimated that he only had enough munitions immediately available for a few days' hard fighting. He had only a small central reserve under his direct control. The vast number of various captured weapons had no reserves available at all – i.e. what the front-line unit had to hand was all they would get. This was not the only problem; the widespread inexperience of Rundstedt's men, and the lack of ammunition available for the weapons that they operated, conspired to create a perfect storm. As night follows day, one can expect inexperienced troops to rapidly expend their ammunition. With very few, if any, reserves available, he could expect his munitions to be rapidly depleted in any firefight.

In addition, the state of the West's static coastal defences was poor. It would perhaps be more accurate to say that they were non-existent. Work had not yet begun on what would later be known as the 'Atlantic Wall', and the few solid defences that were in place were either captured from the French in 1940 or very much ad hoc. In any case, the defences were nothing more than utterly insufficient. However much he may have wished things were different, Rundstedt would have to make do with what little he had.

Chapter 2

The Dieppe Division:
302nd Infantry Division

Since Operation Sealion, the planned amphibious invasion of Britain, had been called off in 1940, the section of beautiful Normandy coastline on which the town of Dieppe lay had always been of little concern to the Germans. Any soldier stationed here was a very lucky man, and not just for being spared the intense combat of the Eastern Front. The wonderful countryside favoured by holidaymakers, the food and the pleasant weather made a posting to this part of France a gift. Hans Albring, a soldier who spent every spare moment drawing pictures to send back home to his parents in Germany, said simply of Normandy's landscape: 'I see Paradise.'[1] France was not overrun by Resistance fighters, as myth might suggest. In fact, this was very much the quiet side of the war. Indeed, it remained so until June 1944. One of the early beneficiaries of French amenities was the fresh-faced 20-year-old Rudolf Oehus, who was fortunate enough to be quartered in one of the many quaint little villages in Dieppe's surroundings late in 1940. Like most of his recently conscripted comrades, when he arrived in France Oehus had only been in uniform for a few months. The most senior of his barrack-mates had only six months' service under his belt. Serving in Artillery Regiment 295's 7th Battery, Oehus had learned to ride in training, since his unit's guns were horse-drawn, as were the vast majority in the occupying army. At Christmas he wrote a series of letters to his parents. Having grown up in the Lower Saxonian town of Bergen, near Hanover, he was used to far more snow than he saw in northern France. He asked in one of his messages home: 'Is the snow on the ground where you are? We've had frosty weather for two days now, other than that it has been mild.' The young Oehus went on to describe the relative calm of France: 'There hasn't been an air-raid alarm. Somewhere near us a bomb fell for the first time. That woke us, but other than that we've been allowed to sleep.'

Oehus recognized his luck in being in the West. 'Nothing important has happened so far, only that planes come over and drop a few bombs more often', he wrote to his family. 'Other than that, I can't write about anything special. We have it really good here. We don't know how long we'll stay.'[2]

In 1942, the men in Dieppe belonged to the 302nd Infantry Division. By all accounts, they continued to enjoy a good life as an occupying force. The typical daily schedule was leisurely compared with that of most soldiers on active service. For one artillery unit, the day started at half past six. Fifteen minutes' physical exercise preceded coffee at quarter to seven. Four hours of drill, exercises or maintenance led up to a two-hour lunch at midday, followed by another four hours' work. From six o'clock in the evening the men enjoyed free time, at which point they could apply for short-term leave. The midday meal normally consisted of either goulash and potatoes or a hotpot of meat and vegetables. Also at midday, the men were also given extra rations of half a kilogram of bread, 40 grams of butter and 80 grams of sausages for making their own dinner. Three times a week, they were given jam or honey substitute instead of butter and sausages at lunch, with soup provided for dinner. Fresh fruit and vegetables were always freely available on the open market. If one was willing and able to pay a bit more, much more variety was available on the underground market. Dieppe's black market was partly operated by the Germans – Corporal Müller, whose job was to manage the German canteen in the Hotel Royal, ran a clandestine shop, with a Private Pandel assisting him. At Müller's little enterprise one could buy a pair of stockings to send home for 100 francs, or 5 Reichsmarks – this was an artificially advantageous exchange rate set by the Germans. Müller was also selling plums at 7.50 francs per lb. For those who fancied a tipple, a bottle of French red wine was available for 20 francs, or, for a special occasion, cognac for 60 francs. A newly-recruited German private's basic monthly pay was 120 Reichsmarks, equivalent to 600 francs.

It does not seem that the German leadership cared much at all about their men's widespread involvement with black market activities. So well provided were the occupiers with basics like toothpaste, paper and sweets that the German soldiers often sent them back home, where such things were scarcer. The soldiers' wives and girlfriends regularly enjoyed deliveries of stockings and underwear, much of it undoubtedly bought on the black market. Perhaps, though, their significant others would have been less pleased to know that the men at Dieppe regularly enjoyed the services of their own brothel. Other more respectable entertainment included a 700-seat cinema which showed films daily at 7 o'clock, with an extra showing at 4 o'clock on Saturdays. Without exception, the cinema was packed to the rafters. Friedrich Waltenheimer, stationed in Dieppe, used the same words as Hans Albring to describe his French occupation: 'It was a paradise compared to Russia.'[3] He was right.

Whilst those servicemen privileged enough to be stationed in the Dieppe sector during 1942 may have enjoyed a lifestyle unimaginable on the Eastern Front, their military situation was dire. Just one German division, the 302nd Infantry, was charged with defending a 40-mile stretch of coast from Sotteville-sur-Mer in the far west to the mouth of the Somme in the extreme east. The 302nd was commanded by 53-year-old Major General Konrad Ludwig Benno Haase, an unremarkable general who was relegated to the command of this poor-quality 'static' division. Little more was expected from him and his men than to occupy the Dieppe coastline and maintain German control. Tactical flair was neither demanded nor expected. Haase was not an imposing figure; he wore thin round spectacles on his bulbous nose, and his double chin betrayed the significant weight that he carried. His hairline was receding, and from the front only a thin line of hair was visible. Haase had joined the Imperial German Army as an artillery officer cadet in 1908, gaining his commission as a Second Lieutenant a year later. The First World War brought him promotion to Captain and an Iron Cross 1st Class, but he was not one of the select few officers who were retained in the Weimar Republic's new army, restricted to 100,000 men under the Treaty of Versailles. Haase turned to civil law enforcement instead and became a police officer in 1919. This seems to have given him a second wind; only five years later, he became chief of Dresden's police force. After varied police duties, he was recalled to Army service in Hitler's new Wehrmacht in 1935 as a regimental commander. In late 1939, he was assigned to command the 164th Infantry Division while it was being formed in Germany. He then briefly commanded a reserve unit in Poland, which brought him promotion to General. After this brief posting, he was given command of the short-lived 365th Division in late 1940 for Polish occupation duties. He impressed his superiors in this post

– one performance review noted that he was 'tireless' and 'quite good intellectually' with 'healthy ambition'. Overall, he was rated 'very good'. He was consequently recommended for another divisional command, and on 12 November that year he finally transferred to the 302nd Infantry Division as its commanding officer during its creation in north-eastern Germany. He received his final promotion to Major General on New Year's Day 1942, and for his services thus far was awarded the War Merit Cross 1st Class with swords.[4]

The Dieppe area was well known to Haase's men; they had been stationed there ever since their promotion to combat-ready status in May 1941. The 302nd Infantry Division was formed using largely captured equipment, in order to alleviate pressure on German war manufacturing capacity. This consisted mostly of repurposed French arms left over from the conquest in 1940. Some old Czech and French tanks captured in 1938 and 1940 had had their turrets removed and were used as static armoured artillery. Almost all the vehicles assigned to the defence of the 302nd's sector were captured French models, as were the artillery pieces, and they had few heavy weapons – only a small number of light mortars would ever be at the division's disposal in battle. In view of its static role, it had neither a reconnaissance detachment nor bridging equipment for its engineers. Furthermore, the long logistics and transport 'tail' behind the front-line units was almost nonexistent, as the division's units were expected to remain in the same location. Only one signals company served the division's communications needs. One German officer summed up the design philosophy for this kind of division: 'a) Maximum combat strength with minimum numerical strength, to be achieved by giving up all mobility. b) Abandonment of the bulk of the supply troops ... c) Assault gun batteries and infantry equipped with bicycles ... assigned to the division as mobile combat units.'[5]

Shortage of fuel meant that there was very little opportunity to conduct meaningful and realistic training; despite the fact that the division possessed very few motorized assets that required fuel in the first place, this was a serious problem considering the raw recruits being delivered to France to replace the veterans sent to the East. Without the benefit of motorized transport, most of the reserves assigned to the defence of Dieppe would utilize old bicycles. Significantly, there were a number of forced conscripts within Haase's division. Few of these men were fighting fit. One Pole, Bronislav Wesierski, was so physically frail that he collapsed on his arrival in Germany for training. Being called up into the Wehrmacht was not the first time that Private Wesierski's services had been forcibly enlisted. Before donning a German infantryman's uniform, he had been compulsorily sent to a German boot factory, along with 400 other Poles overseen by two German foremen. Not only did the manager scalp more than half his wages, but he and his fellow countrymen received half the food ration of an equivalent German worker – in addition to missing out on a monthly litre ration of schnapps. Speaking Polish was forbidden in public; a fine of two weeks' wages could be levied on anyone caught doing so.

These units were hardly the fighting fit legions of stormtroopers that German civilians saw in their weekly newsreels back home. As the 302nd's quartermaster later put it, 'In no way was the division adequately fitted out for the task assigned to it.'[6] Nevertheless, the men of the 302nd Division would perform reasonably well on 19 August. After the war, a German veteran testified that 'we had about 60 per cent of our troops who were experienced in battle, nearly all officers or non-commissioned officers. The rest were not fully experienced but had been trained in coastal defence. But they were attached to units which had fought before, so when it came to the battle there was no psychological crisis. Everything worked out marvellously just as we'd exercised. Even the youngest got accustomed very quickly.'[7] Drilling over and over again is the classic way to keep otherwise inactive soldiers busy and motivated, and certainly Haase had had the time to do so, having commanded the division since its inception and arrival in Dieppe in May 1941.

The division also ran regular invasion exercises. One in October 1941 was remarkably prescient in predicting how determined small teams could climb cliff faces until then thought to be impassable. A year later, the British Commandos would do exactly that. Still, these exercises just as regularly exposed the weaknesses inherent in the poor motivation and drive found in low-quality infantry. During the October exercise, for instance, a lone man in civilian clothing was allowed to walk around freely at night and record the various divisional insignia on artillery guns, vehicles, bunkers and the like. He was even spotted observing the division's military grounds and installations using binoculars. Although he was spotted, nobody could be motivated to question this strange man as to his intentions. He was certainly not taking part in the exercise.[8] He may have just been a curious Frenchman, but he could well have been an Allied spy. Whoever this unidentified figure really was, this egregious lack of security demonstrated to General Haase the task he had on his hands. By August 1942 matters had scarcely improved. Just a week before the Allies came to Dieppe, Haase inspected a night march unannounced. What he saw was, as he understatedly characterized it, 'unmilitary' – a shabby collection of co-drivers fast asleep, passengers wrapped in blankets despite the warm summer weather, men sitting on top of field kitchens, shirts hanging out with buttons undone and collars turned upwards. If the division was not mentally prepared for action, then it was even less physically prepared. It possessed only nineteen dedicated anti-tank guns, most of which were small 37mm types. Its complement of thirty-three anti-tank rifles was a third of the nominal quantity. The sub-machine gun situation was even more woeful, at a quarter of its intended strength.[9]

Chapter 3

Anticipation

Despite the fact the German coastal defenders were hardly sufficiently supplied with men and materiel, they were fully aware that the Allies might attempt to scale up their raiding programme in summer 1942. German commanders recognized that instead of Commando raids like John Frost's 120-man Operation Biting, they might well have to face a large-scale landing by a whole division or more. First and foremost, political and diplomatic events reinforced this view. Alongside the Anglo-American-Soviet Lend-Lease agreements, Foreign Secretary Anthony Eden and Soviet Foreign Minister Vyacheslav Molotov had signed the Anglo-Soviet Treaty on 26 May. This would commit the two powers not only to a military alliance, but also to a political one. With ever-increasing cooperation between East and West, it was strongly suspected in Germany that Britain would feel obliged to engage in military action in Europe.

Joseph Goebbels, Hitler's Reichsminister for Public Enlightenment and Propaganda, was eager to exploit any opportunity to lampoon his adversaries. Goebbels has deservedly received much attention from historians, but there was a far less well remembered figure at play in Germany's war of words. Otto Dietrich was Reich Press Chief and Goebbels' right hand man, charged with finally deciding how the German press should report the war news. Dietrich was the ultimate link between the Reich's journalists and Hitler's inner circle, and he saw himself as such. Under Dietrich's leadership, each day at the Propaganda Ministry, a press conference took place to issue binding instructions to German newspapers, dictating to them how the day's war news was to be reported. Seen from the outside, the Ministry was an imposing building on central Berlin's Wilhelmstrasse; indeed, it had been expanded considerably since the Nazis had taken power. Inside, however, the new Propaganda Ministry was a mostly functional series of offices, archives, film projection rooms and an auditorium. The 'press conferences' that took place in the Propaganda Ministry's corridors were not press conferences as those living in democracies understand the term; no journalist was permitted to critically interrogate the Nazi government on its policies. This would have been an absurdity in a totalitarian dictatorship. What the Nazis meant by a 'press conference' was rather simpler: the assembled journalists were told what to say and how to say it. Sometimes they were directed to use certain phrases or even specific words in their newspaper articles.

Dietrich's instructions were distributed in daily press packets called *Vertrauliche Informationen* or 'Confidential Information'. Normally, these injunctions ran to about three pages. The *Vertrauliche Informationen* contained specific 'Daily Watchwords'. Called *Tagesparolen* in German, these were lengthy series of bullet points which dictated how a specific event should be handled in the press. Generally, there were three or four stories considered important enough each day to receive their own *Tagesparole*. The 'Confidential Information' guidelines were handed out at the daily press conferences, which were mainly attended by Berlin journalists, due to their proximity to the Propaganda Ministry. Those who worked further afield were sent the guidelines by teleprinter. Importantly, specialist advisers and representatives from other government organs such as the Wehrmacht or Foreign Office attended regularly in order to inform policy.

Though the Propaganda Ministry was headquartered in Berlin, Reich Press Chief Dietrich often found himself outside the capital. He regretted the fact that he did not have much time to personally direct Germany's wartime propaganda effort, once telling an assembly of pressmen in Berlin: 'I have always nurtured personal contact. The journalist, I know, cannot work by regulation, but rather his own conviction. Unfortunately, we cannot often come together. Daily contact is created by the *Tagesparolen* of the press conference, which I myself lay down. They are an invisible connecting piece between you and me.'[1] The guidelines, watchwords and press conferences were all designed to create a unified journalistic weapon against Germany's enemies, be they foreign or domestic. Importantly, this was a force whose every word could be controlled. As Goebbels explained before the war, the overarching goal for the press was to make the German population 'think uniformly, react uniformly, and place themselves body and soul at the disposal of the government'.[2]

The very day after Eden stood up in the House of Commons to announce the Anglo-Soviet agreement on 11 June, Dietrich made plain in Berlin how the Nazi press should treat their enemies' mutual diplomatic efforts. Normally, the press conferences were daily events, but they would be held twice a day if events were moving quickly. Churchill's visit to Moscow was one of these critical moments. Dietrich duly proclaimed in his *Vertrauliche Informationen* brief on 12 June: 'The new English-Soviet agreements are to be portrayed as trivial compared to the military situation, and as a sign of England's willingness to listen to Bolshevism.' The link between the military and political themes of the war was made all the clearer during the next day's press conference: 'The London agreements are the same hollow boasting that the Anglo-Americans and Soviet Russians present when military success is lacking. Instead of military victory they present treaties to pull the wool over the eyes of their populations.' These words may have represented pure rhetorical bluster, but they also demonstrated a simple truth; the Germans understood perfectly well that politics and war fighting were intertwined.

When Churchill travelled to Washington a few days later for his third meeting with Roosevelt, Dietrich was likewise eager to turn this into a sign of Allied weakness: 'Churchill's sudden departure is evidence of four problems: the opening of a Second Front, the question of transports, strategy in the Near and Far East and deliveries to England, Soviet Russia and China. The trip is an alarming expression of the great dilemma in which Churchill finds himself.' Speaking to his audience of assembled journalists, he made their mission in this new phase of Anglo-American cooperation crystal clear: 'This is an attempt to distract attention from the military defeats of the Allies on all fronts. The objective of our news output is to quash this propagandistic manoeuvre through constant repetition and ruthless exposure of England's precarious position ... The unity of Churchill and Roosevelt is not a sign of strength, rather it is a sign of desperation.'[3] The Nazi papers took Dietrich's words to heart with rapier-like force. People reading the *Fuldaer Zeitung* in central Germany saw on their paper's front page the headline: 'They Are Investigating Their Defeat: A Sign Of The Wehrmacht's Victories – Churchill's Journey An "Inspirational Moment".' Austrians perusing the *Völkischer Beobachter* ('People's Observer'), the Nazi Party's official newspaper, were told that Churchill was now 'before his master for the third time'.

The front-page headline was equally dismissive of the Prime Minister's initiative: readers saw 'Churchill's Lightning-Quick Visit To Roosevelt – An SOS', in giant lettering with red underlining.

Whether they were civilians at Goebbels' Propaganda Ministry or generals stationed in France, the Allies' enemies were right to make the connection between military and political events. Matters were soon to become even more critical on the Eastern Front, where the vast majority of the Wehrmacht was deployed. On 28 June 1942, Hitler's summer offensive for 1942 began and achieved phenomenal initial success, with some armoured formations advancing a startling 30 miles on the first day alone.[4] With Hitler's armies closing in on the great city of Stalingrad, it was also clear that the compulsion for the Allies to act in the West would grow ever more acute. To this end, Hitler personally sent a circular telegram on 9 July warning that German success on the Eastern Front might well provoke reckless action by the Allies in the West: 'Our rapid and great victories may place Great Britain before the alternatives of either staging a large-scale invasion with the object of opening a second front, or seeing Russia eliminated as a political and military factor.'[5] Essentially, this was a recognition that political matters could force the Allies' hand in the military sphere.

On the other side of the Channel, Churchill was vexing his Chiefs of Staff with all kinds of schemes for large-scale landings in France and Norway. The Prime Minister was desperate to provide some kind of relief to his allies in the East. One should not forget, either, that it was not just Churchill's Soviet allies who wanted early action in the West. The Americans, with Chief of Staff of the Army George C. Marshall at their head, were insistent on an invasion of France as early as 1942 or 1943, on the basis that the shortest route to Berlin ran through France. Ultimately, Chief of the Imperial General Staff Sir Alan Brooke managed to fend off the absurd idea of a cross-Channel invasion in 1942. Nevertheless, Churchill was undeterred in his wish to commit British troops in the West. How far Churchill was motivated by his allies' views and not by Britain's own relative passivity in this period is hard, perhaps impossible, to judge. Suffice it to say, however, that the Germans were well aware that even though a divisional-scale raid or invasion might not make sense in purely military terms, such a venture was very much a possibility in summer or autumn 1942. No longer would they have to worry merely about small-scale Commando raids. Hitler's generals were justifiably concerned with the question of a land-sea-air operation involving thousands or even tens of thousands of men.

Rumours of such a landing were commonplace in German-occupied France throughout 1942, and German units were constantly receiving reports to that effect. These intensified after Operation Chariot. The war diary of the German Naval Staff noted that 'the experience gained at Saint-Nazaire … shows that Great Britain possesses the determination and the facilities to attack along our extensive coastline more frequently and on a greater scale than before … The Naval Staff [therefore] gives directives for the reinforcement of coastal defences: employment of naval forces, use of mines, employment of other naval weapons along the coast [and] setting up of new coastal batteries.'[6] Even Hitler was not immune from indulging in such rumours. His own high command's war diary noted on 10 April, little more than a week after the attack on Saint-Nazaire, that 'the Führer has information from abroad to the effect that the English and Americans are planning a big surprise.' As to the details of what this great surprise might be, Hitler remained silent. A month later, intelligence from the Foreign Office reached Hitler's headquarters at the Wolf's Lair, predicting that a landing on Denmark's western coast was 'imminent'. Further reports in support of this possibility caused the Führer so much concern that he dispatched reserves from Germany to defend Jutland's coast. Commander-in-Chief of the Luftwaffe Reichsmarschall Hermann Göring considered sending more aircraft to southern Norway to defend both Denmark and Norway. His air commander in Norway believed that if the Allies landed at all in Jutland, it would be 'madness' if this did not form part of a much larger operation, perhaps stretching to Norway and/ or the French Channel coast.[7]

Göring was also keen to raise his subordinates' awareness of the Allies' landing capability. In a conference on 16 May 1942, the Reichsmarschall impressed upon his air commanders in the West that a British landing could happen at any time, and that any forces under Luftwaffe jurisdiction – in the Wehrmacht this included airborne forces – should be used against such an attempt. Göring was no fan of inter-service cooperation, tending instead to maintain his personal control over Germany's air forces, but in this matter he urged cooperation both with the Army and Kriegsmarine. At Dieppe, another warning circulated around 302nd Division in mid-

June: 'According to a reliable source, the British intend the installation of a second front in Belgium and France prior to 22 June. This is confirmed by other reports which indicate that preparations for an invasion are being carried on in England at high pressure.'[8] The British had, intentionally or not, contributed to these rumours. In June the BBC had broadcast warnings to the French population, urging them to evacuate the coastal areas of the country because the Allies were likely to attack.[9]

The Kriegsmarine increased the regularity of its reconnaissance missions in the Channel, and suggested that a reserve of U-boats be held at very high readiness to respond quickly to an attempted landing. Raeder agreed with Rundstedt that Admiral Karl Dönitz's submarines should be available 'as far as the operational picture allows', with the explicit caveat that none would be deployed in or around the Channel.[10] The dominance of Allied aircraft and the Royal Navy in the Channel made this decision an easy one to take. Against the advice of his generals, including his Army Chief of Staff Franz Halder, Hitler decided to reinforce the West with two full SS divisions (*Leibstandarte Adolf Hitler* and *Grossdeutchland*, although the latter remained in the East). Although most landing warnings circulated by German intelligence were spurious, sometimes they did come close to the truth. One agent working within the Foreign Office gave an assessment in July that 'a large-scale landing operation of American and British troops on the French Channel coast, starting from the south coast of England, is to take place during the month of August.' Whoever this spy was made much the same assessment as many post-war historians have regarding the raid – that the precarious military position of the Soviets would provoke an Anglo-Americans landing in France.

Large-scale amphibious operations require very specific sea and light conditions in order to proceed. These only occur a few times a month. Therefore, if one could recognize these occasions and put coastal defences forces on alert at the right time, the probability of defeating an assault would be massively increased. In working towards this goal, the Wehrmacht experienced a rare, small but significant instance of inter-service cooperation. In mid-July, the OKW requested a report from Erich Raeder's Kriegsmarine high command staff as to what times and conditions would be best for landing on the Channel coast. The Kriegsmarine stated that there were four conditions which could be used to predict an amphibious landing. Firstly, the absence of current. Naturally, fast currents made boat and ship handling extremely difficult, and as a result any landing would be best conducted when these were absent. Secondly, the Kriegsmarine regarded high spring tides as of considerable benefit to the attacker, because transports and landing craft could then approach much closer to the landing beaches. They did note, however, that this was not necessarily a key factor if troops and supplies could be disembarked quickly. Thirdly, the Kriegsmarine staff judged that an assault about two hours before daybreak would give cover of darkness while landing but also give the troops on land some daylight. Their final condition was an obvious one known to all military planners – moonlight. Quite correctly, the Germans knew any landing conducted during a full moon phase would negate the benefits inherent in a pre-dawn operation. Therefore, a moonless (or at least half-moon) night would be preferable.[11] Based on these prerequisites, the Wehrmacht as a whole could now prepare to face landings with a rough idea of when the danger periods were.

So concerned was Supreme Commander Field Marshal Rundstedt at the thought of a possible landing that just over a month before the Dieppe raiding force took to sea, he gave two new orders to all German units in the West. These were his 10th and 13th 'Basic Orders' (*Grundlegende Befehle*). These were essentially standing, permanent orders that laid out German conduct in the West, and they would ultimately define the Germans' methods of operation at Dieppe. Basic Order Number 10 appeared in early July and laid down a core element of Rundstedt's strategy – that he would try to defeat the enemy before they reached land: 'It must be our goal that the enemy assault shatters … if possible before, or at the latest after reaching the coastline.' This, though, was an ambitious aspiration when one considers how materially weak the Germans' western defences were. Rundstedt admitted it was likely that, in spite of this aim, the enemy would make landfall in force. Thus, the coastal defences were to hold their positions at all costs as a delaying action until reserves could arrive. 'Every half-hour that a higher command can use can be decisive', Rundstedt told his men.[12]

Basic Order Number 13 appeared at the end of July 1942 and was more focussed on expected enemy behaviour. For years the Wehrmacht had prepared for British Commando raids on a foolishly ad hoc basis, with no concrete idea of what they could expect from a super-raid on Dieppe's scale. Now, though, they had a document which they could use to plan a defence which was based on studied analysis of predicted Allied behaviour – if the British or Americans came to the shores of Europe en masse, what could the Germans expect, and how should they react? Answering these questions was the driving force behind Rundstedt's decision to write Basic Order 13.

Basic Order 13, although it carried an understated title, fundamentally changed the way things were done by the Germans in occupied Europe. For the first time, with the newly recognized threat of a large-scale landing attempt in France, Belgium or the Netherlands, the Wehrmacht's higher echelons were taking that threat seriously. Rundstedt began Basic Order 13 with a stark message: 'The likely enemy methods are currently unknown, but it is certain that he will use every conceivable means to achieve success. We must be ready and use every possible counter-measure.'[13] Considering what came later during the Dieppe raid, Rundstedt's analysis bordered on the clairvoyant. What concerned him most was the role that air power could play in a landing on a contested coastline. With their speed and versatility, aircraft were well suited to supporting a coastal landing. They could not only control the skies, but also exploit freedom in the air in a ground attack role. 'At his landing point, the enemy will fight for air supremacy, then turn the mass of his air force against defences on the ground.' Amongst other measures, Rundstedt mandated that every wagon in a supply train, or every vehicle in a reinforcement convoy, was from then on to mount some kind of anti-aircraft weapon. In Rundstedt's words, 'a single AA machine gun in a convoy as was common previously is no longer enough.' Basic Order 13 went so far as to compel German soldiers to use their rifles and sub-machine guns against low-flying aircraft in the absence of proper anti-aircraft weaponry. This may seem futile, but small arms could be effective against aircraft if the man on the ground was very lucky. Rundstedt noted the example of a Corporal Doras, from the 321st Division on the Dieppe division's right flank, who succeeded in shooting down one aircraft and helped down another during an air raid. He went on to write that 'it has not been easy to make battle-experienced troops use their personal weapons against low-flying aircraft instead of taking cover. This is even more difficult with inexperienced units. Here, nothing is achieved without the constant effort and the example of all commissioned and non-commissioned officers. The responsibility is yours. You must know this. Your failure costs the blood of your men.'

Air power also brought with it the ability to bring infantry to the battlefield via glider landings and parachute drops. Though the term 'airborne' has come to be a catch-all description of airmobile soldiers, it refers, technically speaking, to infantry dropped by parachute, whereas 'air-landed' refers to those who are delivered via gliders which actually land in enemy territory. Impressed by German successes with airborne and air landed infantry during the 1940 campaign – most notably their *coup de main* at the Belgian fort of Eben Emael, Churchill had directed the War Office to form an equivalent British unit. Now in mid-1942, Britain's airborne forces, which would form the famous maroon-bereted Parachute Regiment on 1 August, were a serious worry for Rundstedt. The ability of paratroops and glider-borne infantry to land behind the lines and wreak havoc in the rear caused him great concern: 'The enemy on his island has held multiple airborne exercises. The purpose of these exercises is to practise blocking chokepoints, occupying bridges and structures to the rear of fighting units, taking airfields and raiding officers' staffs as well as depots, all hand-in-hand with the amphibious troops landed on the coastline.' Rundstedt's worry was justified; 302nd Infantry Division at Dieppe, for example, had conducted an exercise/wargame in April during which a battalion of German infantry, posing as British parachutists, had managed to land five miles south-east of the town, take it, and embark on simulated landing craft sent to extract them, all within five hours.[14]

However, Rundstedt also clearly identified the considerable downsides of employing air-landed troops and parachutists: 'The weak point of airborne troops lies in their necessarily long time spent in the air, their large drop zones and the time needed to form cohesive fighting units.' Therefore, German doctrine would rely on a 'ruthless' drive right into the Allied drop zones in which the enemy could be 'annihilated, before he can emerge as a fighting force and use his air-dropped heavy weapons'. For this very reason, Rundstedt had already signed an order which divided coastal areas into districts. Units were assigned to each district, tasked with planning responses to parachute or glider attack. The idea behind this was simple: if air landings were sighted, the units in the district where the landing was taking place could offer an immediate response during the enemy's moment of weakness.[15] OB West was not the only man in German uniform thinking about the threat posed by paratroops. Writing the Kriegsmarine's response to Hitler's Directive 40, Raeder noted that airborne troops posed a real risk to his precious naval coastal artillery.[16] Since they could be dropped far inland, airborne forces could rapidly attack artillery battery positions placed further to the rear. What is more, they would naturally attack from the rear, where there would be fewer defensive fortifications.

In his Basic Order, Rundstedt did not confine his thinking to aerial matters. He also noted the very real complicating factor of artificial smoke, which he warned would be used to shield any landing force when it was approaching the coast. Moreover, he made sure to raise awareness of the threat posed by armour. Though amphibious tanks had never been used before, Rundstedt had the foresight to warn his men: 'We cannot let ourselves be surprised. All heavy weapons must have armour-piercing ammunition to hand.' In light of the fact that the West was starved of resources, he was forced to concede that the anti-armour rounds could not be used liberally: 'These may only be used against armoured vehicles. Every round of this precious ammunition used against other targets will be missed dearly when the real armour comes.'

There had hitherto been considerable interest in learning how the Allies might bring armour to a German coastline – so much so that the Germans had an article from a 1941 issue of *Life* magazine translated and disseminated amongst coastal units. The article was nothing more than a puff-piece, showing all-action American heroes storming Lake Pontchartrain near New Orleans during an exercise, but the Germans clearly were concerned enough about amphibious armour to take note.[17] In December 1941, 302nd Infantry Division had received and distributed a pamphlet entitled 'Tactics of British Landing Operations', which warned that the British were capable of landing armour in the very first wave of an amphibious assault. On the back of this warning, Major General Haase attempted to acquire six more anti-tank guns for his front-line units.[18]

Rundstedt's Basic Order 13 was a surprisingly insightful document, especially in the hindsight of history. His acute awareness of both the strengths and weaknesses of airborne forces, still very much a novelty when he took up his position in the West, showed a level of insight possessed by all great captains in military history. However, it is striking what Rundstedt did not include in his Basic Order. Despite being ostensibly a joint force commander, a position supposed to come with responsibility and command authority over all forces in the occupied West, he included no details on how the Luftwaffe or Kriegsmarine should react to a large-scale landing, or what they could expect from their adversaries. Bluntly put, this was due to his powerlessness over naval or air forces. Since he had no authority in these domains, they were simply omitted from his survey. The lack of control that Rundstedt enjoyed over some of his own men and equipment was undoubtedly the greatest single weakness the 66-year-old OB West was forced to endure.

The lack of interest in and occasional downright opposition to operating cohesively with the other services was a pervasive trend in the Wehrmacht. Cultural aversion to what would today be called 'jointery' was evident at the very top of Nazi Germany. Hitler's High Command of the Armed Forces (*Oberkommando der Wehrmacht*, OKW) offers clear evidence of this fact. OKW was intended, much like Rundstedt's command in France, to be an integrated joint services organization which would involve the Army, Kriegsmarine and Luftwaffe equally in its decisions. When it was founded in 1938, Hitler personally assumed command of the Wehrmacht in its entirety, replacing General Werner von Blomberg, whose wife had been revealed to have posed for pornographic photos. But even this early form of joint direction was by all accounts a failure. OKW was a small, weak organization. It did not even have control over the whole armed forces, as the British Chiefs of Staff Committee did. The problem was exacerbated by the strains of war, and by 1942 the Army had taken total control in the East, with OKW in charge of all other theatres. Not surprisingly, this erratic command system led to squabbling between individual commanders over men and resources. The only man who could resolve such disputes was Hitler himself, who had since December 1941 been Chief of Staff of the Army. Throughout the war, OKW represented nothing more than an instrument of Hitler's personal will. Field Marshal Wilhelm Keitel and General Alfred Jodl, as OKW Chief of Staff and Chief of Operations Staff respectively, were mere 'yes men'. Even within OKW, the three component arms were far from equally represented. In 1942, for example, Luftwaffe officers assigned to OKW were outnumbered five to one by Army officers. No Luftwaffe officer of one-star rank (RAF Air Commodore or American Brigadier General) or above was employed there, in contrast to seven Army and two Kriegsmarine representatives of at least that seniority.[19] OKW went without a single permanent General-equivalent Kriegsmarine representative for three years from the outbreak of war.

As head of Germany's air force, Hermann Göring likewise rejected outright any serious cooperation with his land and naval partners. His oft-quoted boast that 'everything that flies belongs to me' perfectly epitomized his complete lack of interest in collaboration with his Army or Kriegsmarine counterparts. Unsurprisingly, he never agreed to cooperate meaningfully with the Kriegsmarine. Naval aviation – airframes dedicated to duties at sea – hardly existed in the Wehrmacht. To the limited extent that it did, it was owned and operated by the Luftwaffe – jealously guarded all the way by Göring. Unhelpfully, the Luftwaffe's chief was almost completely ignorant of naval matters. Consequently, Raeder's constant attempts to set up some kind of naval air force fell on deaf ears. These two very different men detested each other. While Raeder abhorred Göring's intransigence in hoarding aircraft, Göring despised what he saw as Raeder's interference in air matters. In his memoirs, after decades to consider the matter, the former Admiral of the Fleet launched a scathing personal attack on his long-dead rival:

> Of all the men close to Hitler, however, Göring was the one with whom I had my most violent battles. We were perfect opposites, both personally and ideologically. While he might have been a brave and capable flier in World War I, he lacked all the requisites for command of one of the armed services. He possessed a colossal vanity which, while amusing to some, and pardonable if it had been associated with other more significant qualities, was dangerous because it was combined with a limitless ambition. His penchant for show, and the exaggerated luxury in which he lived, set a bad example for the Luftwaffe.[20]

Raeder was in a strange position, since his Kriegsmarine did not own any operational aircraft carriers, for which a naval air arm would primarily have been suited. Britain's Fleet Air Arm, for example, operated first and foremost from aircraft carriers. The vast majority of operations out at sea from land airbases, such as reconnaissance and anti-submarine warfare, were handled by the RAF's Coastal Command. Nevertheless,

Raeder still desperately craved direct naval control over at least some aircraft, to take advantage of the speed and reach that air power provided. Considering Göring's general apathy towards the maritime domain, this was a reasonable request.

This pernicious Kriegsmarine/Luftwaffe dispute aside, there were more fundamental deficiencies in how the Wehrmacht's three services cooperated (or did not). Most absurd was the fact that the Luftwaffe's commander-in-chief held the special rank of *Reichsmarschall*, equivalent to a six-star general officer above every Army and Luftwaffe field marshal or Kriegsmarine admiral of the fleet. This made him technically superior to every single serviceman in the Wehrmacht, even Wilhelm Keitel, who headed OKW – nominally the Wehrmacht's High Command. In Hitler's Germany, one thing above all was certain: a personal relationship with the Führer guaranteed certain privileges within the Reich. For Göring and Raeder, both beneficiaries of a close association with Hitler, this meant that neither the Luftwaffe nor the Kriegsmarine would ever be subject to the orders of a single joint commander in the field. There existed no body which could force their hand. The only person who could do that was the Führer, and he was perfectly content to sit back and use his divide-and-rule philosophy. The US Army's official historian put it best, surmising pithily that 'the only unity of command in Germany rested in the person of Hitler'.[21]

Beside the thorny structural issues created by command culture, there remained the inescapable fact that the West was treated by the Germans as an unimportant theatre. Dominated by low-quality divisions, France was also used to rest and recuperate divisions that had fought in active combat. This brought about an inevitably dire state of affairs. On an inspection visit to the Channel coast in mid-1942, Admiral Raeder saw at first-hand the deficiencies of manpower and equipment across France's coastline. During his visit to the north, he was presented with requests for a heavy battery of several guns at Dieppe and Le Havre, which lay at the mouth of the Seine. Without the means to resource both places appropriately, Raeder decided to grant Le Havre its request. Dieppe, on the other hand, he later noted, was 'not so important'. On the western French coast at Brière, one of the four guns available – all of which were captured French models – went completely unmanned due to a personnel shortage. A battery of two 200mm guns at Brest, upon inspection, was found to have a shocking fire rate of as little as one round every five minutes. Raeder found critical failings within the leadership as well. In one case, he came across an officer, still actively serving, who was so mentally unstable that he was refusing to eat. As head of the Wehrmacht's naval service, he was justly concerned that the Kriegsmarine possessed not nearly enough means to give adequate warning before a large-scale raid. Of particular concern was the lack of patrol boats. Additionally, he had to rely on inter-service cooperation for air reconnaissance, because naval aviation was controlled by Göring's Luftwaffe. Even then, only a handful of Heinkel 111 reconnaissance planes was available for sorties in the Atlantic. In April 1942, for example, there had been only four mission-ready aircraft. Raeder felt that it was the fundamental weakness of reconnaissance and early warning which had led to the success of the Saint-Nazaire raid in mid-March.[22] He believed improvements in this area above all would prevent another similar operation from succeeding.

Raeder was the Kriegsmarine's commander-in-chief, but to deal with matters in the West in more detail he created the position 'Naval Group Command West', which held direct operational command over all naval units operating in the West. For most of 1942 this post was held by Admiral Alfred Saalwächter, who had been heavily involved in the German invasion of Norway two years earlier. Saalwächter was a submariner by trade, having commanded three U-boats in the First World War. By 1939 he had risen to high command, and in that year he and his career survived a brief investigation by the rather clumsily-entitled 'Office of the Führer's Commissary for the Observation of the Overall Spiritual and Ideological Education of the NSDAP'. In short, this was the government office that could exclude from public life persons who did not display enough loyalty and affiliation to Hitler's ideals. Fortunately for Saalwächter, he passed this purely political test, partly because he had worked well with his local Party branch in the past.[23] Now in 1942 at Naval Group West, Saalwächter commanded all naval units that operated in and around Western European waters, excluding the Norwegian and German coastlines. Importantly, his remit did not include U-boat fleet operations, which took place far out into the Atlantic. Saalwächter had gained great credit through his planning and executing of Operation Cerberus, the so-called 'Channel Dash' by the pocket battleships *Scharnhorst*, *Gneisenau* and *Prinz Eugen* in February 1942.

Raeder's uncomfortable partners in the Luftwaffe were led in France by Hugo Sperrle, commander of Luftwaffe's Air Fleet 3. Field Marshal Sperrle was a large, imposing figure. His gruff expression, coupled with the monocle often worn in his right eye, served to effectively intimidate those around him. Since 1940, Air Fleet 3 had been tasked with defending the airspace of France and the Low Countries. In this, Sperrle's airmen had proved extremely capable. Late in 1941 Air Fleet 3 was the first to take delivery of Germany's new Focke-Wulf 190 fighter/fighter-bomber aircraft. This was an outstanding radial engine design, and Eric 'Winkle' Brown, Britain's most notable test pilot, stood in awe of its speed and manoeuvrability when he had the chance to fly a captured model: 'The FW 190 [had] a performance equal, if not superior to that of the current Spitfire IX, her very high rate of roll making her a formidable aerobatic aircraft.'[24] During 1942, the fighter pilots of Air Fleet 3 proved their worth. Between January and mid-June 1942 RAF's Fighter Command had lost 259 aircraft in return for 58 kills in operations over occupied France, many of them to FW 190s. This success came despite Air Fleet 3 not having an integrated air defence system like the one found on the British side of the Channel and used during the Battle of Britain two years earlier.

A curious quirk of the German command system was that, while Field Marshal Sperrle and Admiral Saalwächter were the Luftwaffe and Kriegsmarine's overall operational commanders in the West, they had no Army equivalent. In fact, as the overall theatre commander, Field Marshal Rundstedt had direct operational control of all land units but not aerial or maritime ones – control of these was vested purely in Sperrle and Saalwächter respectively. This relationship created a situation where, in effect, Rundstedt's orders to Luftwaffe and Kriegsmarine would only be implemented if Sperrle or Saalwächter agreed. They were under no obligation to follow his instructions, even when confronted with an imminent or ongoing coastal landing.

The Luftwaffe suffered as much as its Army and Kriegsmarine partners from the failure to agree on a unified command structure. Quite apart from this, the Luftwaffe in France were doctrinally unprepared for coastal defence. There was no German doctrine specific to coastal defence to base preparations on, above all because Germany was primarily a continental land power. At their core, pre-war German ideas of air power were chiefly concerned with its offensive use in a land campaign, like the invasion of France in 1940 or the Soviet Union since June 1941. In these tasks the Luftwaffe was a superb tool for giving ground troops close air support and making interdiction strikes further behind enemy lines. This was quite different from defending a coastline, however. One reason for the lack of concrete plans for how air power would be used to defeat a landing lay in the absence of joint thinking in the Wehrmacht. While Gerd von Rundstedt as overall Western commander was focussed increasingly on coastal defence in 1942, this was not the case for Sperrle's air forces – they were more concerned with the RAF's repeated fighter sweeps over northern France. Sperrle and Rundstedt's unwillingness to discuss a joint air battle plan meant that none was ever devised. Nonetheless, there were two general principles baked into German air combat philosophy which would guide the fighter and bomber forces during a landing; firstly, fighters could best support friendly ground forces through intercepting enemy aircraft. Rather than attempting to support the troops on the ground directly, fighters would focus on shooting down enemy aircraft. This would indirectly support the ground war by neutralizing enemy bombers and their all-important fighter escort. Secondly, the Germans believed that, in general terms, attacks on ground targets outside friendly artillery range should represent the predominant effort of ground strike by fighter-bombers and bombers. Though this mentality left less visible support for the German boots on the ground – Allied units in close contact with German forces would consequently not receive as much attention from the Luftwaffe – it followed from this that units behind the lines, logistics elements, artillery and combat reserves, would come under air attack. In a coastal defence context, this would entail a focus on the warships and landing craft of an amphibious force, not the men on the beaches. This had the added benefit of reducing the likelihood of friendly fire from German aircraft on their own ground troops.

Chapter 4

A New Siegfried Line? The Myth of the Wehrmacht's 'Steely Rear'

With commitments on so many fronts in 1942, on land, at sea and in the air, Hitler's Reich was in no position to supply the West with the men and materiel needed to mount a solid defence against a concerted invasion effort. However, the German public did not want to hear about Germany's strategic headaches. Even in a dictatorship, maintaining public morale nearly three years into war remained crucial. Indoctrination in the strength of German arms and men was key – even if an attack came in the West, it would be quickly defeated with no effect whatsoever on the great campaign against the Bolshevist Soviets. A key goal of Goebbels' press campaign in this period was to prepare the men and women of the Reich psychologically for a large-scale landing in the West, to convince them that the so called 'Watch in the West' (*Wacht im Westen*) was invincible. To that end, the journalist Hans Wamper was invited to tour the defences on France's Channel coast in July. Near Calais, he described a unique view: 'From up high, our view of the water extends to England. The view is especially good. We can recognize England with the naked eye. We can see the radio towers and barrage balloons at Dover.' What really caught the war reporter's eye was what he saw on the French side of the Channel: 'Time and again, our view becomes fixed on what is to our right and left. Made of iron and concrete, armed with the best weapons, a defensive line of unimaginable size and integrity has arisen here.' Concluding his report, Wamper had a final message for those Germans, military or civilian, who might be worried about the so-called 'second front' encircling Germany: 'This front is more solid than ever – the Battle Line "Atlantic", the bulwark against England.' This could not have been further from the truth, but it was comforting to German ears all the same. Another newspaper report on 8 August similarly boasted of a 'vast defensive front that stretches from the North Cape to the Bay of Biscay'. It continued: 'We know that others have an obsession with the Second Front, which will supposedly take the heat off the Bolshevists. Every German knows that this is an illusion.'

It was not merely in the public realm of newspaper articles that Germany expressed confidence. Whatever the material and military situation may have been, in private talks German leaders told their Axis partners that all was well. Hitler was no exception. In a letter dated 4 August to his fellow dictator Benito Mussolini in Rome, he devoted a great deal of space to the issue of a possible second front in 1942. The Führer wrote to Il Duce:

> I consider this Second Front, Duce, as something utterly ridiculous. Since, in the democracies, the majority has the decisive voice, and with that comes basic human ignorance, one must always reckon with the possibility that the madmen will win the upper hand and try to open a Second Front ... Should the English and Americans really undertake this insane venture they will be surprised and outgunned, which, at least from 1942 onwards, will exorcise any wish for a repetition of that experiment on the European Continent once and for all.[1]

In a meeting with Japanese Ambassador Lieutenant General Hiroshi Ōshimam, the Reich's Foreign Minister Joachim von Ribbentrop discussed the chances of a large-scale landing in view of the Allies' precarious military position. Speaking in the north-eastern Polish village of Sztynort (known to the occupying Germans as Steinort), Ribbentrop told Ōshimam, 'Perhaps the English will now make some landing attempts in the West – we are even counting on it because Stalin has extorted this from Churchill, maybe with the threat that he will sign a separate peace with Germany otherwise.' The Foreign Minister then used a phrase pregnant with meaning for the British. 'At any point suitable for landings, we are prepared ... Any landing would simply mean a new Dunkirk.'[2]

Despite clear German overextension, the Allies were not confident of victory in 1942. By the end of June, General Erwin Rommel's Panzer Army Africa was at El Alamein, perilously close to the crucial Suez Canal. Army Group South seemed irresistible in its march towards the oil-rich Caucasus region of the Soviet Union. For the Allies, any map of Europe and Africa looked ominous. In the face of these worrying German advances, Churchill arranged a visit to Stalin in Moscow on 12 August. He arrived from Tehran in an American B-24 Liberator bomber, escorted by Soviet fighters high above, at 5 o'clock in the afternoon. A key part of this first meeting of the two warlords would be a discussion of the second front question. Crucially, towards the end of the first day's talks, Churchill hinted that he might be able to satisfy his Soviet ally's wishes with 'a raid of France on a large scale in order to seek information and to test the German resistance'. As a sign of his desperation to appease Stalin, he went on to admit that the British 'might lose as many as 10,000 men on this operation, which would be no more than a reconnaissance'.[3] This kind of 'sacrifice operation' had been discussed in London before, but this was the first time that Britain's wartime leader had gone into such detail during open discussion with the Soviets. It was undoubtedly a form of appeasement, although Churchill would certainly never have used that 'dirty word' to describe his offer to Moscow.

These details were of course unknown to the Germans, but German propaganda would not pass up the opportunity which Churchill's first visit to Stalin presented. Reflecting the 'strong man' nature of its own totalitarian despotism, the Nazi party line as dictated by Reich Press Chief Dietrich was necessarily personal. In a predictably petty slant, he directed German papers to point out that Stalin did not meet Churchill when he landed at the airport. Thus the *Hamburger Anzeiger* dutifully reported: 'When Churchill arrived in Moscow, as in Washington he gave his V-signal to the assembled crowd with his two fingers. Clearly, he believed he was pleasing them with this "victory sign". The Bolshevists misunderstood Churchill's outstretched fingers, because they believed … they meant the Second Front.' In a painfully prophetic brief to his pressmen on 8 August, Dietrich asked the Reich's journalists to cover the Anglo-Soviet Moscow Conference with the following approach:

Whenever there is a crisis for England and its allies, Churchill travels abroad. When he visited France, Dunkirk followed. When he visited Washington for the first time, Hong Kong fell. When Churchill travelled to Washington for a second time, Tobruk fell.

> If Churchill is visiting Moscow today, a new crisis is approaching. Churchill is always the herald of catastrophe.[4]

Dietrich could not believe his good fortune when the Dieppe raid ended in calamity less than a fortnight later.

As their adversaries were conducting heated diplomacy, the Germans were distinctly aware of the amphibious threat to their European coastlines. This is exemplified by the case of Hans Detlef Teske. Teske was born in 1924 in what was then Stolp, a small German town on the Pomeranian Baltic coast. Later, his home town was given to Poland as the country's border shifted westwards after the war, and it was known from then on as Słupsk. By his own admission, Teske was too young to remember Hitler coming to power in 1933, but he enjoyed what the Hitler Youth gave him when he joined in 1934. He especially appreciated the camping trips to western Germany and the opportunity to go hill climbing, because Pomerania was so flat. By the time war came in 1939, he was an apprentice in his father's printing shop in Stolp. When he was called up for war service in August 1941 as a 17-year-old, Teske wanted to join the parachutists but was refused permission by his father, who had served as an infantryman in the First World War. 'The infantry is bad enough, but parachutists are even worse', he told his youthful son. The young Teske played along for a while, but requested a transfer to the airborne forces as soon as he was put in uniform, in defiance of his father's wishes. After ground training he qualified as a parachutist. The trick when jumping from a three-engined Junkers 52 transport, he learned, was to jump forwards towards the wing, allowing the wind to carry you clear. Otherwise, your parachute cables might snap on the aircraft. However, thanks to Hitler's ban on parachute operations after the near-disaster on Crete in May 1941, Teske would never make a combat jump. After finishing training around the turn of the years 1941/42, Teske was posted to Normandy as a member of the 5th Parachute Regiment, which would sit in reserve and await an Allied landing.

After several postings around Normandy, in August 1942 Teske was posted to Brécy, a small village on the south-eastern end of the Cherbourg Peninsula. He and a small motorcycle section were stationed in a disused workshop on coastal alert. He became particularly fond of the omelettes served at the local café, and made sure to eat one every day. Eventually, he went there so often that the owner had an omelette ready for him as soon as he stepped through the door. But an invasion alarm on 16 August shattered his routine and tranquillity. 'We had to take the motorcycles out and left them on the roadside', Teske later recalled. He and his comrades then found a new home at the side of the road in a muddy ditch: 'We were in full uniform day and night. We were not allowed to take our shoes off [in case] they didn't fit when you tried to get into them.' What really struck him as out of the ordinary was the fact that, for the first time, he was given live ammunition for his rifle. The only other time this had happened was during John Frost's raid on Bruneval in February. 'Normally we were practically unarmed in France. When we went out we didn't have any ammunition, and when we went for marches we had rifles but no live ammunition in them. This time we realized something was going on.' Well into his later life, Teske believed steadfastly that the German high command knew that the Dieppe raid was coming: 'We were sleeping there in the ditches for three days and three nights, and that's when the British landed in Dieppe. They were three days late!'[5] That Teske's unit was placed on the coast and given live ammunition for the first time during their alarm on 16 August demonstrates a more concrete point: the Wehrmacht took the more general possibility of a large-scale raid or even an invasion of northern France incredibly seriously. At the start of August, Rundstedt had taken the decision to temporarily forbid civilians from holidaymaking or German servicemen from taking leave in coastal areas.[6]

Teske was not the only one thinking about landings in August. Hans-Paul Liebschner was stationed in Dinan in eastern Brittany. His job during his 'very pleasant occupation' (as he described it) was to carry post between Dinan and Dinard using a donkey and old two-wheeled French cart. He managed this despite, by his own admission, not knowing a donkey's 'one end from another'. He told an interviewer after the war that near the beginning of August he was sure something was going to start, but that 'nobody knew what or where'.[7] In reality, the Germans had no foreknowledge whatsoever of any Allied amphibious operation in August 1942. It is only with hindsight that a sudden deployment towards the coast became meaningful. The reality was that no Germans at any level of command had any concrete and actionable intelligence from any source that indicated a specific raid on Dieppe on 19 August (or near to it). German units were moved to and from the coast all the time, and the kind of alarms that Teske experienced in his ditch at the side of the road were common in France during 1942 – there was nothing out of the ordinary here. It just so happened that on 19 August all the warnings and alarms actually portended something. On the last day of October 1942, the Kriegsmarine War Staff diary even mentioned an agent who had apparently 'predicted' the August raid a week in advance.[8] Once again, this was an instance of information only becoming meaningful with perfect hindsight. A German veteran of 302nd Division who emigrated to Canada after the war summed things up well when speaking on Canadian television in 1967: 'We were prepared for the great unknown; that's what we were there for – not to await something certain.'[9]

Chapter 5

Facing Up Across the Channel

The raid on Dieppe, codenamed Jubilee, was supposed to be a simple one. The operation was planned as a temporary 'seize and hold' of Dieppe and its surrounding area involving the troops of six nations. A force of over 6,000 men was to land across six beaches in the early morning, take Dieppe and advance inland up to four miles, capturing the small aerodrome and the town of Arques-la-Bataille. This is where Allied planners believed German divisional headquarters was housed. Once a defensive perimeter around the town had been secured, the port would be destroyed using explosives laid by sappers. Commencing at around midday, the forces would conduct an orderly withdrawal, taking captured prisoners and invasion barges with them. Ideally, the withdrawal would be completed before evening, thereby preceding the arrival of significant German mobile reinforcements.

The bulk of the force, and those who would undertake the main assault, consisted of the 2nd Canadian Division under Major General John Roberts. These were all volunteers, as domestic political pressure had compelled Prime Minister W. L. Mackenzie King to allow Canadian conscripts to stay at home if they so wished. Canada's French-speaking population would not have stood for forced service overseas, though it is notable that many French-Canadians were at Dieppe. The main beach in front of the promenade was split for Jubilee's purposes into two parts; the eastern half was codenamed 'Red' and the western, 'White'. The Essex Scottish and Royal Hamilton Light Infantry Regiments would land here. To their left was 'Blue' beach in front of Puys, allocated to the Royal Regiment of Canada. To their right, the South Saskatchewan Regiment and Queen's Own Cameron Highlanders would take 'Green' beach at Pourville, which lay on the west flank of Dieppe as Puys did on the east. Significantly, the Canadians in front of Dieppe town (at Red and White) would have armoured support from the Churchill tanks of the Calgary Regiment. Critically, these had not been specially adapted for beach conditions. British Commandos (3 and 4 Commando) were to secure Dieppe's flanks. The latter would include a small party of US Rangers, itself a unit set in the Commando mould. Free Poles serving in the RAF, and those aboard the destroyer ORP *Ślązak*, came with them. Free French fighters served on small anti-aircraft gunboats, and New Zealand, Czech, American, Polish, Norwegian, Belgian and French airmen joined the British pilots of the RAF in the air in this truly multinational force.

In the skies, the British hoped that the Luftwaffe would be sucked into a massive air battle in which the RAF could not only destroy hundreds of German planes, but also draw additional air strength away from the Eastern Front. Close air support for the ground element would be provided by Boston bombers and cannon-armed Hurricanes. A flight of twenty-four American Flying Fortress bombers were tasked with making a high-altitude attack on the Abbeville-Drucat airfield – 35 miles east of Dieppe – at a set time about five hours after the initial landing. The air element was massive, commanded by the Air Force Commander Air Marshal Trafford Leigh-Mallory. On 19 August he would have command of a grand total of sixty-seven squadrons, fifty of which were fighter cover squadrons. These were to provide an 'air umbrella' under which the force could safely and freely operate. Preparing such a huge air offensive was a monumental logistical challenge. In the days and weeks prior to Jubilee's launch, the RAF had concentrated masses of fuel and ammunition in No. 11 Group's area in South-East England. Staggeringly, no fewer than 10m rounds of .303 ammunition and 712,000 gallons of 100-octane fuel had been accumulated within 11 Group in preparation for the air effort.[1]

At sea, the Allied force was commanded by Captain John Hughes-Hallett of the Royal Navy. Allied planners had decided against bringing battleships or even cruiser-level support because of the risk from German bombers, so naval fire support was limited. The ground force would have to make do with the relatively small 4-inch guns of the eight 1,000-ton Hunt-class destroyers escorting the naval force, as well as HMS *Locust*, a small river gunboat with one 4-inch gun. Further protection came from a swarm of small, fast and agile patrol boats that would reach the French coastline before the main naval group. German minefields in the Channel would be dealt with by 9th and 13th Minesweeping Flotillas. The naval force comprised a great variety of landing craft in which to bring the landing force to shore. The troops and their landing craft would be carried across the Channel in converted civilian ferries like HMS *Prince Charles* and HMS *Princess Astrid*. These weighed in at several thousand tons and would stay well back from the beaches, instead allowing the smaller landing craft to bring the troops all the way to the beaches. Facing this great international force were the men of the German 302nd Division. On 19 August, it was positioned much as it had been for the last few months. Like most German divisions of the low-quality 'static' type, the 302nd consisted of three infantry regiments (equivalent to a British or American brigade). These were the 570th, 571st and 572nd Infantry Regiments. The great length of the division's coastline meant that no continuous line of resistance was feasible. It had therefore been set up with various 'points of resistance' at vital locations.

The principal point of resistance was Dieppe proper, and so it was classified as a 'strongpoint'. This meant the division devoted a significant portion of its resources to the town and its immediate surroundings, stationing the best part of 571st Infantry Regiment in the Dieppe strongpoint, headquartered on the western headland near Dieppe castle, which proudly stood, as it had done since the fifteenth century, on the high ground to the west of the town. Only one of the regiment's battalions was left in reserve, at Ouville to the west. Two companies of engineers were also stationed within Dieppe itself; although their primary role was certainly not to close with and kill the enemy, they were trained to fight as infantry when required. Additionally, a healthy portion of the division's own field artillery was located within the town. These were not the coastal batteries over which there had been so much wrangling with the Kriegsmarine; rather, they were 302nd Division's own organic artillery support. Static field defences littered the seafront. Pillboxes and a lengthy 2ft-high sea wall dominated the beach in front of the town. Barbed wire ringed Dieppe, and searchlights stood ready along the coast and in the inner port area. One house had been demolished on the west side of town to make room for a dual-purpose anti-aircraft and coastal defence gun. On the eastern side of the main port entrance, four rows of dragon's teeth guarded the exit from the beach. Although the Germans did not have the means to construct proper concrete fortifications, the field defences they had built created an essentially continuous line of defence across the width of Dieppe. Not to be ignored in Dieppe's centre were the port commandant and his protection company of 72 men. Another 200 men manned the Kriegsmarine signals centre, port control and other stations within the harbour. Between Berneval and the main town of Dieppe was the village of Puys, rendered 'Puis' in some accounts. This lay in front of Blue beach, and though it was a distinct settlement separate from Dieppe town, the Germans considered it part of their central Dieppe 'strongpoint', and it was ringed with barbed wire.

As 571st Regiment formed the centre of 302nd Division's line, 572nd Regiment formed the right. This included the village of Berneval, where stood much of the Germans' coastal artillery – four 105mm and three 170mm guns of 770 Army Coastal Artillery Battery's 2nd Troop (written as 2/770 Battery). The defensive positions at Berneval were much less densely occupied by infantry than those in Dieppe proper; only one small picket group of one non-commissioned officer and nine private soldiers was committed here, though the crews of 2/770 Battery's guns could act as infantry if their position came under direct assault. Essentially, the Army's heavy guns at Berneval were expected to defend themselves. The effectively impassable ground in front of the village justified this disposition to a certain extent. Aside from a short section of barbed wire, an observation post and a handful of pillboxes, the coast in front of Berneval was bare. The village was a particularly valuable position, containing a Luftwaffe radar station. Accordingly, around a hundred Luftwaffe personnel were stationed in the village at the time of the Dieppe raid. Entrusted with neutralizing this position was 3 Commando. Like 4 Commando's 'Orange' beach in the far west, 3 Commando's 'Yellow' was split into two parts, labelled 'Yellow I' and 'Yellow II'. Yellow I lay in front of the eastern part of Berneval, with Yellow II to its west.

The western flank of Dieppe was relatively weakly defended, with only a scattering of minor units from 571st Regiment making up the defence. The most important 'point of resistance' here was in Quiberville village, through which the River Saâne flows. Here was 'Orange II', the eastern section of Orange beach where 4 Commando would land. One infantry company of 571st Regiment as well as a machine gun section were located there. A short distance to the east was 'Orange I', which lay directly in front of the essentially undefended village of Vasterival. Further down the Saâne was the village of Ouville. This housed the 571st Regiment's regimental reserve, placed here so that it could respond to threats on a broad front. This reserve included most of 571st Regiment's 1st Battalion, as well as a precious anti-tank unit of company strength. Significantly, 302nd Division had little anti-tank capability. Weapons and munitions were few and far between. One company (a unit containing around 150 men) in 571st Infantry Regiment possessed only one medium anti-tank gun.

In 1942 the town looked remarkably like it had done two years earlier. Germany's war situation simply did not allow the urgency in construction that would have been required for strong, permanent battlements. When Reichsmarschall Hermann Göring visited Dieppe with Field Marshal Sperrle in March 1942, the former noted that there had been significant work on low-grade field fortifications built by the men with their own basic equipment such as shovels, spades and barbed wire. However, heavy fortifications built by specialist engineers were still generally lacking, though OT (Organization Todt) was present in Dieppe and had been working on light fortifications. Some of these workers would be killed during the raid, despite the fact that, according to the laws of war, they were non-combatant civilian engineers. Wooden fortifications were common, but the shortages of material in 302nd Division's area of responsibility were acute. In an effort to help, the Reichsmarschall enquired why the men did not simply use wood from the forest. After some discussion, this was agreed, though the deputy CO of 571st Infantry Regiment hastened to request that fruit trees were not cut down; his men were fond of eating what grew on them. Göring's solution to a shortage of iron was simple: break up Dieppe's houses and take it from there. The Reichsmarschall promised that he would use his considerable political influence to make this happen.[2] Around the time that Göring visited Dieppe, plans were drawn up for 'reinforced field works', or steel-reinforced concrete fortifications.

An anti-tank wall along the beach was one of the few significant structures built in the two years since occupation began. One noteworthy change to the landscape was the flooding of two rivers at towns to the west of Dieppe; the Scie at Pourville and the Saâne at Quiberville. The Germans had done this in order to restrict any amphibious force's movement shortly after landing. The lack of fortification development at Dieppe and coastal positions like it was the symptom of one inescapable fact: namely that in 1942, Hitler's Wehrmacht was fighting on so many fronts that the West, a zone of relative inactivity, was nothing more than a sideshow – perhaps even less than that. Attacking the Soviet Union in June 1941 without neutralizing the threat from the British Isles was a monumental strategic blunder, as was declaring war on the United States in December 1941 without any means of bringing violence to continental American shores. In short, the Germans' own strategic folly had stretched the Wehrmacht to its limits.

Due to their scarcity, any anti-armour formations were vitally important to Major General Haase at division HQ. The Germans could not rule out the use of armour by the invaders even in a technically challenging amphibious assault. On 6 December 302nd Division received guidelines on combating British landing operations – these included the confident claim that the British would land armour in the first wave of any large-scale assault. Haase, realizing that this would not give him time to bring up anti-armour reserves from other units, requested six extra anti-tank guns for his men.[3] Later, Dieppe Port Commandant Commander (*Fregattenkapitän*) Wahn conducted tests of armoured vehicles during an anti-invasion exercise in early 1942. Wahn found that a landing with any kind of heavy armoured vehicle like a tank would be near to impossible because of the pebbled beach, which trapped his test vehicles and rendered them immobile. He concluded simply, 'Now we know the British cannot land here with tanks.'[4] Consequently, 302nd Division did not feel obliged to mine the beach, nor were any heavy anti-tank guns stationed there on a permanent basis. Nonetheless, it would have been foolish to ignore the armoured scenario entirely, and rightly, the Germans did not do so.

Just east of Quiberville along the coast stood the lighthouse at Phare d'Ailly. Although there were no infantry stationed here, this point was incredibly important to German defensive plans. For one thing, the lighthouse served as a crucial aircraft reporting centre, meaning that headquarters would have early warning of approaching air raids. A naval radar team also found themselves within the lighthouse's 'point of resistance' defensive network. Moreover, the structure served as an observation post for the coastal battery about three quarters of a mile to the rear. At Varengeville, 813 Battery consisted of six Krupp-made *Kanone* and sixteen 150mm guns of First World War vintage. It was distant from any infantry support, and though both Army and Kriegsmarine officers had known about the precarious position of 813 Battery for some time, they could not convince their high command to commit the men necessary to relocate it. In May, to prove his point, divisional commander Haase had organized a mock Commando-style attack on the Varengeville battery, using some of his own troops to simulate the enemy. In this exercise the 'Commandos' were able to take and destroy 813 Battery with little trouble. Still Haase could not gain agreement to move the guns at Varengeville to a more defensible location.[5] As the Kriegsmarine held tactical control of Army coastal artillery guns, 813 and 2/770 Battery came under the command of Sea Defence Commandant, Seine-Somme, Captain Hans-Udo von Treschkow, who was headquartered in Le Havre. Captain Treschkow's most important duty on 19 August would be deciding whether his guns should engage targets at sea or on land.

At the higher divisional level of reserves, 302nd Division had placed an entire infantry regiment, the 570th, in the rear at Eu, which lay 17 miles east of Dieppe, just landward of the port town of Le Tréport. The men of 570th Infantry Regiment were the closest and readiest reserves available to Haase in case of an amphibious landing, but they were not especially mobile. It is a basic tenet of military tactics that reserves are held back from the front line so that they can remain flexible and respond to threats at any point. This demands speed above all. However, there was limited transport available due (above all) to the low priority of France as a theatre of war in German eyes. Most of the division's 'mobility' was decidedly makeshift. In 302nd Division's infantry companies, for instance, all heavy battle equipment was loaded onto improvised metal wagons drawn by two horses. Each infantry company used bicycles as personal transport. The rear area around Dieppe was relatively well supplied with motorized vehicles ready for use, but even these had been commandeered from the Organization Todt civilians completing construction work in the town. The only dedicated, purpose-built transportation available to 302nd Division was 2nd Transport Column in Boscrocourt, near where 570th Regiment was stationed at Eu to the east of Dieppe. Indeed, on 19 August, the battalion would ride on 2nd Transport Column's vehicles westwards on their way to reinforce Dieppe. Some arrangements for transport bordered on the comical. One anti-tank unit had been outfitted with bicycles, and so had been named the Anti-Tank Company Cyclist Squadron. Even those not fit for battle were pressed into service, so desperate was Haase for manpower. He included 117 wounded men from

St Aubin Hospital in his official order of battle, adding slightly to his reserve strength.

As a divisional commander, Major General Haase reported to his superiors at Corps level. In 302nd Division's case this was LXXXI (81st) Corps under the command of Lieutenant General Adolf Kuntzen, headquartered in Rouen. As a Corps commander, Kuntzen had responsibility for three divisions: Haase's 302nd centred around Dieppe, as well as the 332nd and 711th to the west; 302nd Division therefore stood at the extreme right of LXXXI Corps' area of responsibility. In Kuntzen's Corps-level reserve, the most relevant to the Dieppe sector were two battalions of the 676th Infantry Regiment. These were part of 332nd Infantry Division to the 302nd's left. Additionally, the 81st Tank Company was quartered in Yvetot, a town approximately 25 miles south-west of Dieppe. This unit consisted entirely of captured tanks left over from the 1940 conquest of France. Between the Corps level and Rundstedt at OB West stood Fifteenth Army, commanded by General Curt Haase. He was not to be confused with Konrad Haase commanding 302nd Division, so German soldiers nicknamed Fifteenth Army's Haase 'the Big Haase', while 302nd Division's was 'the Little Haase'. Fifteenth Army had responsibility for all units across the entirety of the Le Havre–Pas de Calais coast. 'Big Haase' was a somewhat odd character. He was sixty years old and prone to making rather erratic pronouncements to his troops. During the period of tides which would favour an invasion, from 10 August 1942, he gave a particularly strange Order of the Day to the troops, filled with exclamations like 'Fear does not exist!', 'I have looked into your eyes! You are German men!' and 'Them or us!' Concluding his address, General Haase told those under his command that 'the German Army has in the past received all kinds of tasks from the Führer and has always carried them out. The Army will carry out this task too. My soldiers will not be the worst!' One might have expected him to say something slightly more encouraging. Nonetheless, Haase ordered this particular message distributed as far down the command chain as possible, and placed in open areas so that every man could read it. British intelligence officers crafting a character analysis of the elder Haase noted that in photos that 'he would easily pass for ten or fifteen years' older than his actual age. They surmised that this was the reason for his being given a command in France, where not much action was expected.

They commented on his hysterical Order of the Day, concluding that 'Big Haase' had 'all the characteristics of an old and worried German General, who, fearful of losing his job, seeks to pacify his master by most unmilitary invocations of his name.'[6] Perhaps they were right, as the old and worried general lost his command in December 1942 and died in February 1943 of heart disease.

If much more powerful armoured support was required, 10th Panzer Division under the command of Brigadier Wolfgang Fischer stood ready near Amiens, south of Le Tréport. A few months previously, 10th Panzer had returned from the Eastern Front for rest and recuperation. Despite this, it was still a formidable formation and one of the few out-and-out armoured units in France. In addition, the motorized SS Division *Leibstandarte Adolf Hitler* was located near Paris, in the process of being converted into a Panzergrenadier division. Though it was located at the French capital, *Leibstandarte Adolf Hitler*'s mobility gave it great operational range. The division paraded with its new trucks down the Champs Élysées in August, and Hitler was particularly proud of his namesake division's drive through Paris. 'In order to give the French population an image of the real situation and to put the proclamations of the British radio and secret broadcasters in the right light', he boasted to Mussolini, 'I have had the *Leibstandarte* go through Paris, which is today a strong armoured and motorized infantry division with around 22,000 men.'[7] But Hitler was overly enthusiastic – the *Leibstandarte* had not yet been fully converted. Only in November would it be renamed *Panzergrenadier Division Leibstandarte SS Adolf Hitler*. One man who was particularly pleased with this refit was 19-year-old Herbert Schröder. Having grown up on a farm in the tiny village of Hohengörsdorf south of Berlin, he had had enough of dealing with horses, which were ubiquitous in the Wehrmacht, and to his joy, he became a driver. For Schröder, being a member of one of the few high-quality formations in France was a great honour. In a group of more than thirty candidates for places in the *Leibstandarte*, he was one of only three to be selected: 'It was a great thing! There was nothing negative about it. We were sent wherever there was a fire. We were an elite unit … We had young people who had no wife or children. They were easier to "conduct" – they had no [other] relationships.'[8] However, *Leibstandarte Adolf Hitler* was the exception rather than the rule. Its high standards and the great *esprit de corps* found within all SS divisions was absent throughout the poorer-quality divisions in France, especially the 'static' ones guarding the coastline such as the 302nd under Major General Haase.

On 19 August 1942 the forces of Field Marshal Hugo Sperrle's Air Fleet 3 were spread across France, Belgium and the Netherlands, as they had been since 1940. Sperrle's most powerful fighter units within range of Dieppe were the 26th and 2nd Fighter Wings, or *Jagdgeschwader* (commonly abbreviated as JG). As per Luftwaffe doctrine, these were each split into three groups called *Gruppen*. Each *Gruppe* normally had responsibility for three sub-units, each called a *Staffel* (plural *Staffeln*). A *Staffel* was the rough equivalent of an RAF squadron – i.e. it was the Luftwaffe's most basic tactical and organizational building block. All in all, a Luftwaffe JG operated approximately 130 aircraft each – up to 30–40 airframes per *Gruppe* and roughly twelve aircraft to each *Staffel*. JG 2 and JG 26 were equipped mainly with the superb Focke-Wulf 190 fighter-bomber, which had first appeared over French skies late in 1941. Exceptionally for a Luftwaffe *Geschwader*, both JG 2 and JG 26 included two special-purpose *Staffeln* on top of their standard strength. Their 10th *Staffeln* were both dedicated FW 190 ground attack units, which could carry bombs under their wings. Additionally, their 11th *Staffeln* were both *Höhenjagdstaffel*, or specialist high-altitude flights. These did not fly with the standard FW 190 because of that aircraft's poor high altitude performance. Rather, the 11th *Staffeln* flew the ever-trustworthy Bf 109, which was more suited to high-altitude combat. As a result, the fliers of JG 26's 2nd *Staffel* were nicknamed the 'Abbeville Boys' by the RAF after their home airfield near the mouth of the Somme. JG 26 could call no less a character than Adolf Galland, a former commander and one of Hitler's greatest flying aces with at least 100 victories in the air to his name. Succeeding him in the *Geschwader* during August 1942 were his two brothers, Paul and Wilhelm-Ferdinand who, although not sharing their sibling's extraordinary talent for aerial combat, were solid fighter pilots. The Galland family would claim two kills on 19 August – one for each brother. Taking into account aircraft not fit for service due to maintenance, on the morning of 19 August Sperrle would have 230 fighter aircraft of all types available with which to defend Dieppe.[9]

Complementing Air Fleet 3's fighter strength was Bomber Wing 2, known to the Germans as *Kampfgeschwader 2* or simply KG 2. Like

Sperrle's fighter forces, his bombers occupied a broad front across occupied Western Europe. KG 2 was exclusively equipped with the Dornier 217 medium bomber, with the entire *Geschwader* operating around 100 of these. Known affectionately as the 'flying pencil' for its particularly long and thin fuselage, the Do 217 was an older but still effective bomber type. A detail that would be important on 19 August was the fact that KG 2 was a night bomber force not accustomed to operating in daylight. Ever since the end of the Battle of Britain in summer 1940, the Germans had launched insignificant nuisance raids against the British Isles. KG 2 had been the main bomber force responsible for these ever since the *Geschwader* had relocated from the Eastern Front in 1941. Elements of KG 40 and KG 77, flying Ju 88s and Do 217s, also took part in Dieppe's air battle. The bombers had significantly greater range, and on 19 August some would fly from as far afield as Belgium and the Netherlands. For reconnaissance purposes, Sperrle possessed Reconnaissance Squadron (*Aufklärungsgruppe*) 123. This was nominally a *Geschwader*-level unit, but like all Luftwaffe reconnaissance units it possessed fewer airframes than even a single fighter *Gruppe*. Reconnaissance Squadron 123 operated only twenty-one aircraft of all types in July 1942.[10]

At first glance, this collection of military might seem formidable, but Air Fleet 3 was in fact severely depleted. Sperrle had about a third of the aircraft normally allocated to an Air Fleet in the Luftwaffe, and he was particularly weak in terms of twin-engined bomber aircraft. Not only this, but Sperrle's air forces would have to fly in from all over Western Europe to join in the air battle over Dieppe. The area around Dieppe did include an aerodrome, which had in the past housed fighter forces, but in August 1942 there were only miscellaneous aircraft such as air-sea rescue planes stationed there. Significantly, however, the airfield was protected by a sizeable anti-aircraft 'flak' force, in addition to a reporting section which would plot both friendly and enemy aircraft during Dieppe's air battle.

Chapter 6

Eve of Battle – 18 August

So, at sundown on 18 August 1942, the Dieppe Division was in place. All was quiet. Fifteenth Army, which controlled every German division from Le Havre to Calais, had mandated an increased state of readiness for the period from 10 to 20 August. This meant that at night every single defensive position had to have a duty officer awake at all times. Fifteenth Army was expected to take the brunt of any Allied assault, and since May 1942 it had possessed six 'Cases', or pre–planned operational responses that could be implemented at a moment's notice. One covered the Netherlands, two covered the French Channel coast and another two focussed on the Atlantic Coast; there was even a further plan in case the Allies invaded the Iberian Peninsula. Alhough there was an official state of readiness within Fifteenth Army on the morning of 19 August, that does not mean it was necessarily heeded. In La Maison Blanche at Pourville, a house so large that it was more like a mansion, a party of German officers billeted there had broken every possible rule by staying up well into the night drinking, in celebration of a comrade's promotion. They had invited some young Frenchwomen to participate in the festivities, and several had even been persuaded to stay the night.[1] One consequence of Haase's increased readiness order was that the front-line infantry were supposed to sleep in their fatigues, though this was quite often ignored. Nor did these measures extend to the other services. Even during the operation of Fifteenth Army's blanket readiness order, the Luftwaffe had taken no significant special precautions, and had continued its regular practice of granting leave to its personnel in the evening. Nor were its planes made ready for instant take-off by pre-fuelling or pre-loading with ordnance. Considering that it took around two hours for a squadron-sized unit to be fully bombed-up, this was a serious oversight.

Over the course of the previous thirty days, a total of 2,503 raw recruits had been transferred to Haase's division in place of the grizzled veterans sent to the east, a figure which represented about a fifth of the division's full fighting strength. Yet there had been precious little time to adequately train these fresh-faced replacements in the intricacies of coastal defence duties.[2] The majority of these recruits were not Germans, but Poles. They had had at best a month's training, at worst not more than a fortnight's. Consequently, they were not well motivated; above all, they wanted to see the war come to an end so that they could return home. Polish soldiers widely ignored the order to sleep in their uniform during August's period of increased readiness – why endure discomfort to assist the very same people who had invaded and brutally occupied their homeland? To prevent the Poles conspiring as a collective, their German masters attempted to split them up. However, because 302nd Division had so often been reinforced with foreign conscripts, this ambition often fell by the wayside. Many sections – three or four of which formed a platoon – consisted of one German NCO and nine Poles. Private Otto Samulewitsch's section included only three Germans, one of whom was a priest. Five of the others were Polish, one was Belgian and another Czech.[3]

As these defenders looked out to sea, the coast appeared calm. French civilians had that very day thought a spot of relaxation was in order and gone swimming in the sea. Flying over the gorgeous countryside surrounding Dieppe, Luftwaffe bombers were returning from southern England; even at this point in the war, the Germans persisted in occasional nuisance raids on Britain. Once they had landed back in France, the bombers' maintenance and refuelling was conducted at the usual relaxed pace. German fighters were travelling to or were already at their night dispersal airfields, so that they were not concentrated in the same place in case of an Allied air raid. On the ground, Lieutenant Hermichan and Sergeant Wilius of JG 26's 3rd *Gruppe* were celebrating, each having shot down a Spitfire in a skirmish over the Channel that day.[4] Best of all, these were both confirmed victories ready to be painted on their aircraft. At midnight, Admiral Alfred Saalwächter at Naval Group West put an E-boat fast patrol squadron stationed at Boulogne on half an hour's notice. He could see just as well as Haase that conditions were favourable for a possible invasion. These were the only significant naval forces available in the Channel on 19 August. Another E-boat unit would have been available had they not been laying mines in Lyme Bay along England's south-western coast the previous night. These were now refitting and unavailable for action. Dieppe port was as a matter of course protected by a small band of harbour protection boats, but these represented nothing more than a thin tripwire. All that was expected of these tiny craft was to fire their alarm rockets when an enemy force was spotted, and afterwards beat a hasty retreat. They were hardly combat platforms, being equipped merely with a machine gun or two. Unbeknownst to the Allied force preparing to leave their home ports in England, at 2100 a small German five-vessel convoy, protected by two sub-chasers and a small minesweeper, had departed Boulogne on their way to dock at Dieppe. By early morning the next day they would be nearing their destination.

Captain Hans Ditz was an artillery battery commander attached to the 302nd Division. He had only recently been reassigned to take command of four guns situated on Dieppe golf course, on the high ground between the main town and Pourville. Ditz later remarked that a golf course was the perfect place to put a gun position, as the rises and troughs needed to protect it were ready-made. His men were quartered in a stable which had previously been occupied by a flock of sheep. As an officer, though, Captain Ditz enjoyed rather more luxurious accommodation – he was given a room in a nearby golfing hotel by a fellow officer in the Luftwaffe. Several hundred metres in front of the golf course, right on the coast of the western headland, was Ditz's observation post. From here he could observe targets that his inland guns could not see directly, and direct fire against them. Ditz, suitably impressed, wrote later: 'It was the best observation post that I had in my service as a fighting soldier. Here, we were like kestrels sitting on a church tower, the whole world sitting deep beneath our feet.' At midday on the 18th Ditz went out riding with another artillery officer to see a mutual friend for coffee and cakes. It was a long but pleasurable ride, not least because of the glorious sunny weather. Alas, their friend was out on manoeuvres, and so the two thirsty officers rode rather dejectedly back home. Ditz was fatigued by the whole episode and quickly found his way to bed.[5] Also turning in for the night was Georges Guibon, a former hotelier resident in Dieppe. He had been writing a meticulous diary of the occupation and sat down to write his entry for 18 August, recalling a conversation he had overheard between a couple of German soldiers that day – they had been discussing the air raid on Rouen the previous day. 'The Tommies are coming', the soldiers insisted, pointing to the sky. 'Some say the English are going to land', the Germans continued, 'they have to land – they can't do otherwise.'[6]

In the cloak-and-dagger world of espionage, a great game of deception was afoot. On Rundstedt's orders, German intelligence had for months been leaking false information to their adversaries on the other side of the Channel, in what they called a *Gegenverbindungsspiel*, literally 'counter-connection game'. These *G-Spiele*, as they were known, were an important tool in the German intelligence arsenal. By placing their own operatives in Allied spy networks, the Germans could feed their enemies false information. The *G-Spiel* system was in full operation before Dieppe. A few weeks before the raid, on Rundstedt's orders, a German double agent had reported to Allied spies back in Britain that the German vehicles in Dieppe were painted with the symbol of a white church topped by a small tower. This, the German operative slyly suggested, was some kind of unit identifier which could be used to determine which German division was quartered in the town. Of course, there was no unit displaying such an emblem anywhere near Dieppe – 302nd Division's emblem, for instance, consisted simply of two crossed swords. This kind of disinformation was commonly employed in *GV-Spiele*, but most significantly – and misleadingly for Allied intelligence – was the carefully chosen language used in this false report. Whoever this faceless agent was, he was a master of deception. When he made contact with England, he used the English word 'nave' to describe the fictional church emblem he had supposedly seen. This, however, was intentionally misleading. While 'nave' does indeed mean the central interior section of a church or cathedral, it can also mean 'barque', a multiple-masted sailing vessel. Indeed, 'nave' stems from the Latin *navis*, meaning 'ship', and 110th Division's emblem, with its large, white Viking sailing boat, fitted this interpretation perfectly.

No doubt partly as a result of this clever game of deception, Combined Operations Headquarters' intelligence officers, led by an RAF wing commander, wrongly concluded that the German 110th Division was stationed in Dieppe. They mistakenly believed that 302nd Infantry Division had been stationed at Dieppe but had moved to the Eastern Front midway through 1942. They rated 110th Division as 'potentially a high quality field-force division'. It was indeed a good-quality division, but it was in fact 1,500 miles away wrestling with the Red Army in the immense Battle of Rzhev in front of Moscow. One can only speculate how much greater the defeat at Dieppe would have been had a high-quality mobile division like the 110th been present.[7] Also, it was not just the Germans in France who would be surprised by Jubilee. British agents embedded in the northern Normandy area remained blissfully unaware that a massive raid was about to be launched straight towards them. Although their pre-arranged task in case of a landing was to support the military effort through (amongst other methods of disruption) blowing up railway lines, London had not involved its spies in France in the operational planning.

Part II

19 August, Day of Decision

Chapter 7

Confusion: 0430–0700 hrs

The first inkling that the Germans had of Jubilee came an hour before dawn. At 0430 hours German time, a small group of ships approaching Dieppe from Boulogne, designated Convoy 2437, was just five nautical miles north-west of its destination. Commanded by Lieutenant Wurmbach on the 300-ton submarine chaser *UJ 1411*, Convoy 2437 had so far enjoyed a peaceful and routine trip. Stars were still visible through the light cloud in an otherwise clear early morning sky. This day, 19 August, was to be the hottest of the month, with a morning temperature of 19° centigrade rising to 24° in the afternoon. A gentle breeze blew from the south-west at between six and ten knots, and high tide was at 0503. The merchantmen were lightly armed, with nothing more than small 20mm cannons between them. Slightly punchier were the 88mm guns carried by the two 300-ton sub-chasers, *UJ 1411* and *UJ 1404*. Wurmbach commanded the former, while Sub-Lieutenant Max Berner captained the latter. Described by some of his men as 'unusually stupid' for an officer, Berner was also an heedlessly callous individual. When one of his men lay sick in Norway, Berner had said to him, 'Hurry up and die, then they'll send us your relief!' The escort was completed by a minesweeper, *M 4014*. The worst this small band of seafarers expected to face was a nuisance attack by British fast attack boats, as was typical in the Channel. At half past the hour, the sub-chaser's crew detected peculiar anomalies off to starboard on their sonar screens, and *UJ 1411*'s crew quickly hurried to their action stations. At 0448, lookouts on the convoy's starboard side saw strange outlines on the horizon. Gradually, the silhouettes of small craft grew larger and larger, heading straight for them. The three patrol boat escorts fired star shells. With the immediate area now bathed in light, the convoy could see as plain as day one of these British boats bearing down on them. Almost immediately, a hail of fire from the German convoy hit the British intruder, causing it to burst into flames. More fast boats appeared to starboard and came under equally heavy fire.

The action was confused and frantic. It took place at such close quarters that *UJ 1411*'s crew were in a position to lob four hand grenades at their enemies. *UJ 1411* had a particularly eventful encounter, her crew registering several hits on a large landing craft as well as other vessels. Despite his marked inferiority in both firepower and numbers, Wurmbach decided to press home the attack. With battle smoke fogging up the waters, he launched depth charges as an improvised projectile, hoping in vain to hit the enemy, more by luck than judgement. With his crew's standard weapons, however, Wurmbach later claimed to have sunk two fast patrol craft. Time and again, though, *UJ 1411* was forced to turn away, making smoke for cover, as the return fire was simply too strong to handle. *UJ 1411* alone had expended over 300 37mm rounds and 800 20mm cannon shells, as well as 3,000 machine gun rounds and four grenades.[1]

While *UJ 1411* managed to escape, others were less lucky. The other sub-chaser in Convoy 2437, *UJ 1404* commanded by Max Berner, was hit multiple times and knocked out of action, burning ferociously. HMS *Brocklesby* later scuttled the smouldering wreck after twenty-five of her forty-four crew had been rescued and made prisoner. The others perished, including Berner himself. Ironically, Berner had deliberately pushed for assignment to a sub-chaser command in the Channel – he had been desperate to win an Iron Cross First Class, something which came to pass only shortly before 19 August. When Wurmbach eventually made his decision to withdraw he wisely ordered his men to cease firing, so that their position was not betrayed to the countless RAF aircraft overhead. All the other vessels followed suit, except for one. In the inevitable confusion of battle the crew of *Franz*, one of the coastal motor merchantmen under escort, did not realize that their comrades had turned tail. *Franz* and her crew continued alone on their way to Dieppe, oblivious to their isolation.[2]

From their position in Berneval to the east of Dieppe, a small section of German infantry heard the sounds of battle out to sea at 0445. The crew of a Luftwaffe radar station in the village rushed to man their equipment. Minutes later, Admiral Otto Schultze, the Commanding Admiral of France, received the following brief teletype message: '0450 hrs 4 nautical miles off Dieppe – attack by surface naval forces on convoy'.[3] As early as 0352, a Luftwaffe sea-radar station in Pourville had already picked up the Allied ships approaching Dieppe. This contact was relayed by the Luftwaffe personnel there to their naval superiors at the radar plotting centre in Boulogne. Fortuitously for the approaching raiding force, this contact was assumed to be Convoy 2437 transiting from Boulogne to Dieppe. In any case, the Kriegsmarine harboured a distrust of the Luftwaffe and the information it provided – hardly a new problem.[4] The Germans' picture of events was further confused by the collision of Convoy 2437 with the patrol boats guarding the eastern side of the Allied raiding party.

One minute before dawn, at 0530, Major General Haase at 302nd Division headquarters reported the action off the coast to his superiors at LXXXI Corps. Despite this, most of 302nd Division was not at an increased state of readiness; the men still believed the sounds of gunfire to be coming from a standard small-scale coastal skirmish, a common event in the Channel. While this was happening, the first shots from coastal artillery were being let loose. Just to the east of Dieppe, at Puys, artillery opened fire on a group of fast patrol boats that had approached the coastline. Two emergency signal flares fired by observers in Dieppe shot into the half-light sky.[5] These came from one of the three harbour protection boats and the 11-man naval signal station on Dieppe's eastern cliffs. The signal station challenged some of the approaching craft by light signal, but to no avail. After firing off their warnings, the three picket boats hurried into the safety of Dieppe harbour, which they managed to do unscathed. Just like Lieutenant Wurmbach's *UJ 1411*, their radio sets were not functioning, so they were unable to raise the alarm through the proper channels. Even so, the patrol boat captains had the impression until well after 0600 that this action was just another convoy attack, though a bit closer to the coast than usual.[6] Some infantrymen complained later that they had not been given enough warning, and that the alarm had not been raised early enough.[7] Ideally, the noise and visual signals should have instantly roused the men from their sleep, but this did not happen. In the heat of the moment, the flares and sounds were not heeded as they should have been by 302nd Division's men. Many, especially those to the west of Dieppe, remained blissfully unaware of what was happening just a short distance away. Soon, Allied aircraft began bombing Dieppe, using Bostons and Hurricanes in a close air support role. One German warrant officer later described this opening scene: 'At first light, English fighters and bombers suddenly appeared and covered the city and most of our coastal defences with bombs … But our bunkers, trenches, barbed wire and other defences were well constructed, and from these positions we [later] fired our weapons.'[8]

As night turned to day, British fighters attacked *Franz*, the lone coastal motor vessel now totally isolated and without support from its escort only a short distance from the French coast. Soon, now with a massive Royal Navy task force bearing down on it, the little German boat was hit multiple times in the stern by a British patrol craft, starting a fire on board. It had been roughly two hours since *Franz*'s crew first caught sight of Jubilee's forward elements. Only now did the crew disable their sole 20mm weapon and jump overboard, swimming for the coast and praying that they would avoid the bullets and shells flying all around them.[9] During this sideshow action, Convoy 2437 had been very fortunate. The Polish captain of ORP *Ślązak* had heard the convoy battle but believed the firing to be coming from the shore, thereby sparing the merchant ships and escorts from complete annihilation. As *Franz*'s crew abandoned ship, the sun could finally be seen above the horizon.

As it happened, other than *Franz* and *UJ 1404*, all other vessels in the German convoy survived their encounter with the massive Jubilee force and disengaged at about 0730. Convoy 2437 – minus *Franz* and *UJ 1404* – reached Le Tréport at 1000. The merchantmen sheltered in Le Tréport's harbour, while *UJ 1411* and her accompanying minesweeper motored on and at 1230 finally reached the safety of their home port Boulogne, having claimed (plausibly or not) to have shot down two bombers and a fighter on the journey home.[10] Even after the surviving ships had transmitted the customary immediate contact reports, German staff officers sitting at Admiral Raeder's supreme naval headquarters still believed, due to a complete breakdown in communications, that they had lost the entire convoy, as they first assumed. This was despite the fact that Le Tréport port authorities had reported sighting the returning convoy on its return journey eastwards.[11] For almost the entire battle, Raeder and his staff back in Germany would remain completely detached from what was going on in France.

Even though many men of 302nd Division could hear the sounds of the convoy battle coming from the north-east, especially after 0500, there was still no official word from high command. Having received no orders, some Germans decided simply to ignore the possibility of enemy action. One of those hoping for another quiet morning was Private Bronislav Wesierski. Like all the Poles fighting for the Germans at Dieppe, he had been forcibly drafted and spoke little German. At 0500 he had been woken up in the casino by a corporal who had heard the shooting out to sea. Wesierski's section then turned out in full battle dress in front of the building a quarter of an hour later, but with still no word from their superiors they returned to their bunks. After fifteen minutes, the section turned out again, this time for good, and took their positions in a trench just behind the casino.[12]

Just after dawn, naval shells began landing on the edges of Dieppe. The Allied fire plan called for direct fire on the beaches with delayed fuses at first, using a 50/50 mix of high-explosive and armour-piercing shells. Later, the destroyers would shift their fire to areas just behind the main Dieppe beach.[13] At 0550, exactly to plan, 4 Commando on the extreme western flank of the force made landfall near Varengeville. Approaching the skyscraper-like cliffs, they met no resistance whatsoever. The Germans considered these cliffs to be utterly inaccessible, and so had placed no forces there in their defence plan. With no enemy in front of them, the Commandos rapidly moved inland under the command of Lieutenant Colonel Lord Lovat. Their objective was 813 Army Coastal Artillery Battery, codenamed 'Hess' by the Allies. Hess's isolation from the rest of the Dieppe defence, and the fact that the Commandos had scaled the seemingly unconquerable cliffs in front of it, did not bode well for the ninety-three Germans stationed there.

3 Commando on the extreme eastern flank had intended to land simultaneously with Lovat's 4 Commando. Their target was the 'Goebbels' battery of 2/770 Army Coastal Artillery Battery, at Berneval, which boasted a potent array of four 105mm and three huge 170mm coastal guns. Eliminating this massive firepower from the German defence was 3 Commando's sole task. The random encounter with the German convoy had scuppered that plan, though. Worse still for the British was the fact that most of 3 Commando was scattered at sea and did not land. Their commanding officer, Lieutenant Colonel John Durnford-Slater, architect of Britain's first-ever Army Commando unit, was travelling back to England while his men were landing. Only at 0610, twenty minutes

late, did 3 Commando's landing craft finally reach the shore. Unlike the men of 813 Battery in the far west, 2/770 Battery in the east was fully aware that action was imminent. Ten minutes later, this landing would be reported to 302nd Division's headquarters.

Finally at 0600, more than an hour after Convoy 2437 had made first contact with the enemy, Major General Haase ordered his division to its battle positions. Men all around Dieppe roused themselves from their beds. The blank magazines normally kept in the division's weapons were for the first time switched for live ones. Today, 302nd Division's men would have the unexpected chance to play their part in the war. Despite this general alarm, some lower-level posts still remained oblivious to the approaching danger. However, this would do the Canadians no good. Half an hour later, Rundstedt's headquarters finally received word of the ongoing Dieppe battle, meaning that all German forces in the West would now be on the lookout for further simultaneous landings. At this early stage, there was no way for Rundstedt to discern whether the attack on Dieppe was an isolated operation or part of a wider invasion. OB West delayed somewhat, but eventually decided to pre-emptively warn 10th Panzer Division and 1st SS Division *Leibstandarte Adolf Hitler*, stationed near Amiens and Paris respectively.

The two Commando units that had landed were merely in support of the main Canadian effort stretching all the way from Pourville just to the west of Dieppe, across the main Dieppe beach, to the village of Puys on the main town's eastern side. By the day's end, these brave Canadians, including their armoured support, would be almost entirely annihilated. At first, all seemed to be going well for the men huddled in their landing craft. Although captivity ultimately awaited them, they were not to know this. There were all manner of craft carrying 2nd Canadian Division's men – the French-Canadian Les Fusiliers Mont-Royal would later go ashore sheltered inside unarmoured wooden craft. As the initial wave approached the shore, the RAF's bombers dropped 100lb phosphorus smoke bombs. The great white curtain that this created would shield 2nd Canadian Division as it moved towards land. To their left near Berneval a phosphorus bomb landed on a German ammunition dump, and an awesome spontaneous firework display erupted, with thousands of rounds of ammunition, grenades and flares lighting up the early morning sky.

The Royal Regiment of Canada was the first Canadian force to land. They did so at Blue beach in front of Puys village, just to the east of the main town, at around 0610. The Germans here were by now fully alert. Presented with barbed wire, a 10ft sea wall and a hail of machine gun fire, there was no advance inland. Not only this, but the sheer cliff walls around the Puys beach – only about 250m wide – provided perfect positions from which German pillboxes could rake the helpless Canadians with fire. In the words of one Canadian officer present, 'In five minutes' time they were changed from an assaulting Battalion on the offensive to something less than two companies on the defensive being hammered by fire which they could not locate.'[14] General Curt Haase at Fifteenth Army agreed, writing subsequently that his enemy 'found himself in a hopeless position as soon as he came ashore'.[15] Wisely, the Royal Regiment had brought Bangalore torpedoes with them – these were long, thin explosive charges used for the demolition of wired obstacles – but the German position was commanding. Barbed wire blocked any possible routes around the wall, and even if the attackers reached the relative cover offered by the sea wall – as some miraculously did – they would still be exposed to the enfilading fire of the German pillboxes situated at each end of Blue beach. This meant that the weapons on each side could fire along their longest axis, i.e. they engaged the Canadians from side on. Being exposed to enfilading fire is the worst tactical position for any military formation to find itself in, other than being completely surrounded. As if all this was not bad enough, 'B' Battery of 302nd Division's divisional artillery was located directly in front of the beach on which the Royal Regiment had landed. Although the battery's guns were not set up to fire at the land targets below them, it made itself indispensable to the defence in another way. In the next few hours, 'B' Battery would fire a thousand rounds at the ships and landing craft that were making a desperate attempt to reinforce the men stranded vulnerably in front of Puys.[16] Almost from the start, the Royal Regiment was a doomed force. Their task had been to advance on the eastern headland, but these military plans were irrelevant to the men trying desperately to survive the hail of gunfire. Their position was wretched. As Terence Robinson's colourful account of the slaughter at Blue described it: 'Puys was the abattoir where the Germans learned how to dismember, dissect and decimate the anatomy of invasion, how to rip out its heart with clawing fingers of fire.'[17]

The Canadians with the best luck on 19 August were the men at Green beach at Pourville. Much like the German positions elsewhere, Green beach was flanked by an east and west headland. These areas of high ground dominated either flank. Not only did the headlands provide height for the defenders, but they also allowed the Germans to build concrete bunkers inside the cliffs themselves. These positions were impossible to outflank and hidden from the Allies' otherwise flawless aerial reconnaissance. First into the breach were the South Saskatchewan Regiment, or SSR. During their approach, a bright green flare shot up in the air from the German-occupied coast. This was a prearranged signal for defensive fire from coastal artillery. Fortunately for the Canadians, the German defenders were by no means fully ready and prepared – failure in radio and telephone communications meant that many were simply unaware of the scale of the oncoming Canadian assault. At 0550, the SSRs landed in front of the village, having achieved a reasonable degree of surprise. Only shortly after landing did they begin taking fire. Even now, there was still no general alarm at Dieppe and, especially to the west, many Germans were blissfully, almost comically, unaware of what was happening less than a mile away from them.

Despite a measure of local tactical surprise, the Canadian attackers encountered an unavoidable geographical obstacle. The River Scie ran through the eastern side of Pourville, dividing the valley neatly into two. This would have been perfectly manageable, had the Germans not deliberately flooded the Scie to make crossing incredibly difficult. Inside Pourville was a single bridge, which would serve as the Canadians' only crossing point unless they decided to swim (as some did). Further south, Appeville village possessed another river crossing, yet this would require a significant advance inland to reach.

Ultimately, the goal of those landing at Green was simple: to secure the western flank of the main force and advance to 302nd Division's headquarters, which Allied intelligence officers believed was in Arques-la-Bataille to the south. As things turned out, no Canadian would ever advance far enough inland to discover that 302nd had some time ago relocated its HQ. In fact, Haase would be coordinating his division's response from Envermeu, fully ten miles south-east of Dieppe. Near Pourville there was an Organization Todt camp with 400 civilian workers. Upon hearing the unmistakable sounds of battle, most of them fled, and many did not return for several weeks. Those that stayed faced the Canadians. According to military law, OT was a civilian organization, thus its workers were non-combatants and it was a war crime to view them as military targets. Complicating matters was the fact that, despite an order from Rundstedt, OT workers in and around Dieppe wore a swastika armband. This condemned the workers remaining in Pourville to some horrible reprisals from the Allies, despite their non-combatant status. One man was stabbed in the chin then killed with a shot through the stomach. Others had a string wrapped tightly around their shoulders and neck, then passed down their backs and connected to their outstretched thumbs held at waist height, in such a way that any arm movement would result in strangulation. Pourville was the only place where the Allies held ground for a significant length of time.[18]

Soon after the landing at Green, German artillery shells began landing along the coastline. Thankfully for the Canadians, the Germans in their observation posts could not observe the fall of shot accurately due to the persistent artificial smoke, so the shooting was sporadic. This does not mean that it was not ferocious. One battery, 302nd Division's 8th, fired off forty rounds in ten minutes. Captain Hans Ditz was one of those directing fire onto the SSRs. He had been woken up by the Luftwaffe officer friend who had offered him a room at the golfing hotel and who now told Ditz that the sounds of fighting had been heard out to sea. Ditz decided to abandon any hope of more sleep and slowly trudged down the wooden steps to the door, on his way to his observation post on Dieppe's western headland. He had barely reached the ground floor when his left ear picked up the faint sounds of explosions – their direction could only mean Pourville was under attack. Ditz now ran just under a kilometre to his post, where he saw five green flares shoot high into the sky on his left side – the prearranged signal for defensive artillery fire. The artillery captain quickly ordered a pre-determined barrage against Green beach, and another against Dieppe's main beach for good measure. 'Anyone attacking Pourville would surely be up to some mischief in Dieppe as well', he later said. At his observation post, with two other men beside him, Captain Ditz began to observe more and more small craft coming towards him, far beneath their position high up on Dieppe's western cliffs, and he recalled:

The black became a dark grey, which became lighter and lighter. And then suddenly we saw them, all three observers at once. They did not come from the front, where we had expected them, but from our near-left side, tiny at first, then growing rapidly, like families of ducks swimming about, each with a large lead boat in front and three smaller boats on each side. More and more of these wedges appeared, which then grew together again into larger wedges, all in the direction of the Dieppe beach. We didn't have time to count, because now we had to open fire. We saw enough to know that a superior force was composing itself to fall on us. When our shells hit the water, however, we were greatly disappointed. We saw no hits, everything was swallowed up without a trace by the wind and waves, so that it was impossible to zero in on the enemy fleet. If only we'd had German ammunition! Then we could have used time-delay fuses, so that the shells that ricocheted off [the sea surface] and exploded in the air would have shown us the way. But with our Czech ammunition we couldn't get any ricochets. So we had to wait, teeth clenched, until the landing fleet came close to the shore, where we were pre-aimed and could get hold of them. But even that proved to be a wonderful illusion. Suddenly, the individual wedges began to lay smoke, and the favourable wind carried the fog in front of them so that they were soon completely hidden from view.

Several RAF fighters overflew Ditz's battery throughout the day. One strafed his position with 20mm cannon shells to no effect. Others dropped a series of bombs which missed by well over 100 metres. Like most other commanders at front-line positions on 19 August, Ditz was totally unable to communicate via field telephone as the lines were dead. The sole message that he did receive was a warning that enemy armour had broken through and was advancing towards his position.[19] This report, of course, was utterly false.

While the SSRs were still struggling in the outskirts of Pourville, half an hour late at 0650, on the point of daybreak, the Cameron Highlanders under Lieutenant Colonel Gostling arrived. There was no question of surprise now. The sheer undeniable strength of the German defensive positions on either side of the town proved their worth. Almost as soon as he had jumped out of his landing craft, Gostling was slain by fire from a machine gun in a pillbox built into the eastern headland. His deputy, Major A. T. Law, assumed command. For the French locals, the arrival of the Canadians was confusing at first. The Mallet family owned a house in Pourville's surrounding hills. They had heard the vague sound of aeroplanes, but were used to it by this point in the war. Mme Mallet had got up early at half past six to accompany some friends to Appeville train station, from where they would travel to Rouen. She was awake in time to observe a dogfight between two planes, and watch as the loser was shot out of the sky. She called her husband to see what all the commotion was about. Suddenly, two figures with flat helmets appeared almost directly in front of their front door – soldiers they naturally assumed to be German. Neither of them being experts in military equipment, one said to the other, 'They must have changed their helmets during the night!' Only later would the couple realize that they were looking at the flat Brodie helmets worn by the Canadians.[20]

From the moment they stepped onto land, the South Saskatchewans and Camerons faced the inevitable consequences of the confusion inherent in all warfare. While Green beach was nearly all located to the east of the River Scie, the Canadians actually landed mostly on its western side, thanks to the low morning light and slight fog. This might have been nothing more than an inconvenience, but the Germans' decision to flood the Scie essentially split the attacking force in two. Those forces tasked with attacking the hill up to Four Winds Farm would have to delay their advance inland, as they were forced to cross the small bridge in Pourville's outskirts before moving in on their assigned objectives. Canada's official historian of the Second World War, Colonel Charles Perry Stacey, concluded gloomily that 'the delay thus caused nullified the effect of the surprise that had been obtained, and was probably fatal.'[21] Four Winds Farm was perhaps the most important target in this sector, as the high ground it sat on dominated the entire area, and it would provide a superb position for observation and artillery fire until it could be neutralized. The Germans had in the previous few months been busy with construction on top of the Four Winds Farm hill, and as a matter of course the position there was ringed with menacing barbed wire.

Just in front of this hill lay a precious Luftwaffe 'Freya' radar station. Freya was a type of air early warning that was in some respects more advanced than Chain Home, the British equivalent. Freya stations were normally manned by three men. Their range varied, but the device could detect aircraft at distances of around 125 kilometres. Importantly, this system was good at detecting enemy aircraft, but not at providing a detailed firing solution – its radar did not have the fidelity required to accurately pinpoint targets for anti-aircraft or anti-shipping guns. This made Freya quite different from the Würzburg gun-laying radar captured in Operation Biting in February 1942. Surprisingly for such a high value target, and like most installations of its type, the Germans made little effort to camouflage Pourville's Freya station. It was not hard for RAF reconnaissance planes to spot – a great array of aerials stuck straight up in the air about 12ft high, forming a bulky square shape. Pre-raid observations had already gleaned a significant amount of precious intelligence; it was clear that this radar station could be immensely valuable to the Allies, and an attempt to gain physical access to it would be worthwhile. For this reason, the South Saskatchewans would assault the position on 19 August. In addition, Flight Sergeant Jack Nissenthal, a radar expert from the RAF, would be taken along dressed in a Canadian Army private's uniform. He was tasked with evaluating the equipment after its capture. However, the radar station was shielded by multiple machine guns, barbed wire and, most significantly for the unfortunate Canadian infantry, 100 yards of perilously open ground to negotiate.[22]

The assault on the main Dieppe beach went in at 0620, with the first nine Churchill tanks arriving ten minutes late. German coastal batteries, by now fully aware of the oncoming assault, caused serious casualties; 302nd Division may have been a poor quality division man-for-man, but its undeniable strength lay in the copious amounts of artillery, both coastal and inland types, that it could call down on coastal targets. 'D' Company of the Royal Hamilton Light Infantry, on the far right flank of the Canadian assault, was almost entirely wiped out before it reached land. Casualties would have been far worse had it not been for the dense fog on the morning of the 19th and the artificial smoke dropped by the Boston bombers and fired from Allied ships. A German infantryman fighting just in front of Red beach described the start of the main landings: 'And now all hell broke loose. Thick artificial smoke from the destroyers drifted towards the land. It shrouded the little landing boats that came in at high speed and in large numbers towards the coast.' He had nothing but praise for his comrades, remarking: 'Our artillery fired incessantly

… you could clearly see a transport ship sink, and another shared the same fate just in front of the Casino.'[23] Throughout the battle, German coastal artillery batteries would concentrate on destroying targets at sea. Cannon-armed Hurricanes tried desperately to keep the German heads down with strafing attacks, but the effect was only ever temporary. The scene in front of Dieppe was much the same as at Puys. As soon as the landing craft dropped their ramps, a vicious hail of machine gun fire was aimed at the attackers. This came from strong, defensible positions on the cliffs flanking the beach, in addition to those directly opposite the beach. A formidable row of pillboxes lined the sea front. Unsurprisingly, the insignificant pre-landing shore bombardment from the Hunt-class destroyers had done little damage to the Germans' static defences. The only cover to be found was behind either the sea wall or one of the vehicles that 2nd Canadian Division brought with them. These even included some Daimler Dingo armoured scout cars. There would be no need for these on 19 August, since only a handful of Canadians would ever manage the hundred or so metres off the pebbled beach.

The story of Red and White beaches is a sorry one. The German defences guarding the main beach seemed unaffected by the insignificant Allied bombardment. Jubilee's air plan called for only eight Hurricane ground-attack squadrons to be employed, most of them equipped merely with 20mm Hispano cannon. Those Hurricanes that were loaded with bombs – the so-called 'Hurribombers' – could only carry at most 500lbs' worth of ordnance. Another four squadrons of Douglas Boston twin-engine bombers could carry somewhat more ordnance, but this was hardly a significant increase. This critical lack of bomb-carrying capacity per airframe, coupled with the paucity of Hurricane and Boston squadrons dedicated to ground attack, meant that air attack never became a real concern for the German defenders. A woeful total of just 270 sorties were launched in direct support of the land forces, either before or after they made landfall.[24]

A single German company (7 Company) manned Dieppe's seafront – a strength of roughly 150 men. The company manned four heavy machine guns, two heavy mortars and two three-man flamethrowers, though the latter were not brought into action. From the houses behind the promenade, snipers picked off the Canadians below and in front of them at will. On the west mole, a French tank turret converted to an anti-tank gun had a free arc of fire across the entire landing area. The Essex Scottish, on Red beach, were closest to this gun and suffered horribly. Multiple waves of tanks landed on Red and White, attempting to provide some kind of armoured support. Many were swiftly knocked out by artillery and anti-tank gun fire, and in many cases the large stones and smaller shingle on the beach became stuck in their tracks, rendering them immobile and helpless. The Churchills' tracks were incredibly weak and brittle, and they ripped off violently after being hit even with smaller-calibre weapons. This made the Canadian armour extremely easy to immobilize. A German senior NCO near the promenade described the scene in front of Dieppe: 'Only two tanks managed to get within 50 metres of the first houses at the beach. Here, they broke down with mangled tracks. The others barely got across the stony beach and were finished off by our artillery. English destroyers, fast craft and the landing craft took the first houses under heavy fire, where naval and flak units were located.'[25] After the late arrival of the first armour, a steady stream of LCTs arrived at the beach to unload their Churchills as well. By around 0710, an hour after the first infantry landed on the beach, all twenty-nine tanks in ten landing craft had reached shore. Many craft were beached and unable to return to their transport ships, or were simply destroyed by artillery on their return journey. The defenders possessed six 37mm and one 47mm anti-tank gun, but these were all but useless against the Churchills' heavy armour. Only hits to the tracks had any effect.

Despite all the odds, fifteen Churchills managed finally to traverse the main beach and reach the promenade. However, these fortunate few merely came up against the other obstacles erected by the Germans in Dieppe town. Tank traps and roadblocks were impassable without the aid of sappers, who were stuck back on the beach still fighting for survival amidst punishing fire from all sides. With no better option, most returned to the beach in support of the boots on the ground. This was a stroke of luck for the defenders – the Germans had very few troops behind the first row of houses in the town, perhaps as few as one single company. The German infantry had no handheld anti-tank weapons and relied on anti-tank guns and coastal artillery to deal with the Churchills. Troops at the Port Commandant's HQ resorted to throwing grenades and satchel charges against the Canadian armour. If those tanks had been able to get into the streets with even a scattering of infantry support, the German position would have become untenable. All in all, the Germans were very fortunate on 19 August that their enemy became extremely immobile upon reaching the shore. Even the Churchills, the precious armoured support for Red and White beaches, were quickly stopped either by German gunfire or by their tracks coming off. This put paid to any hope of a breakout, meaning that the Canadian armour would eventually and inevitably fall victim to the German guns. As it turned out, only after their surrender would the infantry of 2nd Canadian Division see the streets behind the promenade.

It is hard to exaggerate how dominant the German position in front of Dieppe was. The east and west headlands, the two sections of high cliffs immediately on the town's east and west side, were perfect firing positions. Firstly, they had the advantage of height; not only did this allow for easy observation, but it also made it much harder for the Canadians below to return fire. Secondly, as we have seen, the headlands' position in line with Red and White beaches provided a textbook opportunity for enfilading fire. An artillery gun dug into a 3 x 4 metre cavern in the western cliff was particularly menacing. To the left of this gun was another 37mm anti-tank gun.

Every possible weapon was turned on the powerless Canadians below the headlands. One German fighting in the town remembered looking up to see that 'over at the eastern headland our machine guns were rattling. It was the crew of the Navy Signal Station, the eyes of the Port Commandant. Unfazed, the signalmen persevered in their especially dangerous and exposed position. It wasn't enough for them to simply observe and pass on their reports to their superiors. No, they manned their machine gun and ceaselessly held the enemy on the beach. One of them shot, another fed the gun's belt, another observed. It was like that until the battle was at an end.'[26] Throughout the day, the German defenders ruthlessly exploited the advantages offered to them by the topography. The signal station was only defended by an 11-man team led by Petty Officer Wilhelm Heinz, a reservist who had been a postal secretary in civilian life.

Although the Germans were in a tactically dominant position, it was not necessarily a pleasant experience for the men on the ground. Georges Dauzou was a 19-year-old civil defence worker in Dieppe, trained to perform the role of an ARP warden in Britain. Awakened by the sounds of battle, he put on his helmet and armband and slung his gas mask carrying case over his shoulder – one could never be too careful. A German soldier led him up Parmentier Street on Dieppe's eastern side to a gun position just behind the esplanade. There, he found a man lying prostrate before him, apparently injured. In fact, Dauzou found that the man was dead, and he beckoned to his German companion to help him carry the dead man, grabbing the lifeless body by the boots and expecting his comrade to take the shoulders: 'But nothing … I raised my head and saw him. He looked at me with distraught eyes, a trickle of blood running down his temple.'[27]

Once the initial landings across all six beaches had been made, the German response was quick. Evidently, the Allied force flung at them was not merely a small-scale Commando raid like those that had come before. The sheer scale of the forces involved made that plain. At 0620, the Luftwaffe at long last made tentative moves towards action. Two reconnaissance fighters, piloted by Lieutenant Sternberg and Sergeant Crump, took off from Abbeville to reconnoitre the area. Simultaneously, JG 2's first *Gruppe* scrambled from Triqueville, south of the Seine estuary. Ten minutes later, JG 26's fifth *Gruppe* did the same from Abbeville.

Rundstedt, at his headquarters at Saint-Germain in the outskirts of Paris, was monitoring the developing situation extremely closely and with considerable concern. He did not yet know how large the Allied effort might become. Were these the opening stages of the attempted liberation of France? At 0630 he issued his first appreciation:

It cannot yet be estimated whether the operation is of a local character and what strengths are involved. But because there have been simultaneous landing attempts at several localities (for the first time!) on a front of 20–25 kilometres and in daylight it is possible that the landing is a major effort. Moreover, [it is] not known what is behind. The possibility of an attack at another point is still open! Situation still unclear.[28]

Back in Dieppe, the first reserves arrived in the immediate battle area. A cyclist platoon began to occupy positions on the western edge of town at Four Winds Farm, on the slope that overlooked Pourville. They would occupy this high ground for the rest of the battle, ensuring that the German defenders enjoyed good observation of the entire battlefield. Shortly afterwards, Major General Haase despatched a staff officer to Ouville, instructing 571st Regiment's sole uncommitted battalion to move in on Pourville from the west, through the town of Hautot. Unfortunately for them, however, the seemingly simple 4-mile trip would not be so easy, for many of the men in 1 Bn 571st Regiment were equipped with bicycles. Hailed as a silent, mechanically reliable alternative to mechanized or motorized transport – which the Germans in France lacked anyway – bicycle-assisted mobility proved a curse rather than a blessing. Mounting their bicycles outside their barracks in Ouville as they had practised time and again, all went well at first. First the right legs and then the left pushed the pedals in perfectly drilled motion. It was only as the bicyclists set off that a rather comical scene ensued. Carrying all the extra ammunition and stores, the small and weak bicycles simply could not take the strain. One after another, the men's 'battle chariots' collapsed under them, causing an entirely avoidable delay to their joining the battle. This picture repeated itself everywhere around Dieppe. One later report estimated that as many as 60 per cent of the German bicycles collapsed, leaving their helpless riders stranded.

In Pourville, the Camerons and SSRs were making some progress. Forces from Green beach had captured the town and were now fanning out in an attempt to secure a defensible perimeter. Having moved through the built-up area, the Camerons' stand-in CO Major Law pushed through the forest on the eastern side of the valley, and forces pushed west to capture the high ground on the western cliff. To the east, Lieutenant Colonel Merritt commanding the South Saskatchewans had inspired his men to cross the bridge spanning the Scie, a natural choke point which threatened to halt the advance from Green beach before it had started. By all accounts, bodies littered the bridge, and some Canadians simply avoided it by swimming the river instead. Having reached the eastern side, a party travelled along the coast road to capture the Freya radar station. However, the massed machine gun fire that greeted them when they arrived forcefully dissuaded them from advancing any further. Moreover, the open ground between them and the station ruled out any kind of flanking manoeuvre. Flight Sergeant Jack Nissenthal would not get his eager hands on the Germans' radar equipment. Moving south-east up the hill on which Four Winds Farm stood, the Canadians were initially successful but soon became stuck. A line of barbed wire ran north to south along the slope up the hill, impeding their progress. At the hill's summit lay a circular trench defence system with multiple machine guns; truly, this was a menacing position.

Unfortunately for the Canadians climbing up to Four Winds, they had little or no gunfire support from the navy. They did request help, but the fall of shot from the destroyers' guns could not be accurately observed due to the abundant fog and smoke that lingered everywhere. In any case, the relatively small 4-inch shells fired by the Hunt-class destroyers were not the kind of fire support the infantry really required. However, the Canadians did manage to destroy a 47mm anti–tank gun and kill its crew. Later, at 0800, a brief battle report reached 302nd Division, stating that an artillery piece and heavy machine gun had both been destroyed as well.

Even at this early stage, Major General Haase was able to make a rough appraisal of the tactical situation. Dieppe and Puys were sufficiently defended and required no immediate reinforcement. Berneval, on the other hand, was a weak point. 3 Commando's landing craft had been scattered by the convoy collision, and most never landed. Several did touch down on Yellow I at around 0610, but the men were struggling – and ultimately failing – to navigate the wired, mined and booby-trapped gorges leading inland. However, the western side was somewhat different. The exits from Yellow II had no such obstacles, and a small party from a single landing craft had made reasonable progress. Comprising no more than twenty men and officers, they were led by Major Peter Young.

An interesting quirk of the battle on 19 August was that throughout the day, German wireless radio intercept stations were able to read British messages sent in plain text by Morse code. Initially, when the Allied naval force broke radio silence, creating an incredibly loud signals environment, German signals intelligence operators did not realize what was going on. A listening station at The Hague was the first to pick up the Allies' electronic signals, and since the signals were so strong, the station at first concluded that the Dutch coast was under attack. As the battle wore on, the Germans began to intercept more and more Allied communications. Lieutenant Kaltcis, an intelligence officer based at The Hague, later wrote cheerfully to a friend that 'the Dieppe business bucked up our chaps enormously. The messages taken – over 150 [in total] and all in clear text

– were wonderful and of outstanding importance to our Command.'[29] Lieutenant General Albert Praun, who by 1945 was the Wehrmacht's head of signals communication, later boasted that Supreme Commander Rundstedt was better informed by intercepted Allied messages than his own fighting units at Dieppe.[30] Although this was surely pure hyperbole, Praun's claim contained a kernel of truth. Inevitably, it was impossible for the Jubilee force to maintain radio silence once the raid had begun; during a short raid, speed was undoubtedly more important than security. As a result, the Germans were able to read unencoded transmissions. However, it is highly unlikely that any intercepted messages were worth much at all during the fighting at Dieppe. Even if there had been significant information contained in these messages, they would need to have been translated and delivered to 302nd Division in time – an impossible task. The constant use of codewords meant that, even if the Germans could intercept and read an encrypted message, it would have been useless to them. In fact, the increased traffic associated with such a large undertaking as Operation Jubilee was detected by German listening stations before the first British or Canadian boots hit French soil; Luftwaffe Corporal Otto Hasibeder was stationed at Deauville, 60 miles south-west of Dieppe, and had noticed early in the morning that a new, crisp Morse code 'sender' was on the air, tapping out references to colours like 'Red', 'Yellow' and 'Green'. Only later did he realize the significance of the dots and dashes he was hearing. Hasibeder was eventually rewarded for his monitoring efforts with a special flight over the 'gruesome' Dieppe beaches, as he later described them.[31]

A further worry for the German defenders concerned Quiberville at the extreme end of the defensive line. Lord Lovat's 4 Commando had moved past the town's weak defences and was now bearing down on 813 Battery. In response, a small part of the German reserves coming in from Ouville were to swing left and counter-attack at Varengeville. Moreover, in a stroke of luck for the Anglo-Canadians, much of the Germans' wired telephone communications had been knocked out by Allied naval gunfire and air-dropped bombs. Adding to the Germans' difficulties, some Canadians around Pourville found wires nailed carelessly to a tree in plain view, and promptly cut them. Unreliable communications had serious ramifications: 571st Regiment fighting in Dieppe town, for example, could only communicate with their divisional commanders through radio, which was less reliable and could even be intercepted by enemy signals intelligence. The Germans made no attempts to repair these lines. Even the signals construction platoon stationed in Dieppe was deployed as makeshift infantry, so they were unavailable for repair and reconstruction work. In addition, the Army's coastal batteries could not receive firing orders from their naval commander – Captain Hans-Udo von Treschkow in Le Havre – for up to two hours after the first shot was fired. In the absence of such orders, the Army's guns opened fire independently.[32]

At 0630, it was still unclear to the Germans whether the landings as then established would be followed up by attacks on an even wider front. The Allies had created a front stretching thirteen miles from Berneval to Quiberville. By now, Haase had already ordered 570th Infantry Regiment's 2nd Battalion to assemble with its motorized transport in Saint-Rémy, near the Bresle estuary. In the adjacent town of Eu, a company of cyclist infantry also prepared to commit to the fight, but Haase was hesitant. Justifiably, he considered further landings within his divisional area a distinct possibility, and he did not want to overexpose his position by showing his hand too early. Therefore, 302nd Division sent a single reconnaissance patrol in company strength from 570th Regiment's 1st Battalion. This patrol would arrive in Berneval from the south-east.

Over Dieppe, the air battle that Air Chief Marshal Leigh-Mallory had been hoping for began in earnest fifteen minutes before the hour. However, it began as it was to go on – with German success. JG 26's 5th *Staffel* arrived over the battlefield at 0645, and Staff Sergeant Heinrich Bierwith opened the considerable German account for 19 August by shooting down a Spitfire from 340 Squadron RAF. To the south, JG 2's 1st *Staffel* claimed three Spitfires and a Boston medium bomber just a few minutes later. Over the course of the next hour, JG 26 would launch patrols from all three of its fighter *Gruppen*, including special high altitude Bf 109 interceptors in its 11th *Staffel*. Complicating the German response was the fact that aircraft had to be brought from far afield. JG 26's 3rd *Staffel*, for instance, was based in Wevelgem in Belgium and only took off at 0700. Moreover, many aircraft were still located at their night dispersal airfields – smaller satellite bases, which ensured that they were not all in the same place if night-time bombers attacked their main airfield. This geographical inconvenience meant that many fighters had to transfer to a coastal airfield to refuel before flying on to battle over Dieppe. The Luftwaffe's commitment over Dieppe would gradually increase until twenty to thirty aircraft could be seen over the town at any one time. There was nothing nuanced about this early stage of the Dieppe air battle – German fighter pilots were told simply to fly to Dieppe and shoot down as many aircraft as they could. Only at 1100 did the bombers join in with attacks on British shipping.

Chapter 8

Action and Reaction: 0700–1000 hrs

At 0700, just over an hour after the first Allied soldier set foot on occupied French soil, preparations for the first concrete counter-attack against the Jubilee force began. A scratch force consisting of a cyclist unit, 570th Regiment's 3rd Company and an engineering company were ordered to push back the Commandos at Berneval in the east. For this purpose, Major von Blücher from the division's anti-tank company temporarily commanded this hastily assembled group, designated 'Composite Force Blücher'. At Petit Berneval, the elements of 3 Commando coming from the eastern Yellow I beach had been stuck ever since landing. However, a small party comprising twenty men and officers from Yellow II, despite having their planned landing ruined by the collision with the German convoy, had somehow managed to make their way towards the German guns. An hour or so after setting foot on French soil, this small band under Major Peter Young began harassing the 2/770 Battery. In response, the gun crews began firing over open sights at incredibly close range, sometimes as little as 200 yards. Despite all the odds, Major Young's men had succeeded in distracting the German guns from their primary task of protecting the beaches. Threatened with destruction, the men of 2/770 Battery understandably did not fire at sea targets, and instead focussed on self-defence. From 0610 to 0845 their guns were silent, except for a few potshots at the Commandos sniping at them. The Germans would be distracted for some time – it took Blücher's reinforcement column over two hours to form up and reach Berneval, and only after 0900 did their attack at Petit Berneval go in.

Even in the heat of battle, surprising moments of humanity still abounded. Jacques-André Lambert was nineteen years old on 19 August and living in Petit Berneval. Despite the obvious danger of crossfire, his father was determined to check on his elderly mother who lived fewer than a hundred yards away. Lambert senior duly left the safety of his underground air-raid shelter and made his way over. Jacques-André's grandmother, however, was dismissive of the suggestion that she should take cover underground: 'Leave me alone with your English and your Germans, I'm making my jams today!' The frail old lady then proceeded to sort plums throughout the day, steadfastly refusing to acknowledge the explosions and general cacophony around her. Her only scare, she later said, was when a stray bullet went through an old wooden chair she had been sitting on only a few moments before.[1]

It was at this stage that the Allies' only unqualified success achieved during Operation Jubilee began to unfold – at 813 Battery in the far west. After moving from Orange beach, 4 Commando had reached their objective and began firing on the battery from all directions. A small 6-man patrol from 571st Regiment's 3rd Company was sent to investigate and soon reported back to divisional command that 813 Battery was under attack and unable to return fire at the Allied ships. The Commandos then began to close in on their objective. At 302nd Division HQ, Haase received the following message just after 0800: '813 [Battery] engaged in heavy close-range combat … Commander seriously wounded, Varengeville under heavy attack.' From a German perspective, the attack on 813 Battery posed two significant problems; first, the guns there were unable to complete their own anti-shipping mission while under direct attack; and second, if the Commandos managed to secure and hold Varengeville they could then threaten the western flank of 302nd's strongpoint at Dieppe. Haase was not to know, however, that 4 Commando had orders to withdraw as soon as they had destroyed the Battery's guns.

Greatly concerned by 4 Commando's seemingly unstoppable advance inland, at 0814 302nd Division issued the following order to 1st Battalion of 571st Infantry Regiment: 'In the event that 813 Artillery Battery be endangered, proceed immediately thereto with a reinforced infantry company for an immediate counter-attack. 3rd Battalion 570th Infantry Regiment expected to arrive soon. If no contact with it, such to be established immediately by motorcycle. Division desires earliest advice on outcome regarding 813 Artillery Battery.'[2] However, in the confusion and fog of war, this order was never carried out, and 813 Battery remained isolated and alone. With few reinforcements, the fighting around the guns at Varengeville was desperate. The gun crews struggled to extinguish fires that erupted when artillery cartridges were hit. A German radio operator, despite being severely wounded, defended his position by throwing back hand grenades which had been lobbed into his bunker. One German account struck a wildly emotional note: '[The] battery was suddenly attacked by men with blackened faces and all but twenty-five men were slaughtered. The guns were blown up by the enemy, and the black-faced men disappeared again.'[3] Casualties were certainly not at the level that this account suggested, but 813 Battery's destruction came as a great shock to the defenders. Eventually, the battery was totally overrun. By the time that Lord Lovat's men had withdrawn at 0830, the guns had been destroyed, with over 50 per cent casualties amongst the crews. Four of these were prisoners taken back to England, some of the very few Germans captured during Jubilee.

Nearer Dieppe, just after 0700, 1st Battalion of 571st Infantry Regiment was ordered to assemble for a coherent counter-punch from the west. In preparation for retaking Pourville, where the South Saskatchewan Regiment and Queen's Own Cameron Highlanders had gained a steady foothold, 1st Battalion was to collect itself in Hautot. This small farming village lay about a mile south of Green beach. The appropriate orders could only be transmitted by motorcycle courier since normal telephone and radio communications were either unreliable or had been knocked out entirely. The Camerons under Major Law had moved to the west side of Appeville (not to be confused with Abbeville). Appeville, though an insignificant little village in peacetime, was a central point in the middle of the Scie valley. It was the site of a crossroads, with crucial roads leading north to Pourville, west to Ouville, east to Dieppe and south to Offranville. The River Scie, too, flowed through the village. German reinforcements would soon be arriving along the southern route.

Reconnaissance elements from a class of trainee non-commissioned officers began arriving in Appeville's outskirts from the east. They reported the strength of the enemy at roughly two platoons, but the Canadians' real strength was several companies, with almost the entire Cameron Highlanders' complement having swept wide through the forests on the valley's west side. The German position at Four Winds Farm, having been quickly reinforced, was a serious thorn in Major Law's side. Any advance up the road running through the valley would have been suicidal, with the German snipers and machine guns dominating from the eastern slope. Additionally, the defenders there counted a threatening field artillery battery amongst their resources. Originally, the Dieppe plan envisaged an advance on the Scie's east bank below Four Winds Farm, but the Germans' strength on the high ground rendered this route impractical. Hence the Camerons' decision to avoid the valley's centre and instead go through the forest on its western side. Crucial to this reasoning was the lack of tank support, as the planned movements had assumed that the infantry would enjoy armoured firepower. Without this, it seemed futile to continue with the scheduled assault below Four Winds Farm. Once at Appeville by his alternate route, Major Law intended to cross to the valley's eastern side and eliminate the defenders at Four Winds Farm.

The Germans did not take the Camerons' incursion lightly. An hour or so after the Germans began moving on Hautot, a brace of horse-drawn 75mm anti-infantry guns crossed to the eastern side of the valley at Appeville and began engaging the Camerons from their southern quarter. These guns were protected against small arms fire by armoured shields. The Canadians' mortars had been destroyed while fighting through Pourville, and without them these mighty German weapons seriously threatened the Allied foothold near Appeville. If Jubilee had proceeded as planned, Major Law could have called on Churchills, which by this time were supposed to have been advancing on the aerodrome in the rear. Clearly, armoured support was not forthcoming. Worse for the Canadians, the 75mm guns were joined by a mortar detachment, though this was later knocked out. The Germans atop and on the eastern slope persisted in harrying Major Law's men from their elevated positions. To the south, 1st Battalion of 571st Infantry Regiment continued to form up to push back the Canadian position, which Haase considered the most serious penetration inland. Elements from Green beach moved through the forest, reaching Hautot's outskirts. The small Canadian presence there would interfere with the Germans' wish to form up in Hautot. Importantly, the Germans sought to delay their counter-push until another battalion, the 570th Infantry Regiment's 3rd, had arrived from the direction of Offranville south of Hautot. After these reinforcements had arrived, the two battalions planned to move north through the valley in a combined assault.

A couple of hours after landing, the main force at Red and White beaches in front of Dieppe was exactly where it had started. The Germans had been seemingly unaffected by the air and naval bombardment, and their static obstacles like the sea wall were holding the Canadians in a kill zone on the beach. In a desperately mistaken decision taken in the inevitable fog of war, Land Force Commander Major General Roberts decided to reinforce failure by committing Les Fusiliers Mont-Royal. So, at 0800, these French-Canadians were thrown, in twenty-six wooden landing craft, straight into the gruesome slaughter endured by their English-speaking comrades. Unsurprisingly, they suffered equally horribly; most of them would not see Canada again until their release from a German prisoner of war camp three years hence. All told, out of 584 officers and men embarked, only 125 returned to England after the operation, with 119 dead. Roberts continued to believe mistakenly that the beaches were open for exploitation. Soon after Les Fusiliers Mont-Royal were sent in, the 360 officers and men of 'A' Commando Royal Marines went into the breach too. But unlike the French-Canadians, the Royal Marines never reached the beach at all. Realizing the hopeless situation in front of him, 'A' Commando's commanding officer Lieutenant Colonel Joseph Picton Phillipps stood up in his landing craft and waved off the approach. For this act of selfless bravery, he received a fatal wound, but his sacrifice saved four of his Commando's seven craft from reaching the shore.

Roberts also ordered an abortive reinforcement of the main beaches with some of his Churchill tanks. His insistence on reinforcing a hopeless situation may now seem to have been utterly misguided, but his decisions were based purely on the information that he was getting from shore. Standing aboard the command ship HMS *Calpe*, he was receiving incomplete and conflicting reports. One signal just after 0900 stated that White beach was under control. We now know that this could not have been true, but a commander must make quick decisions on the spot with the best available information, and this is what Roberts, the Land Force Commander, was being told. Under the circumstances, particularly bearing in mind that visibility was poor due to the Allies' own artificial smoke, his decisions were perfectly comprehensible. To the Germans firing from their ever-dominant stations along the coastline, however, Roberts' reinforcements merely offered more targets – an opportunity to wreak even greater havoc on a doomed Allied operation. After the operation, with time to pause and think, Roberts described in his final report to Mountbatten how destructive the German fire plans were:

The enemy's use of mortars, which were liberally dispersed over the front, was excellent in the extreme and devastating to our troops. They were sited in covered positions with fixed lines of fire and additional control by Forward Observation Officers who were in communication by telephone … Machine guns were well sited in caves, pill-boxes and houses. Some were able to fire directly into the landing craft as soon as the doors were lowered. Extensive use was made of cross-fire, and the enemy was quick to cover with fire any gaps which were made in the wire.[4]

Clearly, the planners at Mountbatten's Combined Operations Headquarters had underestimated or simply ignored how much firepower the Germans had at their disposal.

Georges Guibon, the former hotelier, had been awake for some hours at this stage, having been woken by the sound of gunfire. Ever the inquisitive type, Guibon felt the need to leave his house and investigate the source of the commotion. At around 8 o'clock he stumbled upon a group of German soldiers laden with hand grenades across their belts, firing potshots at aircraft passing overhead. Guibon approached one of them, who told him excitedly: 'The Tommies are here! On foot, on foot!', while stamping his feet.[5] His curiosity piqued, Guibon carried on with his walkabout.

Around the time that Major General Roberts was ordering his ill-informed reinforcement of Dieppe's front beach, a lone Junkers 88 reconnaissance aircraft from Reconnaissance Squadron 123 made a brief and frenetic flight over the Allied raiding fleet. The air umbrella provided by the RAF's Spitfires was so dense, however, that the Ju 88 was unable to properly reconnoitre the scale of the Allies' effort. The crew wisely decided that discretion was the better part of valour and quickly made for home at high speed. Incredibly, amidst all the efforts of JG 2 and JG 26, this was the first dedicated reconnaissance effort by Field Marshal Sperrle's Air Fleet 3. In this minor encounter Air Marshal Leigh-Mallory's fighter umbrella had won an important victory, by denying the Germans proper air intelligence. The German bomber force was painfully slow to get its aircraft crewed, loaded and into the air. A major factor in this was how unprepared its crews were for action. The story of KG 77, a bomber *Geschwader* whose 1st *Gruppe* was stationed at

Creil north-east of Paris, provides an apt illustration. Despite the general invasion warning for the northern French coast, some of 1st *Gruppe's* crews were billeted miles away from their operational airfields. When a call to action stations came through at around 0730, it took more than an hour for transportation to reach these men. One pilot was still fast asleep when it finally arrived. Only at 1000, three and a half hours after the initial alert, did he finally take to the air.[6] The story was similar at KG 2. Only at 0800 did KG 2's sixth *Staffel*, stationed at Eindhoven in the Netherlands, receive an alarm. Even then the unit did not fly straight into action – instead, they were told merely to wait for further orders. Some German aircrew, though undoubtedly aware of gossip that the Allies might test the German defences in France, thought that the idea of a British attack at Dieppe was a rumour at best, or at worst just another exercise. Consequently, many crews did not take the alarm seriously. The night before, many of the *Staffel's* men had been in Eindhoven until late, drinking and enjoying themselves. Unsurprisingly, as a result of all this, it was not until 1000 that a single four-plane flight from KG 2's sixth *Staffel* took off. None of them returned; three were shot down by fighters and the other by ship-borne flak.

On the ground at least, the German defences were beginning to swing into action. At 0900 302nd Division's sole motorized anti-tank company, originally placed in the divisional reserve in the rear, was given orders to move forwards into Dieppe and arrived an hour later. It was, however, not as effective as the Germans would have liked. The very same anti-tank obstacles that prevented the Churchills from gaining access to the inner town stopped the Germans from manoeuvring their 75mm guns to close-range firing positions in front of the beach. Nonetheless, without infantry support, there was no way for the Canadian tanks to destroy the obstacles blocking their path. Eventually, after being stuck forlornly in front of Dieppe for some time, they would be taken out by German anti-tank guns. One German lieutenant later described the scene. Like many German accounts, his does not distinguish between 'British' and 'Canadians': 'It was an odd picture ... when I stuck my nose above the anti-tank wall. Two British tanks were rolling back and forth, searching for a way into the town. But the approaches were blocked, and shortly afterwards the two tanks came under fire from our anti-tank guns.'[7]

All through the battle, copious volumes of Allied artificial smoke hung persistently in the air over Dieppe. The idea of artificial smoke was a simple one: dropped by aircraft or laid by ships, it provided a form of 'soft' cover for the infantry. Though it would not stop a hail of German bullets, it totally obscured the line of sight enjoyed from coast to sea. There being no features at sea, there was no 'hard' cover to hide behind as there was on land. Smoke, if carefully deployed and with the right wind conditions, could temporarily provide amphibious attackers with a certain degree of cover in the perilous transfer from sea to land. For the German artillery overlooking the beach, smoke was a significant hindrance to their accuracy. This inescapable fact not only reduced the German artillery's effectiveness, but also resulted in wasteful expenditure of ammunition. One artillery commander put it well: 'Coordinated fire was not possible. From the very beginning, all [my] guns were hindered substantially by the use of smoke. The smoke at some points became so strong that it was impossible to aim [our] fire.' This did not entirely prevent German guns from hitting their targets. One situated on the higher terrain west of the casino claimed at least three landing craft completely sunk. Others were less lucky. One gun crew inside the Casino and facing out to sea was wiped out by Canadian grenades.[8] In the air, the visibility was so poor that German aircraft at higher altitudes simply could not see their Allied prey down below, and had to waste time and fuel searching for suitable targets. Smoke cover also allowed Captain Hughes-Hallett's ships to get far closer to the shore than they otherwise could have. This cut both ways: while the Germans could not look out to sea, the Allies were rarely in a position to do the reverse. The precious few close air support squadrons that the RAF had assigned were as hindered as their German counterparts – they were, after all, sharing the very same airspace. The Canadian historian Brian Begbie notes in his excellent study of naval gunfire support at Dieppe that, with a few exceptions, in large part due to their own smoke the Allied ships were 'not very effective' as support platforms for their men on land.[9]

For those few Canadians who did make it off the hellish beaches, progress inland was similarly dangerous. A 100m-wide esplanade separated the edge of the beach from the first row of houses facing the promenade. One long row of barbed wire spanned the beach in front of the sea wall, with another behind it. Not only was this space completely open, but it was also covered by multiple pillboxes surrounded by barbed wire. The Casino at the western end of town served somewhat as cover for the assaulting force, as the imposing profile of this building blocked the Germans' field of fire from the flanks and rear. Furthermore, it lay directly behind the wall that the Canadians were so desperate to overcome. Immediately to the Casino's left – as the attackers viewed it – there was also a small break in the barrier. All this allowed small parties of men to exit the beach, despite the horrific fire erupting from the many pillboxes situated in front of it. The presence of the Casino was undoubtedly the greatest structural weakness of Dieppe's frontal defence, and 302nd Division's engineers were planning to raze it to the ground, but this process was not yet complete – by 19 August 1942 only the south-west corner had been demolished. The Casino was not defended at all and was not a strongpoint – no defence works had been laid there except for some light barbed wire and some sleeping quarters.

The Germans made concerted efforts to take back the Casino. As they later recognized, it was the only weak point in their defence. At 0700 the 4th company of the 6th Fleet Detachment under Lieutenant Göbel was ordered to retake it. These Fleet Detachments were not infantry per se, rather they were naval policemen who had guarded the naval craft intended for an invasion of Britain in 1940. Although this invasion never came to pass, throughout the war these detachments helped with order and discipline in German-occupied ports. 4th Company sent twenty-five of its 35-man complement to the Hotel Metropole next door to the tobacco factory. Lieutenant Göbel sent ten men under Sergeant Müller to the Casino – shortly before being shot through the stomach and transported rearwards by car. Sergeant Müller carried on without his officer, and his group made it to a position just behind the Casino. By this time, Canadian Churchill tanks were driving up and down the Boulevard de Verdun, shooting at anything they could see. It was in their attempts to cross the Boulevard to the Casino that Müller's group suffered horribly. Müller and a private were shot through the head and killed instantly, and another man was killed by a bullet through the throat. Some men were not killed by bullets but crushed underneath the Churchills' tracks, almost certainly unbeknownst to the tanks' crews. What remained of 4th Company quickly retreated to the Hotel Metropole.[10]

As it was, the Casino allowed some Canadians to escape the bloody beaches. A couple of hours after landing, a small party of fourteen men from the RHLI managed not only to enter the building but also to cross from it to the first row of houses across the Boulevard de Verdun. Eventually, German infantry intercepted them and by 1100 forced them back to the Casino. A slit trench ran behind the large building, between it and the first row of houses. Here, Private Wesierski's mainly Polish platoon sat unmoving, unwilling to put their lives at risk for their forced German masters, until it was overrun. A grateful Wesierski was taken prisoner along with his Polish comrades.

Even in a life-and-death struggle like those on 19 August, unmistakably human incidents still occurred. In a strange and partly comic episode, a German sergeant inside the Casino decided that he no longer wished to fight, and calmly walked up behind a Canadian private using an anti-tank rifle at a window. The German promptly announced that his willingness to put his life at risk was at an end, and that he wanted to be taken prisoner. He was granted his wish and later left for England as a rare specimen – a German, as opposed to Canadian, prisoner taken at Dieppe.[11] After clearing the building, the Canadians began using the Casino as a firing position against the row of houses opposite them. Another group of eighteen men did likewise later in the day, even managing to clear a house full of German snipers facing the beach. German infantry forced these men to retreat back to the casino by midday. Some sappers managed to place explosive charges on one of the roadblocks preventing the Churchills from reaching the town, but these were never detonated. On the other end of the beach, where there was no such large structure to give them cover, the Essex Scottish only managed one small penetration into the town at roughly 0900. One of their companies had been tasked with destroying the tobacco factory roughly on the boundary between Red and White beaches. In this they succeeded in a fashion – by firing rifle grenades from a distance and setting it alight, the Canadians created a putrid-smelling inferno. 'And the stink of the smoke pall over Dieppe!' Australian Spitfire pilot Flight Sergeant Allen Mawer later wrote in his diary. 'Someone told me later that a tobacco factory had been hit, and I can tell you that all those stories about French cigarettes are true.'[12] Germans occupying the buildings in the immediate area had to be evacuated because the resulting fire was so vicious.

One and a half miles inland at Appeville, and faced with a German build-up right in front of them, the Camerons of Canada pre-empted the coming counter-attack. Realizing his hopeless position, stuck in the middle of the Scie valley, Major Law began an orderly withdrawal at 1030. Withdrawing under contact with the enemy is the most challenging task for any unit in close combat, and the Camerons could have suffered seriously if the Germans had pursued them closely. As it turned out, however, 1 Bn 571st Infantry Regiment acquiesced in the Canadians' desire to retreat. Apart from ad hoc pestering attacks on their rearguard by German reconnaissance patrols, the Camerons attracted little attention as they proceeded north towards the safety of their landing craft. This was a critical point in the battle. Many coastal artillery guns had run out of ammunition completely. As any front-line commander knows, inexperienced and stressed soldiers always use copious amounts of ammunition. In some places the Germans were fighting with small arms alone, but unfortunately for the Canadians and British, their attack had neither the strength nor momentum to exploit this weakness.

Just as the Camerons were making their way back up the valley to Green beach, Major General Haase had left his headquarters at Envermeu and driven to Tourville, three miles south of Major Law's furthest advance. Haase had set up a small command post near the church and was awaiting the arrival of Colonel Klemm, 676th Infantry Regiment's regimental colonel. This regiment was not part of 302nd Division but of 332nd Division, which guarded Haase's left flank. When Klemm arrived, the Colonel was told that he was to lead the counter-attack against Pourville and its beach. Specifically, Haase ordered him to take command of two infantry battalions (1st Bn 676th Regt and 3rd Bn 570th Regt) as well as the 81st Tank Company consisting of old captured French tanks. He was to be supported by several guns subordinated directly to him from 302nd Division's divisional artillery. The force, named 'Reinforced Regiment Klemm', would advance towards Pourville on the west bank of the River Scie. It was expected to arrive at around 1430, just under two hours after setting off. Yet this was far too late to catch the retreating Canadians. Had Klemm's strong reserves acted as aggressively as they should and could have done, the Camerons and South Saskatchewans might have been annihilated before they had time to withdraw. As it turned out, they returned to Green beach via the very same route on which they had come inland. In the aftermath of 19 August, this fact was obvious even to the Germans. One report later noted regretfully: 'A prompt and determined attack towards Pourville would probably have cleared up the situation more quickly and would have helped wipe out an even larger number of the enemy.'[13]

The Germans were now growing increasingly concerned that the Allied effort at Dieppe may have been the precursor to a wider assault on occupied Western Europe. At Evere airfield, just outside central Brussels, all civilians were sent away at 0900, and barbed wire obstacles were set up. Amid enhanced inspection of identity cards, large tree trunks were laid over the road approaches to block access.[14] Rundstedt's staff in Paris called Luftwaffe General Friedrich Christiansen, the Wehrmacht's military commander in the Netherlands, to put him in the picture regarding the events transpiring in France. War inevitably creates uncertainty, and no German commander could be sure that the landing at Dieppe was not a prelude to something much bigger – hence the response not just in France but across Western Europe more widely.

Meanwhile, east of Dieppe at Puys, the Royal Regiment of Canada was facing the dire consequences of poor fire support and failure to achieve surprise. To call their action in front of Blue beach's steep cliffs and gullies a 'battle' would be a grave understatement. It was nothing less than a slaughter. So dominant were the Germans looking down on the poor Royal Regiment, that 571st Infantry Regiment saw no need to even consider reinforcing Blue beach's cliffs. These landings, much like the entire Dieppe operation, had been predicated on the dubious notion that surprise would be achieved on a tactical level. Therefore, as Jubilee's planners reasoned, an advance from Blue beach's incredibly confined space could be achieved with ease. The Canadian bodies now lying all around the Royal Regiment's landing point were evidence of the absurdity of this idea. With only a handful of machine guns manned by a couple of platoons, the Germans were handily defeating upwards of 550 Royals. Such was the dominant defensive position provided by Puys' narrow beach, its high cliffs and almost impassable exits – quite aside from the Germans' own wire entanglements and booby traps. Somehow, the Royal Regiment's men did manage to cut at least one gap through the barbed wire guarding the narrow gully exits. This was despite their position being clearly observed by the dominant Germans above, most of whom occupied the eastern side of the cliffs. Incredibly, a small party of about twenty or so men managed to reach the clifftop and clear two houses, but they could not make any further progress. At 0815 the survivors at the clifftop surrendered. Down below, more brave Canadians on Blue beach tried to make a tentative advance, but in doing so one man triggered a pull-action fuse tripwire. The resulting explosion – generated by a 1kg explosive charge – killed two men, discouraging any further movement. It is almost always foolhardy to state about any military operation that 'it was doomed from the start', but Puys on 19 August 1942 is a prime candidate for such a description. Once the German defenders were aware of the oncoming Canadian assault – and probably even if they had not been – the Royals' attack was bound by all the rules of military action to founder and ultimately fail. As it happened, Blue beach was the first of Jubilee's landing sites to be recaptured. At 0935, 571st Infantry Regiment reported proudly to divisional headquarters: 'Puys firmly in our hands. Enemy lost about 500 PoWs and killed.'[15] So ended the sorriest story of Canada's involvement in the Dieppe raid.

By this time it was clear to Major General Roberts aboard HMS *Calpe* that Operation Jubilee would not be able to secure its objectives. The men on Red and White beach were supposed to be driving on Arques-la-Bataille, 7 kilometres to the south. Instead, they were stuck on their landing beaches barely a few metres from the water's edge. Roberts originally agreed with Captain Hughes-Hallett to begin the general withdrawal at 1130, but requested this be delayed to 1200 in order to make contact with the Camerons and allow for greater RAF fighter cover. A simultaneous evacuation was organized for Green beach at Pourville.

Just to Puys' east, the Germans also held the upper hand, for 3 Commando's attack had been shattered by the encounter with the German convoy. Only Major Young's tiny band of men that landed at Yellow II had made any meaningful progress towards the German guns at Berneval. However, the tactical picture was about to become much more unpleasant for them. At around 0915, Major von Blücher's composite force finally made its way into Berneval, reinforcing the Luftwaffe and artillery personnel. Although the eastern flank of the operation was by no means the strongest, Composite Force Blücher was committed to Berneval as this was where its units could join the battle most quickly. This spelled the end for the Commando attackers stuck in the gorges in front of the settlement – the cyclist squadron and later 3 Company from 570th Infantry Regiment put paid to any breakout from Yellow II. An hour after Blücher arrived in Berneval he could proudly report to divisional headquarters that he had completed the task for which his force had been cobbled together: Berneval was clear of Allied troops, but Major Young, like Major Law at Pourville, had realized the hopelessness of his situation and withdrawn safely to Yellow II. By the time Blücher made his report at 1120, Young and his men were safely on their way back to England. Composite Force Blücher remained active, but its units were split up. The engineering company set to work repairing damage to Berneval's defences; the company of infantry took over the defence of the town; while Blücher and the cyclists withdrew to the village of Graincourt, just behind Berneval. Only at 1800, more than six hours later, would Composite Force Blücher be sent to the rear for rest and recuperation.

Chapter 9

Cruel Attrition: 1000–1230 hrs

Throughout the action along Dieppe's coastline, reinforcements from across France were inexorably making their way forwards to the battle area. By 1000, 10th Panzer Division's vanguard, a reinforced battalion of Panzer IIIs and IVs, had been waiting for over an hour to depart. The order to do so only came just after the hour, and it took until 1045 for the tanks to finally get moving. Further elements followed later. However, it would take some time for 10th Panzer to reach Dieppe, as it had approximately 35 miles to cover. The division would have been able to move off much earlier if not for the farcical unpreparedness of the entire formation. When the original alarm came through from OB West, the division's operations officer was not in his office, and the phone rang unanswered. The division's wireless communications were notoriously unreliable. Not least embarrassing was the division's lack of any maps of the Dieppe area. A motorcyclist had to rush to Lille 80 miles away to obtain them before the commanding officer, Brigadier Wolfgang Fischer, was in a position to start giving orders. Even after his vanguard set off, mechanical breakdowns plagued his unit's progress towards the coast. The Division split into two parts for its journey westwards; some crossed the Somme at Abbeville, while the majority crossed to the south at Amiens.[1]

At this point, Rundstedt's chief of staff, Brigadier Kurt Zeitzler, telephoned General Jodl at OKW and put him in the picture. A follow-up message summed up the tactical state of affairs: 'Enemy landing attempts continue. Army counter-attacking with local reserves. Situation in Dieppe still unclear. High ground on both sides of Dieppe firmly in our hands. Landings at Pourville continue, the situation there unclear.' Throughout the battle, German reserves were able to move towards the battlefield unmolested by the RAF, allowing them to assemble in an orderly fashion for a counter-push against the enemy bridgeheads. Afterwards, Rundstedt expressed utter incredulity at the RAF's complete failure to disrupt German forces moving into the Dieppe area:

The employment of the enemy air force and their tactics were extraordinary. It seems incomprehensible why, at the beginning of the enemy landings, the Dieppe bridgehead and other landing places were not isolated by a continuous curtain of bombs so as to prevent or at least delay the employment of local reserves.[2]

In the maritime domain, Rundstedt now wished to commit U-boats in the Channel to attack Hughes-Hallett's naval force, but commander of Naval Group West Admiral Saalwächter vetoed any and all deployments of his submariners east of Cherbourg. Although a U-boat attack could have caused further losses to the Allies, Saalwächter undoubtedly made the correct call in protecting his sub-surface force. This was for several reasons; firstly, the Allies completely dominated the skies and seas in the Channel, and this made it by far the most dangerous area for any submarine to operate in. The Germans had only once managed a successful naval operation in the Channel: Operation Cerberus, the famous 'Channel Dash', which Saalwächter himself had planned. Almost untouched, the *Scharnhorst* and *Gneisenau* battle-cruisers and the heavy cruiser *Prinz Eugen*, along with their escorts, escaped from France's Atlantic Coast through the Straits of Dover into the North Sea. Secondly, uncharted minefields were a real menace, and might destroy a German U-boat without a second's warning. Thirdly, east of Cherbourg the Channel rarely exceeds a depth of 35 fathoms. This fact robs submarines of their unique ability to manoeuvre in the third dimension and hide below the surface of the sea. Finally, it was unlikely that any German U-boats would have been able to reach the battle area in time, even if they had been committed. For their own protection, no U-boats were based along France's Channel coast, so any orders to move to Dieppe would have entailed a lengthy redeployment. At first, Rundstedt's proposal would have seemed like a perfectly reasonable one: why not pile pressure on the Allies by adding sub-surface attacks into the mix? On closer inspection, however, this idea was not viable, and Saalwächter was rightly dismissive. Flawed proposals like these from Rundstedt, an Army man through and through, served only to intensify the already acute animosity between the Wehrmacht's different services.

While German fighters had been active over Dieppe since the early morning, strafing Allied troops and ships, only at 1100 did the first bomber attack in significant strength go in. The Do 217s of KG 2 reached Dieppe with an escort from JG 26's 2nd *Gruppe*. These night bombers had been on a raid over England the previous night, and since they were not expected to operate during the day they had not been quickly refuelled and refitted after landing – hence the delay in reaching the battle. Like all of the medium bomber strikes on 19 August, this one would be directed against Allied naval forces out at sea. From his position on Dieppe's western headland, artillery Captain Hans Ditz saw first-hand how one such bomber attack bucked up the morale of those fighting on the ground:

> Suddenly, there was a tremendous roar above us, aircraft after aircraft, and soon, to our relief, we recognized the German crosses and the unmistakable figures of our bombers. Hooray! The Luftwaffe had arrived, and how! Our aircraft swooped down like hawks diving on ducks, and soon huge fountains of water were swirling around the boats. The skills that the enemy lead boat used to manoeuvre the falling bomb were admirable. Even so, it was increasingly off course. And, whether intentionally or not, it steered away from the coast. Then, as if by command, all the big boats turned back and their followers got in behind them, and soon the whole mass had disappeared into the mist. And boy did we cheer!

A lone German fighter returned from this attack flying dangerously low straight towards Ditz's position, only just managing to remain airborne. It was heavily damaged, its pilot looking desperately for an emergency landing spot, but his efforts were in vain, as he was simply unable to gain enough height. The aircraft rapidly lost altitude and veered violently just before one of its wings broke off from the fuselage, condemning it to a watery grave. It did not go quietly, erupting in a column of fire taller than the cliff itself. The only remnant recovered was a small impeller lodged at the cliff's base.[3]

The Luftwaffe was not the only airforce playing the bomber game. Half an hour after KG 2's first attack, twenty-four American B-17 Flying Fortresses of US 8th Air Force's 97th Bomb Group made a pre-arranged 'counter-air' strike on JG 2's Abbeville airfield. At 23,000ft the B-17s were too high to be intercepted by the Germans' Bf 109s and FW

190s, which were all occupied with low-level flying over Dieppe. One 109 did succeed in closing in on the B-17s' formation, but it was chased away by the escort Spitfires, unable to claim a victory. Defensive flak, though significant, did not manage to claim any aircraft shot down. The escorting RAF Spitfires reported a great success in the shape of 'many direct hits ... on admin area, and also on southern runway'.[4]

For the Germans on the receiving end, this high-altitude bombing attack was a harrowing experience. One bomb annihilated a tanker, sending it flying up into the air. According to one account, the driver, a young private, was still at the wheel when his vehicle was hit. After travelling a fair distance, throwing its young driver clear in the process, the tanker came crashing back down to earth, burning from every quarter. The private somehow escaped completely unscathed. He even managed to rub his eyes and recover quickly enough to see the black burning remains of the truck he was sitting in only a few moments ago. Another B-17 bomb hit an airfield sickbay, from which the patients had been evacuated only a short time previously. Only the charred, twisted metal beds survived – the wooden structure was a smoking wreck in minutes.[5] Air Marshal Leigh-Mallory would later claim that Abbeville was knocked out as a base of air operations for two hours. Yet the Germans on the ground were perfectly able to carry on taking off, albeit undoubtedly at a reduced rate. Some communications lines necessary for controlling flight operations were knocked out, but casualties on the ground were otherwise light; only two FW 190s from JG 26's 6th *Staffel* were damaged. At 1137, JG 26's 2nd *Gruppe* took off from Abbeville for its fifth patrol of the day, escorting bombers and strafing ground targets.[6]

From the moment that the Allies' boots on the ground had established a front from Orange to Yellow beach, the Germans were well aware that further landings at new points along the coast could not be ruled out – Rundstedt's command indeed warned, and was itself told by subordinate commands across France, that the Allies were preparing subsequent attacks. Just after 1100, based on reconnaissance flights by Reconnaissance Squadron 123, Field Marshal Sperrle's Air Fleet 3 reported directly to Rundstedt the presence of a convoy off the West Sussex coast: 'Twenty-six large transports each of 6,000 tons, three destroyers in convoy. Decks closely crowded with troops.' Of course, 'the Last Prussian' knew better than to believe all of the air reconnaissance reports he received. Nevertheless, he also knew better than to ignore them entirely. Coupled with other reports of transports lying in reserve in the Channel, Rundstedt knew that a much greater Allied effort might be on the cards. Accordingly, he issued an update on the situation to his staff and senior commanders: 'If one brings this reserve into operational connection with the fleet of transports in the rear mentioned [off Sussex], the enemy undertaking may be the beginning of an attempt to establish the "Second Front".'[7] Erring on the side of caution, Rundstedt quickly ordered all of Seventh Army and most of its reserves to 'Alarm Scale II', meaning that they were ready for instant action. Seventh Army covered western Normandy and Brittany.

Anton Roos was a German infantryman who was part of this response. He had worked for Organization Todt before the war and had joined the Nazi party early. Roos was not a young soldier – he was born in 1895 and he and his wife Elizabeth had two sons; Gustav, who was fighting in the Soviet Union, and Günther, who would soon be called up after a stint with the Reich Labour Service. The elder Roos was stationed in Saint-Malo, a small, historic port town on France's Channel coast more than 150 miles west of Dieppe, on the western side of the Cherbourg Peninsula. On being given the alarm, Roos prepared Saint-Malo for battle. He was an administrator, not much of a fighter: he quickly secured his unit's money – as much as 1,500,000 Reichsmarks – and documents in safes, and made the women of the town ready to be evacuated by bus at a moment's notice. It would not be seemly for Saint-Malo's womenfolk to become involved in the possible battle to come. Roos was ordered to safeguard his 1.5 million Reichsmarks until the alarm was over, whenever that might be. Fortunately for him, the secure location chosen was a tavern 20 kilometres in the rear, so he drove over in a truck, cash safely by his side, with a 3-man bodyguard and a full five days' worth of rations. The order to stand down would not come until the next morning, by which time Roos and his escort had managed to devour all the hostelry's food – and no doubt have a drink or two to boot. In a letter to his wife Elizabeth, Roos later understatedly described this experience as 'very pleasant'. There were certainly worse places to spend a night in wartime.[8]

From the time of Rundstedt's alarm order, such was the concern that the operation currently ongoing might not be confined to Dieppe that the entire northern coast of France was put on the highest state of alert.

In fact, the ships off Sussex's coast which concerned OB West so much were nothing more than a 14-strong merchant convoy on its way to the Isle of Wight. However, Rundstedt was not to know this, and he had to take heed of reconnaissance reports that he received, however unreliable they might be. With Rundstedt's vast experience came the knowledge that reacting to a false alarm was far preferable to suffering a surprise attack while unalerted. Seventh Army's men would simply have to put up with being pulled away from their normal, more leisurely routine. In the post-battle analysis, Reconnaissance Squadron 123's spotting of the twenty-six transports confirmed the view of some Germans that the Dieppe operation was just phase one of a wider invasion attempt. These transports, if they had been 'crowded with troops', could well have been used for that purpose. The months of warnings about possible invasion attempts in France created a mindset that erred on the side of caution.

Another typical false alarm came from Fifteenth Army to Rundstedt's headquarters, reporting a completely nonexistent landing 12 miles east of Dieppe: 'At Criel-Plage an enemy company has landed. Counter-attack in progress, proceeding favourably.'[9] Such is the confusion inherent in battle that false alerts like this were common during 19 August. However, the Germans were never distracted from the real threat in the Dieppe area. German worry over new Allied initiatives was not confined to amphibious landings – airborne landings were still at the back of Haase's mind, as well of those of other German generals. To guard against the airborne threat, 2nd Battalion of 570th Infantry Regiment was kept with its transport at the Arques Forest south-east of Dieppe from 1000 hrs. As the battle proceeded to the Germans' advantage, and Operation Jubilee did not result in landings at any other locations, this formation remained uncommitted on 19 August.

Somewhere deep inside northern France, a gaggle of war reporters had gathered to film and photograph a group of female Luftwaffe personnel during their morning physical exercises and to produce a radio programme on the crucial war work that these women – *Luftnachrichtenhelferinnen*, literally 'Luftwaffe female signals communications auxiliaries' – were carrying out. A woman could type and deliver messages just as well as a man could, so the logic went. One of the journalists present was Ulrich Haussmann. Watching these young women was an 'enviable task', he later wrote in a newspaper article. 'Male vanity is a fact that cannot be denied', he conceded sheepishly, for Haussmann and his colleagues were wearing their best white formal dress, as they had been fortunate enough to attend a dance with the *Luftnachrichtenhelferinnen* the previous evening. Now, on the morning of 19 August, two cars sped through the gates of the sports facility. The war reporter subsequently gave a dramatic account of what happened next.

'On the loudspeakers: "The English have landed at Dieppe!"'

'Situation?'

'Nothing concrete yet!'

'White jackets and hats flew into the corner, swapped for field blouses and caps, steel helmet and sub-machine gun in arm. Some film stuck in the pockets and then back to the car. Off we went!'

Unfortunately, the scene was somewhat more chaotic than Haussmann would have liked to admit. For one thing, he and his colleagues were so rushed that they did not have time to change out of their smart white dress uniforms.[10]

Nowhere was the Dieppe battle proceeding more favourably for the Germans than in front of the town. With no cover to speak of, wave upon wave of Canadian infantry found themselves attempting fruitlessly to break through the sea wall, as laid out in Jubilee's grand plan. The Churchill tanks were fortunate to be protected by thick armour plate. Not a single Canadian tank was actually pierced by a German shell during the battle, and none of the tank crew was injured while inside a vehicle. Only by hitting the Churchills' vulnerable tracks could the Germans immobilize them. One 37mm gun was emplaced in a narrow road next to Dieppe's nursing home. Commanded by Corporal Haas – no relation to the divisional commander – its relatively exposed position on Dieppe's streets drew significant enemy fire. Despite this, the gun destroyed one landing craft in the early stages. Although the gun had a large steel shield, this could not provide complete protection – and so it turned out. Corporal Haas was eventually wounded by an exploding grenade, and later died in hospital. Despite being wounded, Lance Corporal Krause took over command. The gun was later disabled for fear that it would be captured if the Canadians advanced far enough By then, Krause's crew had claimed no fewer than five Churchills neutralized.[11]

By 1200 it was obvious to Major General Roberts that Operation Jubilee was doomed. The landing parties at Puys and Berneval had been annihilated, the South Saskatchewans and Camerons were re-embarking on Green beach, and the German 571st Infantry Regiment had successfully protected Dieppe itself. There was now no hope of capturing the town. Only 4 Commando at Orange beach in the far west could call their involvement a success. However, they had withdrawn hours before as per the operational plan. As if this were not enough, over 700 men and 20 Churchill tanks remained unused in their transports. Roberts' only hope now was that as many men could be saved as possible. Saving any tanks or heavy equipment was out of the question.

Thus began a desperate attempt by Captain Hughes-Hallett's landing craft to rescue what remnants they could from Red and White beaches. All ships and boats able to assist laid artificial smoke to cover the approach to shore. The wind blew easterly and towards the beach, which provided visual 'soft' cover until the landing craft had almost made landfall. However, this was not enough. German artillery immediately recognized that a major naval effort was underway and switched their fire from the beaches to the approaching craft at sea. German artillery officers reported an immediate effect on the Allies' anguished rescue attempts. From all around, German shells rained down from the high ground, inflicting punishing losses and forcing many would-be rescuers to turn away. Moreover, the destroyers brought close into the shore to provide covering fire also drew considerable attention. This forced them to break off frequently, leaving the landing craft unsupported. 302nd Infantry Division's 'A' battery, located only a mile inland in between Appeville and Dieppe, having fired nearly 700 shells throughout the day, described the effect of its ruthless bombardment as the withdrawal began: 'Ships shelling shore forced to turn back. Last enemy resistance on beach smashed.'[12] A German soldier in Dieppe town gave a truly desperate picture of events as the abject retreat began:

Our heavy anti-tank guns and artillery took out the remaining tanks that were driving about the beach with direct fire. They were wiped out. The ships off the beach took direct hits and were disabled. In the meantime, we noticed that almost the entire enemy landing force consisted of Canadians; only the ships' crews and the corporals were English. Throughout the morning, our infantry, anti-tank units, engineers and coastal artillery joined the fight effectively.[13]

As the Canadians quickly learned to their cost, the enemy guns dominated Dieppe's waters just as much as they did its shore.

While the Essex Scottish and RHLI struggled to extract themselves from Red and White, so did the Camerons and South Saskatschewans from Green. A short time after the order to evacuate was given, German spotters observed a noticeable increase in activity out at sea. An observation post sent a warning to 571st Regiment fighting in Dieppe town: 'Twenty small boats heading for Pourville, at a distance of 500 to 1,000 metres'.[14] Tactically, the situation was essentially perfect for the Germans. Other than a few excursions from Red and White beaches, Dieppe town remained totally in their hands. Moreover, the dominating cliffs on either side of it ensured that flanking fire would greet any rescue attempt. At Green, the picture was much the same, but with one important difference. The South Saskatchewans, in making their way east of Pourville to capture the Freya radar station, had cleared the eastern headland. Unfortunately, this was not the case on Green beach's west side, which the Germans still mostly held with a small force. Naturally, re-embarking under these conditions would be a terribly costly affair.

It was just around the time that the withdrawal began that news of the raid first reached Hitler's *Führerhauptquartier* headquarters near the Ukrainian city of Vinnytsia, known to the occupying Germans as Winniza. Hidden in Vinnytsia's thick surrounding forest, this headquarters was named *Wehrwolf*. Hitler was particular about this spelling as a play on the German words '*Wehr*' ('defence' or 'weapon') and '*Werwolf*' (werewolf). '*Wehrwolf*' is not to be confused with the more famous Wolf's Lair headquarters located in East Prussia. Hitler had moved to *Wehrwolf* midway through July in order to direct 'Case Blue', the Wehrmacht's summer offensive in the East, and he would stay in Ukraine until late October. Organization Todt had begun work on the HQ in November 1941, and it was still partly under construction in August 1942. Overall, over 8,000 OT workers and 1,000 Russians worked on the site, for a total of 179,500 work days.[15] The whole complex was a striking piece of engineering, comprising everything that a small town might possess, from a barber's shop to a swimming pool. Hitler and his staff occupied twenty wooden blockhouses covering five square kilometres – these were built from untreated wood, as Hitler had complained in the past about being affected by chemical wood preservatives. Security measures were imposing too. Underground guard posts housed Hitler's sizeable security detail, and the trees of Vinnytsia's forest were adapted to serve as observation posts around the perimeter.

On 19 August the Führer was expecting a very special guest from Berlin – no less than his Propaganda Minister and close confidant Joseph Goebbels. After he landed at around 11 o'clock, a young SS lieutenant hurriedly greeted the Reichsminister and rushed to explain what was happening in France. As Goebbels was driven through Vinnytsia, his eye was caught by the 'many pretty, well grown and healthy-looking women', as he later noted in his diary. He was generally impressed with the city, its cleanliness and how much it looked as it would have in peacetime. It was not just the women that Goebbels was impressed by – to his own deluded Nazi mind, the great Führer's presence near the occupied city had clearly rubbed off on its people: 'Most of Vinnytsia's inhabitants know that the *Führerhauptquartier* is right near their city. They don't think of being partisans or saboteurs; rather, they are just proud of having the Führer near them.' So deluded was the Propaganda Minister by his own indoctrination that he appeared to believe it was the Führer's presence which pacified the local population, rather than the brutal Nazi military government. Arriving at Wehrwolf – this was his first visit – Goebbels was impressed by its broader design and larger scale compared to the Wolf's Lair. He appreciated its more comfortable rooms, remarking that it looked at first glance like a traditional East German summer retreat. When he stepped inside the new headquarters' inner sanctum, Goebbels encountered an electric atmosphere amongst the military and civilian staff. Even from what little information had reached Ukraine from Normandy, it was clear that the Dieppe operation was something different to anything that had come before: 'That this English endeavour cannot be compared with the previous "Commando operations" is obvious. They have never before used so many troops and substantial weapons.' He subsequently added, 'What they have up their sleeves isn't clear at the moment, either. The reports that von Rundstedt is sending are incomplete and don't offer a clear picture. Nobody in the Führer's headquarters doubts, however, that the English will be sent home with a massive slap in the face.'

After talking briefly to Julius Schaub, Hitler's chief aide and adjutant, Goebbels went straight to the situation room, where his beloved Führer was conducting the *Lagebesprechung,* Hitler's daily conference with his

OKW high command staff. All those whom Goebbels saw shared in the feverish, even ecstatic mood around the Wehrwolf. As ever, he had no doubt whatsoever where all this energy was coming from: 'Nowhere is there greater optimism than around the Führer.' Upon entering the situation room, the Reichsminister noticed that the Führer was feeling unwell, and he later learned this was the result of a bout of dysentery. As usual, the *Lagebesprechung* covered all areas of concern, especially the struggle around the Soviet town of Rzhev north-west of Moscow. Towards the meeting's end the ongoing Dieppe battle was discussed. The men in the room speculated about the Allies' motivations and considered the possibility that this truly was the beginning of a second front. They learned from British radio broadcasts that the Dieppe force consisted mostly of non-British soldiers – Canadians, Americans and Free French fighters (whom the Germans insisted on calling 'de Gaulle troops'). Always thinking of ways to rupture the Allies' multinational coalition, Goebbels called this development a 'very gratifying' one.[16] In response, Hitler briefly considered shifting the SS *Grossdeutschland* infantry division all the way from the Caucasus region to France – indeed, only a few days earlier, such a move westwards had been cancelled. Ultimately, he was dissuaded from doing so when a cable arrived from Rundstedt stating confidently that the Allied force could be ejected from Europe without further assistance.[17]

After this withdrawal phase of the battle began, the air battle over Dieppe became, if anything, more not less intense. In order to distract German fighters from the main struggle, Leigh-Mallory sent a group of RAF Typhoons on a high-altitude diversionary sweep towards Ostend in western Flanders with the goal of simulating a bombing raid. Abbeville airfield picked up this formation on radar but disregarded it, assuming it to be the feint that it was. No German fighters were sent up to meet the Typhoons. Clearly, the Luftwaffe would not be deflected from their central task at Dieppe, and KG 2's Do 217 bombers continued to strike against targets at sea, most importantly the Hunt-class destroyers guarding the transport ships which carried the landing craft.

At first, the Germans could not be certain that a withdrawal was underway, but all the indicators were there. Just as the Allied landing craft went in to save what men they could, Reconnaissance Squadron 122 informed OB West of 'seven English large naval units', which, most importantly, were 'sighted moving in [the] direction of [the] English coast'. Rundstedt's staff summarized the situation, taking into consideration the naval effort underway in front of Dieppe: 'Everything points to the enemy having recognized the failure at Dieppe and cancelled the operation.' In a painfully precise appraisal of what was to come for those Canadians and British still trapped on the beaches, the commentary concluded: 'This may mean annihilation for the parts of his force which landed.'

Rundstedt grew increasingly confident that his adversaries had been well and truly crushed, so much so that at 1220 he ordered Dieppe's railway lines open for civilian traffic and allowed its French population to return to work.[18] Soon, Dieppe's shops were back to normal, conducting their business as if nothing had ever happened. Rundstedt's relaxation, however, made less difference to the French than he might have imagined. Dieppe's population throughout the battle had seemed generally unperturbed by the commotion. Cars drove in and out of Dieppe throughout 19 August, and some civilian telephone lines remained serviceable.[19] One elderly milkman calmly drove around in his milk float on his daily rounds, and later nonchalantly complained that he could not deliver to the nursery because of the fighting there. In the various rural villages just a few miles behind the lines, farmers continued to work as normal. Contrary to what the Germans had feared and expected, there were no attempts whatsoever by the French population to sabotage or otherwise hinder German defence efforts. In fact, some Frenchmen and women aided the Germans' cause. Soldiers were particularly grateful for gifts of fresh food and drink, while German airmen often found themselves the beneficiaries of generous French hospitality after bailing out or crash-landing. French civil defence personnel, and some civilians, aided the Germans in putting out fires, even at the risk of their own safety. There are no recorded examples of Dieppe's population aiding the Anglo-Canadians, though this is unsurprising considering how little ground the Allies actually occupied. A report from the German state security service (*Reichssicherheitshauptamt*) later described Dieppe's civilians as 'calm and disciplined'.[20]

In part, the French inclination to aid (or at least passively observe) rather than undermine the German defence effort was driven by concern for their own life and property. Nobody is inclined to sympathize with a military force making rubble out of their home town, regardless of which cause they might be fighting for. The Allies, too, avoided cooperation with those whose homes they were attacking, expressly appealing to the men, women and children of Dieppe not to offer assistance to the raiders. Early on 19 August, British radio broadcast warnings to France, urging its populace to play no part in what was to come. To reinforce this message, aircraft dropped leaflets over Dieppe with the following plea:

Men and women of France!

This is a raid and not the invasion.
We urge you to take no part in it in any way and to not do anything that could lead to reprisals from the enemy.
We appeal to your composure and common sense.
When the time comes, we will warn you. Then we will act, shoulder to shoulder, for our common victory and your freedom![21]

These warnings were brought by the Canadian infantry too. Civilian defence worker Georges Dauzou, back from his ordeal at the front line, was now ferrying wounded civilians to a shelter within Dieppe, 100 metres between the esplanade and inner harbour. He had already seen a handful of Canadians running about within the town, and he found another in front of the shelter who pulled out a wad of the small leaflets and told the Frenchman to distribute them. Dauzou refused, however, for fear of German reprisals. Later, Dauzou was accosted by another Canadian and was briefly interrogated about wearing his military-looking helmet, armband and gas mask case. Dauzou explained that he was a civilian, after which the Canadian and Frenchman firmly – but briefly – shook hands. Before leaving, the Canadian gave Dauzou a heartfelt parting message: 'France, I will come back, I love you.'[22]

Evidently, the Allies were so concerned about collateral damage and civilian deaths that they were willing to indirectly inform the Germans that their operational objective was not a full-scale liberation of France (as desperately longed for by many inhabitants). Understandably, however, this message was not taken at face value by any seriously-minded German – such a warning could well be nothing more than a cover for a full-scale liberation attempt. Interestingly, the Kriegsmarine's communications were so slow and ineffective on 19 August that the headquarters of the

Naval Staff (the *Seekriegsleitung*) did not first hear about the raid from their own internal channels, but from intercepts of these British civilian radio broadcasts.[23] Also listening was Joseph Goebbels at the Wehrwolf headquarters in Ukraine. He was anything but sympathetic. As ever, he saw matters from a political standpoint:

> The English are calling on the French to not support this invasion attempt, so that they aren't exposed or get into trouble; new instructions will be given at an appropriate time. In other words, the English have clearly made this attempt, under Stalin's pressure, to build something like a Second Front. They aren't sure about this first attempt so they first want to test the waters. If they are successful, they'll talk about this current invasion as the long-awaited Second Front. If not, they will try to turn it around and say it was a Commando operation.[24]

Perhaps wisely, he elected to simply 'remain silent for now and let our military might play out', as he said afterwards. He would wait until the end of the day before making any definitive public pronouncement.

Undoubtedly in large part due to the calming Allied tone, on 19 August there were generally no openly rebellious acts by the French population of Dieppe, though there were some notable exceptions elsewhere. In Angers, Nantes and other big cities some Frenchmen and women took a great personal risk by listening to British radio broadcasts for news, an act naturally forbidden during the occupation. In Rouen the local population went a step further. Small gatherings took place in the streets, and people spoke openly about – and hoping for – a final liberation from the 'Boche' occupiers.[25] Ultimately however, these minor acts of defiance were insignificant and posed no threat whatsoever to German rule in France. What brief hope the French may have had was crushed when the Dieppe raid ended in abject failure. Rundstedt later commented that the behaviour of the local French population was 'not only unobjectionable, but was absolutely loyal'.[26]

There were some people who evidently did not heed the message. Jean-Louis Steinberg was a young Communist Resistance fighter in Normandy. He was a Frenchman through and through, born to a Jewish mother in Paris in 1922, and he would go on to be one of the founders of French radio astronomy after the war, but as someone with Jewish heritage he was forced to wear a yellow star. At just eighteen years old he felt compelled to join the Communist Resistance. He said later of his decision:

> When I was banned from doing this, banned from doing that, forced to wear a star, eventually forced to observe a curfew, I could see that I was part of a group that was being systematically persecuted. Well, I lived with that. What else do you want to do? But I was outraged, I was appalled. That's how I got into the Resistance, because when you are subjected to treatment like that, there are only two solutions: either you sit back and wait for it to happen and tell yourself that it will end one day, or you fight. Well me, my temperament is to fight, that's the way it is. That's the way it is. That's how I'm made.

By 1942 Steinberg was hiding out at a small farm along the River Orne several miles north of Flers in southern Normandy, having been sent out of Paris by his Communist handlers in case he was caught by the Germans. The farm was owned by a woman with two small girls who had to manage on her own – her husband had been in the French forces before the capitulation in 1940 and was still being held as a prisoner of war. She refused to charge Steinberg the extortionate black market prices – regularly five or ten times more than normal – for scarce farm produce like butter and fresh cream. Naturally, she was only too happy to aid the people fighting the Germans who had taken her husband from her. Despite these small comforts, Steinberg did not seem to mind the grave danger he was in as a resistance fighter, and even appeared to make light of it, saying, 'I was camping like an ordinary Frenchman!' As a member of the Communist Resistance, Steinberg expected to be brought back to France's capital on the eve of the liberation, in order to cause as much disruption as possible to the Germans. His hostess owned a radio and on 19 August she rushed to tell her guest the news: 'The Allies have landed at Dieppe!' After thanking her and her children for their hospitality, Steinberg hurried back to Paris to play his part in a liberation that was not to come.[27]

Just after midday, the first radio broadcast gave civilians in Germany news of what was happening in France. The initial announcement was of course incomplete and lacked detail – it simply told of a British 'landing operation on the French Channel coast' with 'strong air and naval forces'. The broadcast did, however, give an indication of how the battle was proceeding: 'The attack met with immediate resistance, and part of the British landing force has already been wiped out. German counter-measures are being applied according to plan.' Later, these words were repeated by both French and Norwegian radio.[28]

Back in Dieppe, the situation was becoming much clearer. With both the Allies and the Germans now realizing that the battle was over, a new phase of retreat and pursuit began. Reports became ever more optimistic. Rundstedt's naval partners reported at 1230: 'Burning landing craft on the beach. Several tanks still driving up and down, they are being fired at by Army guns which have been run up to the beach. Beach appears to be sealed off.'[29] Whatever the Germans may have thought about their chances, their adversaries persisted in attempts to get their poor, stranded men off the bloody, corpse-strewn beaches. Around this time, Captain Hans Ditz observed a truly harrowing sight just off the coast:

> For some time, I had seen a small enemy ship floating dead in the water, without being able to pay it much attention, because it lay outside of my arc of fire, though I did notice it gradually list more and more severely. I heard loud shouting from that direction and saw that there were many men still on the deck of the sinking ship who were crying out desperately for help. But there was nobody who could help them, if not their own people. Then the ship suddenly gave way. One of my observers saw this happen through the scissors telescope, though I did not, because I was on the telephone to my firing positions. But I did hear the terrified cluster of screams from the crew, and the deathly silence afterwards.

Mercifully, this episode later had a happy ending, as Ditz's men were able to organize a rescue for the crew after they washed up ashore on an inflatable raft.[30]

The huge inferno in Dieppe's skies now came to the fore. If the British ground force could retain their 'air umbrella' in the skies, they would have a free hand in re-embarking the men – at least as far as the air threat was concerned. However, if the umbrella could be broken or at least punctured in places, it would surely mean the end for the entire military force remaining on French soil. Therefore, far from withdrawing his planes, Air Marshal Trafford Leigh-Mallory intensified their protective efforts and thus escalated the aerial struggle between the Luftwaffe and the RAF. In his diary, Georges Guibon took time to describe the scene from his position in central Dieppe: 'A bomber, attacked by the English planes, is hit and falls in flames towards the golf course. The sound of all the bombs exploding at once is appalling. Black smoke rises straight into the air … The smoke coming from the seashore covers the whole town, you can smell the gunpowder, the burnt wood, the noise is still deafening.'[31] At 1230, FW 190s belonging to JG 2 and JG 26 succeeded in shooting down five Spitfires and an American Mustang in quick succession. One of the pilots claiming a confirmed kill was Lieutenant Paul Galland of 8th *Staffel*, brother of Adolf. In this, he was just following in his other brother's footsteps; Wilhelm-Ferdinand had already shot down a Spitfire north of Dieppe, meaning both Gallands in JG 26 could call the day of Dieppe a successful one.

It was not just the Galland brothers who would be celebrating at the end of the day, for the whole German fighter force had enjoyed great success over Dieppe. One important factor was the relatively low altitude at which the combat on 19 August took place. The FW 190 was a weak fighter at higher altitudes, especially since only the early A-1, A-2 and A-3 models were being flown in France at this time in 1942. These versions were powered by various developments of BMW's 801 engine generating 1,540 horsepower. The problem at high altitude for the FW 190 A-1 through A-3 was the weakness in its supercharger, meaning, in basic terms, that as the air going into the engine became thinner (due to increasing altitude), its performance suffered tremendously. This was so much a problem that Focke-Wulf's engineers were already exploring solutions; hence JG 2 and JG 26's inclusion of a special Bf 109 *Höhenjagdstaffel* or high-altitude flight each. When the American Flying Fortresses came to attack Abbeville airfield from way up at 23,000ft, for instance, they could be sure no Focke-Wulf would be there to meet them. However, the centre of gravity in the air struggle on 19 August lay at only a few thousand feet, perfect for the FW 190s of JG 2 and JG 26. In medium and low altitude dogfights the Focke-Wulfs reigned supreme, as they were manoeuvrable and quick to climb and dive. So worried had the RAF been by the FW 190's introduction in the West that they had brought in the Spitfire Mk. IX, which would make its large-scale debut over Dieppe. This was a great improvement over the Spitfire Mk. V, which had taken a beating in earlier aerial combat over occupied France during 1942. Yet only two of the Spitfire squadrons providing the air umbrella flew the improved Mk. IXs, the vast majority using the vulnerable Mk. V. During Dieppe's air battle, the Spitfire Mk. V was outclassed by the superior Focke-Wulfs. By the day's end, a shade under a half of all RAF losses would be Mk. Vs.

It is hard to quantify what really made the difference in Dieppe's air struggle, labelled by Norman Franks 'the Greatest Air Battle'. What turned matters in the Germans' favour? A few explanations come quickly to mind. Firstly, and most obviously, the Germans were fighting over friendly territory, as the RAF had been doing two years earlier during the Battle of Britain. This meant quicker re-arming and repairing times for its aircraft. In addition, the flight across the Channel burned a significant amount of the Spitfires' fuel. Accordingly, they enjoyed much reduced time over the battle space. Flying over enemy-held France also brought land-based anti-aircraft guns into play. Of the RAF aircraft lost on 19 August, one sixth were shot down by anti-aircraft crews; this includes twenty-three Hurricanes out of a total of twenty-six shot down, demonstrating the mortal danger faced by low-flying close air support fighter-bombers.[32] Secondly, the technical superiority of the FW 190 over the Spitfire Mk. V provided an unavoidable edge. Thirdly, on a tactical level, the RAF 'air umbrella' was mandated to stay put over the raiding force at sea and provide top cover. This was their task, and they performed it effectively. But the static and defensive nature of the air cover plan meant that German fighter patrols could pick and choose their fights, only attacking when a favourable position presented itself. RAF Spitfires rarely ventured to pursue German fighters which had entered the umbrella. Fighter pilots in the era of dogfighting needed one thing above all in order to be successful: altitude. With altitude came the ability to convert height into speed. With speed, German fighter pilots could dip into an RAF formation for an attack and quickly dip out again, leaving their adversaries helpless. Coming out of the sun (i.e. with the attacking aircraft between the target and sun) was another typical pilots' trick, rendering the prey blind. These tactics were instrumental in giving the Germans a hefty tally on 19 August. After the battle, Air Fleet 3 believed that more human factors were at play: 'In spite of the enemy's numerical superiority, the [aggression] and better training of the German fighter pilots resulted in very successful operations.' It added that the capabilities of the Spitfire pilots varied greatly: 'Some units showed very good teamwork, kept good formation and were very aggressive. Other formations flew like novices and, aided by the [clouds], it was not difficult to make surprise attacks on them'. This 'Greatest Air Battle' was by no means a one-sided affair, however. It was an incredibly intense struggle for both sides, and the Luftwaffe admitted some RAF pilots demonstrated admirable combat flying skills: 'The well-trained formation weaved a great deal and kept a good watch to the rear. German attacks were generally recognized while the run-in was still being made. When the enemy observed the attack he turned skilfully and attempted to meet it head-on. Other units attempted to escape under cover of cloud.' But this kind of post-match analysis was not what was running through the pilots' heads on 19 August. Dogfighting was a quite frankly confused, frantic and desperate business, and one needed great courage even to think about strapping oneself into a cockpit.

The Germans had been dominant in the air up until the withdrawal began and would continue to be so. Just after midday on 19 August, JG 26 alone had notched up twenty-one confirmed and eight unconfirmed victories, most of them against Spitfires. Their success continued throughout the day. Overall, it had so far been a frantic and intense day for the Luftwaffe. The very high pace of operations was taking its toll on both men and machines. By midday, most pilots had flown three or four times. By the end of 19 August, nearly all would have flown three or four sorties, with some having flown as many as six. Field Marshal Sperrle of Air Fleet 3 had around 230 fighters available and in range, and all of them were being used, with no reserves available. These numbers were hugely exceeded by the more than 1,000 aircraft that Air Marshal Leigh-Mallory controlled. The RAF had not expected an effort half as intense as the Germans were able to achieve. With seventy-four squadrons of bombers and fighters, by midday (German time) the Allies' Air Force Commander had been able to mount a massive undertaking, upwards of 1,300 sorties of all types. This was not something that the Germans could hope to match, so their airmen were not trying to wrest total air superiority from the RAF. That would have been foolish. Rather, they were attempting to gain very local and specific air control where their bombers were flying, so that the latter could carry out their mission.

KG 2's bombers were solely concerned with attacking Allied shipping and disregarded the fighting on land. Consequently, most of the air combat on 19 August took place over the Channel. Only the North American Mustangs penetrated a considerable distance inland, as these planes were charged with tactical reconnaissance for the ground forces. KG 2 was performing admirably under the circumstances which faced it. Having been relegated for so long to small-scale *Störangriffe* (nuisance night-time attacks) against targets in Southern England, the crews of its Dornier 217 twin-engined bombers were eager to make their mark. Their objective was clear: sink as many Allied vessels at sea as possible, big or small. One subsequent report remarked that 'in their uncontrolled enthusiasm, a number of crews sought targets out beyond German fighter cover. These men, who simply wanted to "have a go" and flew into swarms of enemy fighters in full knowledge of what they were doing, showed an exemplary spirit. It was not, however, a wise thing to do and some of the losses which occurred must be attributed to this cause.'[33]

Günther Niemeyer was among those on board one of Air Fleet 3's Do 217s, but unlike the trained crew, he was new to combat flying. In fact, he did not really belong there at all; he was not even a military man, merely a journalist along for the ride. Niemeyer was a well-travelled individual, having reported on Germany's war effort from as far away as Finnish-occupied Liinakhamari, inside the Arctic Circle on the Kola Peninsula. In August 1942, however, he was fortunate enough to be doing his job in a rather more temperate climate. Niemeyer and his Dornier's crew had been woken by the *Staffel* commander, who then rapidly briefed his men. Drawing a large semi-circle on a map of northern France, the *Staffel* leader explained that a large naval force had been detected off Dieppe, and that the *Staffel* had been ordered to strike them. On reaching Dieppe, Niemeyer described the scene in forceful tones typical of a war reporter's. Picking out the identification cross on the side of every German aircraft, he wrote, 'Everywhere black and white *Balkenkreuze* buzzed around.... Suddenly enemy fighters have their teeth stuck into our comrades on our right, the other aircraft in our pair. We parry a few attackers, firing all our weapons. The aircraft to our right seems to have bought it. New bursts of fire shoot past, slashing open the side plate and riddling it with bullets.' Over the Channel, Niemeyer saw another bomber hit, then at a distance the white dots of the crew's parachutes. In contrast, Niemeyer's Dornier made it back to base without a scratch, flying back over the town. On their flight back home, the war reporter described the 'fountains of earth' thousands of feet below him as explosions on land threw soil into the air.[34]

Chapter 10

Pursuit: 1230–1400 hrs

On the ground at Pourville, Colonel Klemm's reinforced regiment was finally ordered to move up the west bank of the River Scie by divisional commander Haase. This came through at 1240. However, it was only expected that Klemm would go into action about two hours later, such was the sluggish nature of the reserves' movement. Elements of 676th Infantry Regiment, with which he was supposed to attack, were only just beginning to arrive in Offranville, three miles away from Green beach. It is difficult, perhaps impossible, to overstate how slowly 302nd Division's reserves came into play. A significant factor in this was that most men had no motorized transport. It was designated a 'static' division for a reason. The leisurely German reinforcement at Pourville, as well as Major Law's wise decision to withdraw pre-emptively, saved the SSRs and Camerons from being annihilated. If it were not for him, Green beach might have looked like Blue, Red or White.

Even so, the men at Pourville suffered in their attempts to withdraw. Since the invaders had not cleared the western or eastern cliffs overlooking the town, the Germans were able to inflict casualties every step of the way. At 1200, the same time that the withdrawal on Red and White began, the British landing craft turned up at Green. Now it was obvious to the Germans that a retreat was underway. LXXXI Corps summed up the situation just before 1300: 'Situation east of Dieppe cleared up … [At] Dieppe, about a dozen tanks shot up. Mopping up on the beach proceeds satisfactorily. To the west of Dieppe enemy still in position at Pourville, counter-attack with two battalions is underway and going well.' HMS *Calpe* approached so close to the eastern headland near Red beach that the Germans opened fire on it with machine guns and rifles. As a result of the German dominance on shore, Hughes-Hallett could only risk one run into shore to pick up the remnants from Green. Despite not clearing a safe perimeter, most of the remaining SSRs and Camerons made their way onto a landing craft. This was thanks in no small part to an outstanding rearguard action led by Lieutenant Colonel Merritt of the South Saskatchewans. Merritt, knowing full well that he and his men would become prisoners of war, held the Germans at bay, allowing others to reach safety. For his actions, Merritt was awarded a Victoria Cross. At 1437, 571st Infantry Regiment finally reported: 'Pourville firmly in our hands.'[1] So ended the briefest of Canadian incursions into France.

It had taken some time, but the war reporter Ulrich Haussmann had finally arrived at the scene of the action after a long drive north. Arriving at the front row of houses, he asked a nearby lieutenant for an update on what was going on. The officer could not tell him much, but had hardly finished when a cry of 'Take cover!' rang out as machine-gun bullets skipped down the street, causing tiny puffs of dust to leap into the air all around. Haussmann then came across a veteran warrant officer, proudly wearing his 1914 Iron Cross, who was in charge of his unit's anti-tank weapons – a collection of Molotov cocktails. With no dedicated or purpose-designed anti-armour weapon, this was the best that could be devised. The Molotov cocktail was a primitive but effective weapon; designs varied hugely, but all were based on a breakable bottle filled with flammable liquid like petrol or alcohol. When the soaked wick was lit and the bottle was thrown against a hard target, the whole contraption ignited violently, causing a fireball and spreading flames. 'With these things', the warrant officer explained proudly, 'even the heaviest caterpillar chain collapses, just like a shattered bicycle chain.'[2] To the east, another team of journalists was rushing to the coastline – these were radio reporters recording the sounds of battle, and they were able to set up their equipment on the eastern headland overlooking Dieppe. An unnamed commentator kept up an excited, but no doubt exaggerated, rapid sports-style play-by-play account of events. He spoke in a passable – but doubtless artificial – North American accent, so that the recording could be broadcast to Allied nations afterwards: 'The British try, they are trying, they are having some trouble – and they're having it right now as we reach the beach. From our spot, not more than 300 yards away from the main scene of action, we have a splendid view. Hell seems to be loose.' The commentary briefly became unintelligible as an aircraft flew overhead, then resumed:

Short flying boats are laying smokescreens. It is hazy about us, chloride stings in our nostrils. Anti-tank guns and machine guns rattle. Those Tommies are being just mowed down. There, one tank burns, there's another one – a third one! A fourth! Hell! One crawls up right in front of us, towards us, fifty yards, sixty yards! It approaches the street. In a desperate wait, bent low, are the British infantrymen. We see them already, very clearly. Most of them have their face blackened. To our left, we see a crew of young German boys, all of them are crouched behind their gun. There goes the shot, oh boy, what a hit! That last chain of the tank is flying off! Yes, now it burns![3]

Now that the tactical picture had turned irreversibly and unmistakably in their favour, the Germans turned to a pursuit. At 1315, Rundstedt issued another appreciation of the situation at Dieppe to his troops, signalling that the Allied foothold in France must be ruthlessly annihilated: 'Now, it is up to us to destroy what can be destroyed. For that purpose every weapon and every barrel must be employed.' Further to this proclamation, Rundstedt ordered 10th Panzer Division to speed towards the coast without regard to forming up as a cohesive unit. They were to drive as hard as possible without regard for their machines: 'Every available weapon must now contribute to complete destruction of the enemy. The whole front on which the enemy had landed must be cleared up in the shortest of time!'[4] As things panned out, however, Brigadier Fischer's tanks would arrive far too late to have an impact; 10th Panzer's vanguard would still be roughly eight miles south of the coast by 1400. This surely disappointed Fischer, who had eagerly rushed ahead to Hautot to scout out exactly where his tanks would intervene.

Although the battle was not yet at an end, preparations were underway for the collection of prisoners. A PoW camp had already been prepared against the eventuality of a large-scale Allied landing, and this was now activated. One need not have read the military theories of Carl von Clausewitz to recognize that politics and war are one and the same; propaganda companies, too, with their multitude of newsreel cameras, were already on their way to the coast to gleefully capture the striking images of a total Anglo-Canadian disaster and broadcast them to the world.

Even at this late stage, some Germans on the ground believed that there was more to come. Captain Hans Ditz, sitting in his observation bunker west of Dieppe, was sure that a parachute or air-landed force was coming to turn the tide. Having been warned time and again about the dangers posed by Churchill's airborne forces, this was a reasonable concern. Ditz's fears seemed to be justified when he saw a group of Boston bombers flying straight towards him. Their twin-engine design made them look just like the transport planes which would be used to ferry parachutists to the battlefield. Ditz and his men prepared themselves for the worst, but instead saw the Allied aircraft open their bomb bay doors and drop strange cube-like shapes almost on top of them. Ditz later remarked that they appeared rather like dice before they hit the ground. 'There was a dull thud', he recalled, 'and out sprang a fountain of white jets that expanded rapidly and soon formed an impenetrable white wall. More of these fountains sprang up all around us, and soon all of us, our firing position and observation post, were enveloped in such a dense fog that we could no longer see our hands in front of our eyes.' For Ditz, though, that these curious packages were smoke bombs and not explosives brought great relief: 'I must confess that it was a great weight off my mind. This could only mean that the Canadians were now trying to re-embark their landing troops and were therefore endeavouring to eliminate all our observation posts.' This blinding smoke remained for over an hour, until a breeze blew it away and finally restored Ditz's vision out to sea. By then, Hughes-Hallett's ships had turned tail.[5]

While the defeated Canadians were coming off Green beach, Red and White witnessed the most humiliating of scenes. Under copious amounts of smoke, landing craft had made one run to pick up survivors from in front of Dieppe at 1200. Some had even been lucky enough to get a ticket home on one of them. For most stuck on the main beaches, however, nothing but the ignominy of captivity remained. Artificial smoke, ironically, had vastly reduced visibility and diminished the value of gunfire support from the destroyers, but as Hughes-Hallett later admitted, 'Without the smoke it is doubtful whether any withdrawal would have been possible.'[6] German domination of the beach and shoreline would make the run-in at midday the sole evacuation attempt. Major General Roberts commanding 2nd Canadian Division was at first adamant that there should be another attempt after the landing craft returned to the ships half an hour later at 1230, but this was rightly judged too risky in the end. From this point on, wave upon wave of Canadian prisoners fell into German hands.

An hour later, 571st Infantry Regiment finally received permission from Haase's divisional headquarters to advance openly on the beaches. One party of Canadians, seeing the writing on the wall, sent a German prisoner towards the town with a white towel to wave about. In a flash, a great mass of Germans jumped onto Dieppe's sea wall and pointed their weapons menacingly at the abject Canadians below. Red and White beaches saw some grievous episodes of human survival. Some men chose to swim out to sea in a desperate attempt to return home. Others had been in the water out at sea for hours, having had their landing craft sunk from underneath them. One captured infantryman relayed his story to a German war reporter, but the German correspondent most likely exaggerated or fabricated the Canadian's language in translation, as was common in the Nazi press:

Many of my comrades died or were heavily wounded in the boats, and these were then sunk by direct hits. I myself was in the water in a life vest for five hours and kept myself afloat on planks. Because I couldn't swim, I was half-conscious when I was finally washed ashore with the tide. I couldn't join in the actual fight any more because of my exhaustion. So I stayed in cover until I was taken prisoner. There was no thought of getting back, as not many of our boats would have made it across. So far as I could see, all of the ships intended for the return had been taken under heavy fire and then sunk. We have none of our belongings, but we couldn't save anything. The shelling on the coast was terrifying – I can say I've never been through something like that before.[7]

Some Canadians escaped capture for a time. Private Jack Kimberly from the RHLI had had three landing craft shot from underneath him as he tried to evacuate the main beaches. When there were no more craft to take him back to England, he swam back to shore:

I landed on the east side of Dieppe harbour, and waited there till dark and then I walked up the coast. I think I walked fifteen or twenty miles, and I was dog tired. [I] crawled into a stone hut the French fishermen had built there and just fell asleep. The next thing I could hear voices, it seemed like they were far away, and I opened my eyes and I saw the ugliest face I had ever seen in my life. It was a German soldier with a rifle pointed right at me saying [to] come out of there, [shouting] '*Raus! Raus!*'[8]

In an undertaking on Jubilee's scale it might have been useful to refer to the agreed upon plan at times, had it gone as intended, and by a great stroke of luck, the Germans captured one of the two copies of the Jubilee plan which had been brought ashore. One of those entrusted with a copy was Brigadier William Southam. Of course, events had transpired so disastrously that the plan had been of no use whatsoever. As the Germans came over Dieppe's sea wall, Southam desperately tried to bury this precious document, which ran to over 100 pages. It was all in vain. An eagle-eyed German officer saw what his Canadian enemy was doing and quickly put a stop to it. This thick wad of paper would prove a great intelligence coup, and would be quickly translated by Rundstedt's staff at OB West. Even more worrying was the fact it laid out in fine detail the policy of binding German PoWs after capture; this was a crime in direct contradiction of the Geneva Conventions. Brigadier Southam's failure to burn, bury or otherwise dispose of the Jubilee operational plan was a terrible dereliction of duty. After the battle, Southam's inaction would have repercussions far beyond his imagination.

The time during which the Jubilee operation could have been termed a 'battle' had long since passed. By 1350, when Hughes-Hallett approached the shore aboard the command ship HMS *Calpe*, he saw to his dismay that the vast majority of men at Red and White had already surrendered. Even if a second evacuation had been possible, there would have been nobody to evacuate. In less than an hour's time, the only men left on Red and White would be the dead. Operation Jubilee's abject closing stages witnessed some extraordinary scenes of mass surrender. One German lieutenant, an adjutant to a flak battery, earned a coveted Iron Cross First Class for reportedly leading a team of four volunteers from his anti-aircraft unit to capture over 200 Canadians. Another man was praised by Supreme Commander Rundstedt for his devotion to duty after firing all his ammunition in a static 37mm captured French gun turret, then proceeding to take a dozen Canadians prisoner and watch over them until relieved.[9] Rundstedt later used two simple, yet entirely apt, words to describe the Anglo-Canadian withdrawal: 'Total chaos'. The German radio crew recorded the scene from their vantage point:

> Wounded are strewn all over the place. German infantry start their counter-attack. Oh boy! You see them? You see them?! Bombers are overhead. Bombs are dropping! Fighting takes place at a very narrow space. The largest transporter is hit, boy oh boy! Smoke mushrooms up well over 500 feet, it blackens the sky. A sheet of fire! Look at that, what is that?! What is that – look, look, look! Over to the right! The Tommies are starting to raise their hands! They're giving up! In front of us, too! Hundreds of them! We don't believe our eyes. It's hardly possible. The fierce battle in the air is still going on. Focke-Wulf fighters and Spitfires are having it out, there are two Hurricanes coming from the sea flying low, towards the beach. German AA guns have opened fire. Tracers fly like strings of brightly-coloured glass pearls. One Hurricane is coming down. He seems to have difficulty to keep halfway level. He seems to be making a forced landing, unfortunately he disappears behind the houses lining the beach. Now we find time and leisure to look around. Hundreds of British wounded are being carried away.[10]

If things seemed gloom-ridden for the Allies, they were about to become considerably worse. At 1400, as HMS *Calpe* approached the coast, two FW 190s from JG 26's special fighter-bomber *Staffel* dived on HMS *Berkeley*, one of Hughes-Hallett's six Hunt-class destroyers. The German planes scored a direct hit amidships with one 1,100lb bomb.[11] So great was the damage that *Berkeley* had to be scuttled by torpedoes from HMS *Albrighton* at 1425. Even at this late stage, the air struggle over Dieppe was as heavy and hectic as ever. Speeding in low at just 1,500ft, Flight Sergeant Allen Mawer described the spectacle from his Spitfire cockpit: 'The air was full of planes and the sea was full of ships. The navy was blazing away merrily and, although the fighter cover was layered up at 5, 10 and 15 thousand feet, Dornier [217] dive bombers were breaking through.' Then HMS *Berkeley* went up 'like a bloody great mine', in Mawer's blunt simile, 'leaving nothing in its place except a huge pool of burning fuel oil.'[12] From the opposite perspective on land, Captain Hans Ditz also saw *Berkeley*'s scuttling: 'Suddenly, a huge black mushroom with a cauliflower-like head rose from the burning ship, its roses turning redder and redder until finally it became a single column of fire. The ship broke apart in the middle, the bow and stern plunging so deep into the water that the broken ends of the middle rose high into the sky. As the thunder of the explosion reached us, the two halves remained in this grotesque position for a moment, then slowly sank, turning on their own axis.'[13]

HMS *Berkeley*'s sinking represented the Luftwaffe's single most significant success on the day. Even after French soil had been cleared of all Allied belligerents, the war in the air continued unabated. Nor would Sperrle's pilots let up even after scoring their victory against Hughes-Hallett's fleet. Shortly after HMS *Berkeley* went down, JG 26's 3rd *Gruppe* took off for its fourth patrol of the day from Wevelgem in western Flanders, Belgium. Their mission was to escort some Do 217s to the Dieppe area. A short while later, it arrived at Dieppe and the bombers began their attack runs out at sea amidst a swarm of RAF Spitfires. Generally, the German bombers had so far been ineffective, since Leigh-Mallory's air umbrella and naval flak fended off any calm, considered and accurate bombing attacks. Placing a bomb on a moving target from a bomber moving at hundreds of miles per hour is hard enough; it is inordinately more difficult when you are being shot at with tracer rounds, which are uniquely discouraging even to the bravest pilots.

Lieutenant Otto Stammberger, flying escort for the Dorniers, later spoke to a German war correspondent about what happened next. As ever, the journalist had no compunction in using dramatic language to spice up his story: 'We were in the middle of them; our formation split up, and a disorderly whirlwind ensued. Finally my pair broke through and sat above the entire assembly. Thus I was able to peacefully seek out two unsuspecting cavaliers who were flying around as though on a joy ride.' Stammberger had been flying with JG 26 for eighteen months without scoring a single victory. Eager to change this, he decided to pounce on this pair of Spitfires below him:

I reached a good position and gave one of them a full salvo. When I rushed past him I saw that his aileron was shot through and his landing gear had dropped. The Spitfire also smoked from the oil cooler. It was obvious that this lad was done for. He fell away and struck the ocean. While I was watching him, I turned around briefly to ensure my own security. There was the other fellow, waiting to give me a spanking. I refused to let him come near, and vanished. Then I fooled around for a while with my wingman until my red lamp showed that my fuel was almost gone.[14]

Delighted with his first ever combat kill, Stammberger waggled his wings in triumph all the way back to base – but air activity continued over Dieppe.

As the Allied naval force slipped back meekly to its home ports in Portsmouth and Newhaven on the southern English coast, 571st Infantry Regiment mopped up the beach and sent the thousand or so prisoners rearwards. Air operations continued far longer than those on land. The Luftwaffe kept on harrying Hughes-Hallett's ships as they made their way home. FW 190s and Bf 109s claimed several kills in the aftermath of Dieppe, and German bombers continued their merciless pursuit of Allied shipping. Increasing cloud cover made it easier for them to slip in and out of the standing aerial umbrella, but these were only nuisance attacks – the Germans knew that they had won a great victory in the air against forces numerically far superior to their own. On the ground, the Germans mopping up the dead and living on Red and White beach could hear the desperate cries of Canadians stranded out at sea. Some had had rescue crafts sunk underneath them, others had swum out on purpose to escape the slaughter on the beach. Some would drown, but mercifully, some of them would be saved. One of their saviours was Captain Emil Hirschfeld. Hirschfeld was certainly the physical type – he was a world-class shot-putter, having set two world records on either side of the 1928 Amsterdam Summer Olympics, at which he had won a bronze medal. The captain ordered his men to save as many Canadians as possible, upon which Warrant Officer Waltenheimer swam out to sea with two lifebuoy rings, managing to return with two thankful rescuees. Hirschfeld and a military doctor found a fisherman's rowing boat which they hoped to use. Unfortunately though, the boat was ill-maintained and was leaking. In an inspired move, the captain and the doctor threw off their uniforms, plugging the holes with the fabric. Waltenheimer then used his uniform as a rope, tying himself to the little fisherman's boat, and went out to sea once again, saving another Canadian who was clinging wretchedly to a sinking landing craft.[15]

Although the ground battle was over, Allied aircraft still occasionally made passes over Dieppe. In one tragic incident, a low-flying Spitfire strafed a German hospital van ferrying four wounded Canadians to a field hospital in the rear areas. The ambulance burst into flames which blocked access to the rear door. Neither the efforts of the driver, nor those of a nearby Flak battery, could save the four Canadians trapped helplessly inside.[16] The radio reporter on the eastern headland commentated on one small dogfight over the French coast: 'There's one of those Spitfires again flying low, hell-bent for shooting with all cannons and machine guns. German AA guns [fire] again from all sides. Focke-Wulf fighters are diving down. Tracer bullets went just over our heads. We keep our noses well to the ground. Oh boy! One Spitfire shows black smoke. There's a pilot [who] seems to have lost control of his plane – too late – he hits the water with a big splash, he's done for.' He then signed off, all the while being interrupted by noisy low-flying Spitfires: 'Now we see the tanks – there seem to be eighteen or twenty of them – all shot to pieces. The crews have all climbed out or they are dead. In the meanwhile the boys that have gained the building over on the beach have been smoked out and they have surrendered. That hopefully-started second front' – he paused once again as a fighter flew overhead – 'has ended as fast as we thought it would, even if some of the Spitfires above us are not convinced as yet!'[17] In the evening, as if to rub salt into the Allies' wounds, on the other side of the Channel the Luftwaffe mounted an attack on Hughes-Hallett's sheltering raiding fleet. In darkness, Portsmouth's harbour was attacked by fifty aircraft. The Luftwaffe claimed two 5–6,000-ton transport ships destroyed, with more probably damaged. This, however, was a typical case of pilot's over-confidence; no Allied ships or coastal installations suffered any damage whatsoever.

Only a little over 1,600 of the 5,000 Canadians who left England made their way back home; this included the men who did not land at all. At 1320, Major General Haase's operations staff told Brigadier Wolfgang Fischer of 10th Panzer Division that his unit's services were no longer required. An hour later, 571st Regiment reported to Haase at divisional headquarters that the main beach was completely clear of the enemy. At the same time, it reported Pourville beach was clear too. Only nine hours had passed since the first Allied Commando set foot on French soil. Now, the only Allies left in France had their hands above their heads. The Germans were triumphant. The Germans had held Dieppe.

Part III

After the Battle

Chapter 11

An Ignominious Defeat

Too often, history is told in raw numbers; lists of casualties killed, wounded, missing and so on. Sometimes this is useful, but numbers alone do not tell the full story of Dieppe, or how great the German victory really was. Statistics and numbers on their own are dry, and cannot show how torrid the raid truly was. However, casualty figures do provide a context which partially explains the rest of the story. Perhaps the most appalling figure was that of prisoners of war (PoWs) taken by the Germans. From a total Allied force of 6,100 men of all nations, the Wehrmacht took over 2,000 prisoner; 1,874 of these were Canadians, not including the handful of men who died in captivity as a result of their wounds. Canada's contribution to the land force at Dieppe was 4,963 men, with the British adding another 1,000 Commandos and Royal Marines. Normally in military operations, the rule of thumb is to assume one man killed for every three wounded. That so many men were killed – proportionately speaking – shows how brutal and bloody the fighting on Dieppe's beaches was. The Canadian losses were especially horrific. Two years after the Dieppe raid, as the Canadian Army fought its way from the Normandy beaches in 1944 all the way into the heart of Germany in 1945, it suffered fewer men captured than on 19 August. That fact in isolation is startling. Of the 4,963 Canadians who embarked only 2,211 returned to England, and as many as 1,000 of these had never even set foot on French soil. A good many of those fortunate enough to return were wounded. More of a human tragedy was the number of men killed in such a militarily fruitless operation. Just a shade under 1,000 Allied soldiers, sailors and airmen died fighting on the 19th. By dawn on 20 August, all told, 3,367 Canadians either lay dead, were captured or were wounded. Major General Roberts' 2nd Canadian Division was essentially destroyed as an organized fighting unit; it would take many, many months of replenishment before the division could even begin to consider itself ready for action once again. The same could not be said for Haase and his 302nd Infantry Division, as the German casualty figures were comparatively minuscule. Including all three services (Army, Kriegsmarine and Luftwaffe), only 297 Germans were killed on 19 August – about a third of the Canadian figure. Almost as many Luftwaffe personnel were killed as Army men – 104 to 115 respectively. These figures are understandable, considering how often the Luftwaffe were forced to defend their own installations along the coastline. All told, only 208 German soldiers, sailors and airmen were wounded. Strikingly, 7 Company, which had borne the brunt of the fighting along the seafront, suffered only sixteen dead and just over fifty wounded. Thirty-six French civilians died during the day's fighting.

The Germans captured a great deal of Allied materiel and equipment. Twenty-seven of the twenty-nine Churchills made landfall, while two were lost at sea. Six Bren gun carriers and a Daimler Dingo scout car completed the list of vehicles that fell into German hands. Of small arms, the Germans captured at least 1,242 rifles, 165 light machine guns, 80 mortars and 60 anti-tank rifles. There was too much ammunition to count.[1] So much explosive material was strewn about that in the coming days the German suffered repeated incidents of accidental detonation, leading to many injuries and some deaths. On 22 August divisional commander Haase forbade any entry to the beaches except to those on official business, on pain of court martial.[2] A week later on 30 August, a colonel and lieutenant from the Army's *Waffenamt* (literally 'Weapons Office'), the agency responsible for creating and testing all German land weapons and vehicles, were killed by an ammunition explosion.

Allied planners had hoped to provoke a great air battle over Dieppe and draw the Luftwaffe into a confrontation in which it would be decimated. However, these dreams were crushed. The Germans ruled in the air as well as on the ground. The RAF and its allied air forces lost 106 airframes, 98 of which were single-engined types. By comparison, the Luftwaffe lost only 48 airframes, 25 bombers and 23 fighters – not including a further 24 which were damaged. Unquestionably, the RAF had suffered a clear numerical defeat. Inevitably, some losses in the air had to be accepted if 2nd Canadian Division and the Commandos were to complete their objectives in and around Dieppe. Broadly speaking, all air power exists in support of land power. However, it is a different question for air power strategists whether these losses would have been acceptable in order to protect the raiding fleet and land forces, though this debate is essentially academic, considering the scale of the Allies' defeat on land.

At sea, the statistical picture for the Allies was equally grim. In addition to the loss of HMS *Berkeley*, a 1,500-ton Hunt-class destroyer, thirty-three landing craft of varying types were sunk. It is impossible to tell how many were taken out by coastal artillery or aircraft respectively, but it is likely that shore-based artillery claimed the majority due to the excellent firing positions they enjoyed for many hours. The Kriegsmarine lost *UJ 1404*, with half her crew captured and the other half killed, as well as several naval infantrymen. In addition, one small unmanned harbour patrol craft was sunk in Dieppe's port.

Dieppe's beautiful waterfront, once an irresistible lure for travellers from all over Europe, now lay in ruins. Across the seafront, the first row of houses were either burning or had already collapsed. The medieval Château de Dieppe, which stood proudly on high above all other buildings in the town, had taken a shell hit. Just below it, the historic Regina Hotel lay flattened. Nevertheless, considering the awesome power of modern firearms, the town got off lightly. Few battles last just nine hours. The Allies had largely been confined to their landing beaches, and the battle was over so quickly that their heavy weapons did not have the time to wreak havoc on this once sparkling seaside resort. Yet this came as little compensation to those who had lost houses or businesses. After a 9.00 pm curfew was declared, some *Dieppois* – as Dieppe's men and women call themselves – did not have homes to return to.

The surrendered Canadians were swiftly led rearwards to a holding area. In a cruel display of their captors' dominance, the French-speaking men of Les Fusiliers Mont-Royal were separated from the main English-speaking body. Not only this, but the Francophones were given Red Cross parcels, while the Anglophones were left wanting.[3] However, these would be the least of the Canadians' problems in the weeks and months to come. With the revelation in the captured operational plan that the Allies had planned to bind German PoWs' hands, it would instead be the Canadians who would find themselves shackled.

After marching despondently southwards, the throng of Canadian prisoners were led to Dieppe's hospital, where the wounded were separated from the unscathed. The latter were held in a field until further transportation by rail could be arranged. There were so many prisoners that a temporary holding area had to be set up inside Envermeu's sports stadium, six miles from Dieppe. The German war reporters and propaganda companies delighted in the opportunity to mine their defeated enemies for stories. Johannes Jörgensen was one of these journalists. Like all German war correspondents, he was willing to follow the Nazi party line to the letter; otherwise, his articles would never see the light of day. Jörgensen portrayed the Allied PoWs not as defeated soldiers, but as pathetic figures worthy of little serious attention. From reading his articles on Dieppe one got the impression that the Allies could not hope to defeat the invincible 'Watch in the West'. As he wrote in one such piece:

Their shock from the unexpected murderous fire of our defences yielded a certain lethargy. Some of them are still nervous wrecks and just can't believe that they – the elite troops of the Royal Canadian Army – fell into German captivity. Others seem to be completely distressed and apathetic. Anyone who saw the beach of Dieppe couldn't hold against the Canadians that they remember the morning hours of 19 August 1942 with a shudder. Many of them had to leave parts of their uniform behind, many wore bread-bags tied with string instead of boots and socks, and there were others amongst them who had covered their bullet graze wounds, scratches and scrapes with first aid bandages.

German papers were not alone in offering this view of the Canadian prisoners. Paris's *Le Matin* published an account in a similar vein: 'When they were picked up they had no idea where they were going or what they were doing. The barrage of gunfire they encountered left them with a terrifying memory. All in all, they are quite happy to have come out of the adventure alive.'

While surveying the Canadians lying on the grass miles inland from Dieppe's coast, Jörgensen also saw the human beings in front of him through a decidedly racial lens:

Walking through the swarm of Canadians, we cannot help but be reminded of the Bolsheviks that we often saw in the East. What a difference. Over there, brutish subhumans, beasts incarnate, ragged, amorphous, yet here we saw good-looking, often blond and mostly tall men who decisively refused every attempt to engage in discussion on military topics. They openly looked us in the eye and didn't have that stubbornly contemptuous, lurking and spiteful glance that we observed so often with the Bolsheviks.

Such ideologically-inspired language served to reinforce the notion that, in spite of the great victory at Dieppe, it was still the fight against Stalin which would be decisive. Indeed, the eyes of the German public were looking eastwards. For them, talk of the grand defensive wall in the West was nothing but a sideshow. Even after the Dieppe raid, it remained so. The rationale here was simple. The Soviets were the arch-enemy of the western, 'Aryan' Germans; they were Slavs, Bolshevists and (if one listened to the Nazi Party) a direct threat to the Germans' homeland. The war in the East was a savage existential struggle, which was not the case in the West.

While surveying the battlefield, something peculiar caught Jörgensen's eye. Taking in the sights of the main beach in front of Dieppe, he noticed little pieces of paper all over the pebbles:

We discovered strange notes, shaped like package labels, scattered all over the place amongst all that had been destroyed, demolished and battered by shells. At first, they were not as interesting to us as the bullet-riddled ships, the destroyed tanks and the countless captured weapons. What were these labels? What was printed on them gave us the answer: 'On His Majesty's Service'. Below that read: 'Prisoner' and 'Captured by ... Place ... Time ...', and the other side had the heading: 'Material'. It went on: 'Taken by ...' and 'Article ...' One didn't have to be a clairvoyant to immediately recognize that these tags were meant to be stuck in our buttonholes should some of us be captured by the Tommies.[4]

These labels were to be used to identify German prisoners once captured. This might have been somewhat humiliating for those unfortunate few to be captured on 19 August, but more significantly, the labels were to be used in conjunction with hand shackles, to stop the German PoWs from causing their captors trouble.

One member of the walking wounded was Corporal Robert Prouse of the Canadian Provost Corps. Only a week previously, Prouse had turned down the opportunity to attend the Canadian Officers' Training Centre in favour of going on the Dieppe raid. When he was forced to surrender right in front of the town, it was an expectedly depressing experience, though Prouse did notice that many of his new captors' lips were trembling. He speculated that this was due to their sudden face-to-face encounter with their Canadian foes. His weapon and helmet were thrown onto a heaped pile. Like all prisoners, he was frisked and his pockets rapidly emptied by greedy Germans, who snatched anything of value, from watches to cigarette lighters. 'We were marched through Dieppe', Prouse later recalled, 'which in parts was reduced to rubble, and French civilians scrambled from air raid shelters to give us the 'V' for victory sign. It was a nice gesture and a hopeful sign for the future, but they were soon chased away.' Upon reaching Dieppe's hospital, which lay just alongside the railway station south of the town centre, Prouse suddenly blacked out. When he came to he found a French nurse staring at him. Prouse did not speak French, nor did the nurse speak English. Yet this did not matter to the wounded Canadian: 'She looked kind and considerate', Prouse later recalled, 'so it didn't make any difference that I couldn't understand what she was saying.' After a while, the walking wounded were transported in box cars by rail to a hospital in Rouen. Those too severely injured to move remained in Dieppe.[5]

An hour or so after the last Canadians came off the beaches, LXXXI Corps provided Rundstedt with a short interim report: 'The enemy's Dieppe operation was smashed in just over nine hours! ... Not only did the enemy lose heavily on land, but he must also have suffered very heavy losses at sea which can merely be estimated. Our own losses seem moderate and compared to the losses of the English they appear trifling.' Even when it became clear that the Jubilee force was overwhelmingly Canadian, the Germans persisted as ever in calling their enemies 'English', regardless of which Allied nation they might hail from. In the early evening, Rundstedt reported the facts of the day to Hitler and his OKW staff in the *Führerhauptquartier* in Ukraine, beginning his message with the proudly underlined statement that 'No armed Englishman remains on the Continent!'[6]

Since ending his conference at Vinnytsia, Hitler had set aside several hours for a one-to-one talk with Goebbels. The Führer and his Propaganda Minister were dear friends and mutual confidants and often spent hours together, without an audience. Others within Hitler's inner circle envied this intimacy. Even Göring, another close and long-term friend, could not hope to match the Reichminister's influence. After the war, he was particularly bitter and vindictive towards the now-dead Goebbels. As he languished in prison at Nuremberg, former Reichsmarschall Göring ranted and raved to an American psychologist interviewing him:

Hitler used to come to my house once in a while for a cup of coffee, and because I led a normal life, he would leave about nine o'clock. I was in the habit of retiring early. However Hitler used to spend practically all of his nights, sometimes until 4.00 a.m., with Goebbels and his family. God knows what evil influence Goebbels had on him during those long visits.[7]

As the Führer and his Propaganda Minister sat over their afternoon meal discussing everything from the colossal battle for Rzhev west of Moscow to the state of Hitler's health, a steady stream of telegrams arrived from France. Even before the battle was over in the early afternoon, they had speculated as to the motive behind the operation. British, American and Canadian historians have argued for decades about what the real objective of and reason for Jubilee were, but for Goebbels and Hitler on 19 August, all was clear; it was the malign influence of the arch-Bolshevik Joseph Stalin which had led Churchill astray. Goebbels recorded in his dictated diary for the day that 'the Führer is firmly convinced that the British Prime Minister started the operation in the West under Stalin's direct pressure.' The two men did not hesitate to insult Churchill on account of his widely-known penchant for alcohol. Hitler told his dear friend the Reichsminister that Stalin was the master, and that 'Churchill the whisky barrel' could not fool him as regards his demands for another front in Europe: 'Certainly, a Second Front has been demanded from Stalin's side, and Churchill must now follow the orders of his Bolshevist chief.' Goebbels was in complete agreement, replying that 'without doubt,

Stalin has put Churchill in his iron grip. He did not let him get away with mere talk, rather he demanded real action. The mad operation against Dieppe is the first instalment.'

During his conversations with Goebbels, Hitler mentioned the name of a German officer who would benefit greatly from the Dieppe raid – Brigadier Zeitzler, Rundstedt's chief of staff. Zeitzler was a Nazi fanatic, who stressed the power of National Socialist indoctrination and willpower above all else. He tried to model himself on the Führer in both deeds and words, going as far to sport the same toothbrush moustache. Hitler was all too impressed. 'Zeitzler has been haring about for weeks in the West and has shaken all the nappers awake', the Führer told Goebbels. He continued: 'That the western area is today in such a fresh and active state of alarm is thanks in large part to him. We need not worry about the West.'[8] Clearly, he was blissfully unaware how patchy his vaunted 'Watch in the West' really was. He did not see the men sleeping into the morning of the 19th, nor did he witness embarrassing episodes like 302nd Division's bicycles collapsing. He was fortunate that the Allies were in no position to launch a 'D-Day' in 1942. Nevertheless, Hitler's false image of Zeitzler's efforts before and during the Dieppe raid would do wonders for this ambitious young brigadier's career.

Another senior officer who had rushed to Dieppe was Luftwaffe General Wilhelm Wimmer. He was responsible for managing, maintaining and defending all airbases in northern France and Belgium. Wimmer had gained a rather less positive impression of Dieppe than Zeitzler. He described a farcical scene of indiscipline he had seen just outside the town, as a small motorized anti-aircraft battery tried to manoeuvre through heavy traffic on a rural road: 'A young officer had command of the battery. Neither the platoon commander ... nor the battery commander were present. The scene was predictably poor and unwarlike. This officer had put absolutely no thought into how he would make the heavy battery and light vehicles move off. How he gave his orders was accordingly confusing.' Despite the fact that this inexperienced junior officer was in a position that he had no training for, General Wimmer clearly had no sympathy for him whatsoever. As time went on, the traffic became ever more muddled and immobile, and despite all the young officer's well-intentioned efforts, his anti-aircraft battery was still exactly where it had started. The confusion 'caused a mass concentration of vehicles', the watching general remarked critically, 'which would have been catastrophic if the enemy had attacked from the air. Any and all traffic was impeded.'[9]

In the late afternoon, as the captured Canadians were being taken from the beaches to their temporary PoW assembly areas, Hitler and Goebbels took a private walk through Vinnytsia's dense woodland. Joining them was Blondi, Hitler's beloved German shepherd dog. Goebbels noticed that the Führer's mood had picked up immensely despite his poor health. Later, he reflected that Blondi was 'that only thing alive around [Hitler] that owns his heart'. After their brief excursion, Hitler began to feel tired and retired to his personal quarters. Goebbels, however, stayed in the *Führerhauptquartier*'s working section to coordinate a propaganda strategy on Dieppe.

One of the German war reporters lucky enough to get a slice of the hot story was Dr Hermann Schramm. Ordinarily, Schramm was assigned to cover the activities of SS units in France. On 18 August he had been in Saint-Nazaire, the setting for Britain's other 'springtime adventure' as he later put it. The next day, while still in Western France, this dedicated ideologue heard vague rumours about some fighting taking place on the north coast. Not one to miss out on a scoop, Schramm raced eastwards through Brittany, Normandy and the beautiful seaside resort of Deauville just south of Le Havre, which the eager journalist was surprised to find perfectly peaceful. Undeterred, he continued eastwards to Rouen, where he finally discovered that the Allies were attacking Dieppe, 30 miles further north. After his grand tour through France, it was not until the fighting was over that Schramm eventually reached the battlefield. In his desperation to get his story published prominently on the front page of some important paper, he used plenty of purple prose: 'When we arrive at Dieppe our fighters are still curving over the site of this mad operation, clearing the airspace of the last British fliers. Looking landwards, a shot-down British bomber blazes with a mushroom cloud of smoke. Burning and shot-up houses, mostly along the coastal road, show the effect of massed fire of the British ships' guns … On a large, burning landing boat, ammunition is exploding.' Schramm described dead soldiers lying in shell holes, surrounded by steel helmets discarded by the men who had been made prisoner. He was careful to explain, however, that the carnage was one-sided: 'The picture of death and terrible destruction only becomes gruesome beyond the [German] wire obstacles, although the rising tide has already washed over most of the sunken landing craft … Between the knocked-out tanks, the dead and wounded, the beach is strewn with bits of equipment – a picture of destruction and total annihilation, for which the term "Dunkirk" was coined two years ago.' Looking for the personal angle that every good reporter craves, Schramm went over to a Canadian. 'Asked what he thought of the operation, a wounded man answered apathetically, "We were ordered to do it." Churchill gives the order and the auxiliary nations are sent to the slaughter. British blood is too valuable for such senseless operations as that at Dieppe.' This vivid and politically motivated description of Dieppe post-battle was exactly what Schramm's higher-ups wanted to see. For this reason, he was rewarded with every Nazi war reporter's dream – his story printed on the front page of the *Völkischer Beobachter*.

It was late in the evening that Goebbels and the others in Vinnytsia finally heard from Rundstedt that the Dieppe battle had been won. Goebbels may have been an evil and despicable individual, but he was a brilliant propagandist and communicator. Immediately after hearing that the military situation was secure, he decided that a new propaganda front should be opened against Churchill and the Allies. He elected at once to publish a special announcement from the Wehrmacht before the day was out. Normally, these *Wehrmachtberichte* (literally 'Wehrmacht Reports') were a routine daily affair, but on special occasions such as this a special announcement, or *Sondermeldung*, could be issued. These reports nominally originated from the Wehrmacht press section, but at moments of great importance the task of writing them could be given to others within the Nazi establishment. They were broadcast on radio at midday and before news programmes, always preceded by a great fanfare and the words: 'From the *Führerhauptquartier*, the High Command of the Armed Forces announces …' In addition, a text version was printed in the Reich's newspapers, invariably on the front pages. For those serving in uniform, it was a great honour for one's unit to be mentioned. The daily report was so significant that commanders would often write rapid preliminary reports so that the information contained in them could be used in the next day's edition. On 19 August, for example, Commanding Admiral of France Admiral Otto Schulze sent a two-page report which mentioned Port Commandant Wahn for his 'outstanding' performance,

Joseph Goebbels, Hitler's Propaganda Minister. (*Bundesarchiv, Bild 101I-811-1888-34 / Wagner / CC-BY-SA 3.0*)

Field Marshal Gerd von Rundstedt. (*Bundesarchiv, Bild 183-L08129 / CC-BY-SA 3.0*)

Field Marshal Hugo Sperrle. (*Bundesarchiv, Bild 146-1977-054-26 / Fischer / CC-BY-SA 3.0*)

Otto Dietrich, Reich Press Minister. (*NIOD*)

The RAF's view of Dieppe on 19 August. (*IWM C 3078*)

An Allied destroyer laying smoke on the day of the battle. (*IWM A 11210*)

The main beach, split into Red and White. (*NIOD*)

An anti-tank gun guards Dieppe's inner streets in case the Calgary Regiment's tanks make a breakthrough. (*NIOD*)

A gun crew enjoy a drink shortly after the battle. (*NIOD*)

General Zeitzler remarked that parts of Dieppe presented a 'picture like Dunkirk'. (*NIOD*)

Animosity between Germans and Allies often disappeared after the fighting was over. Here a German soldier helps his former enemy up the beach. (*NIOD*)

Pictures like this were plastered across German newspapers. (*NIOD*)

The victors meet the vanquished. (*NIOD*)

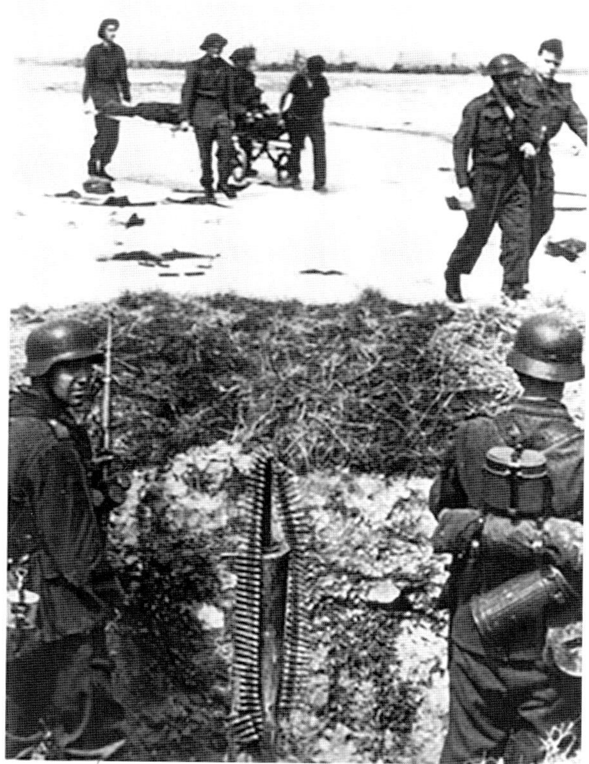

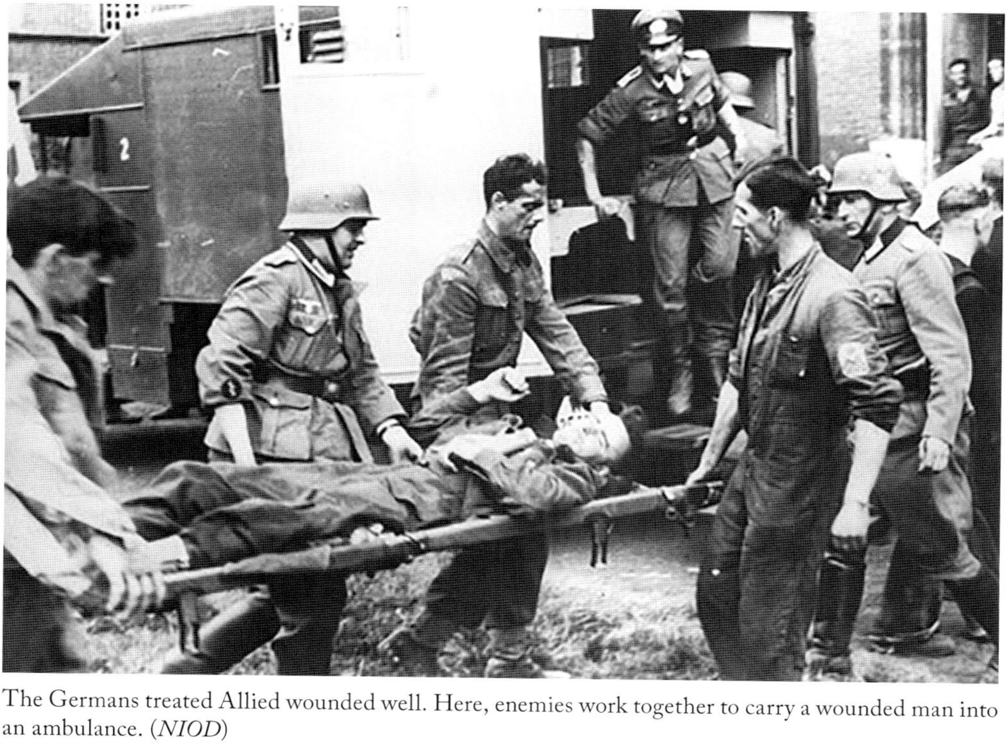

The Germans treated Allied wounded well. Here, enemies work together to carry a wounded man into an ambulance. (*NIOD*)

A band of prisoners taken at Dieppe waiting for transfer to a permanent PoW camp. (*NIOD*)

Helmets and other kit lay strewn over Dieppe for days. (*NIOD*)

Prisoners march away, with Dieppe's harbour cranes providing the background. (*Bundesarchiv, Bild 101I-291-1229-05 / Meyer; Wiltberger / CC-BY-SA 3.0*)

Allied prisoners and their guards in the temporary PoW camp at Dieppe. (*NAM*)

German troops inspect a Daimler Dingo scout car. (*Bundesarchiv, Bild 101I-291-1207-11 / Koll / CC-BY-SA 3.0*)

Lieutenant Epple, from 49th Panzer Engineer Battalion, 10th Panzer Division, takes a break from salvaging Dieppe's Churchills for a quick photo opportunity. (*S. Pallad/Wiki Commons*)

A Churchill tank lying ignominiously in a ditch. (*NIOD*)

Some Germans taking great interest in one of the Allies' huge landing craft. (*NIOD*)

One of the many inglorious images left in Operation Jubilee's wake. (*NIOD*)

Canadians march into captivity. The Château de Dieppe and the high cliff on the western side of town on which it sits can be seen as a backdrop. (*NIOD*)

Dieppe's beach was a hive of activity in the weeks following the raid, with cleaning and salvage operations taking place. (*Fries Museum*)

Dieppe was the first action of the Churchill tank; Hitler called examples like these a 'gift' from the Allies. (*NIOD*)

Rundstedt (third from left) and Haase (centre), along with their respective staffs, review the battlefield on 22 August. (*NIOD*)

The German caption for this image read: 'German soldiers fortify themselves after the battle'. (*NIOD*)

A group of German soldiers outside Port Commandant Wahn's quarters, several days after the raid. (*NIOD*)

The commandant of a PoW camp gives a farewell speech to his prisoners before their departure for Dieppe. (*NIOD*)

One happy French PoW on his way home after two years' imprisonment … (*NIOD*)

… and Canadians making the opposite journey. (*NIOD*)

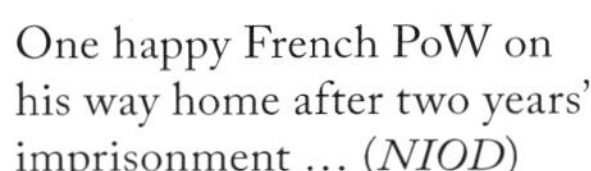

French PoWs play one last concert before being allowed to return home to Dieppe.

Rundstedt handing out Iron Crosses to the Dieppe defenders, an image that was captured for *Die Deutsche Wochenschau*. (*NIOD*)

Jubilant Dieppois on their way home. (*NIOD*)

One of many paintings produced by German war artists to mark the Dieppe victory. This one was painted by Wilhelm Strauss. (*Strauss, Wilhelm, After the Battle, c. 1942, US Army Art Collection*)

in the hope that Wahn's name would appear in a Wehrmacht report – to no avail, as it turned out.[10]

On 19 August, Goebbels took it upon himself to craft a special report before the day was out. He wanted the announcement to reflect his and Hitler's appraisal of the political situation: 'We will make a special announcement that's furnished with cutting political commentary which points to the fact that Churchill's operation came about as a result of Stalin's direct pressure and that it shows unsurpassed amateurism.'[11] As Goebbels began writing the special announcement during the late evening, Hitler rose from his rest to contribute personally. The Führer deemed the day's events so important that he ordered that the announcement be broadcast that very evening. After they had finished their work, Hitler once again invited Goebbels to a private dinner at half past ten. Before they could begin their meal in earnest, the report that they had just drafted came on the radio. They both listened intently as the announcer gave the German people their first news of what had happened a few hours earlier in France:

A large-scale landing of English, American, Canadian and de Gaulle troops in divisional strength as a first wave has collapsed due to the German coastal defence forces with high and bloody losses for the enemy. The landing occurred in today's morning hours against the French Channel coast at Dieppe under the protection of strong sea and air forces, and included the deployment of amphibiously landed tanks. Since 4 o'clock there have been no armed enemies on the Continent. This great success was achieved without the need to deploy any noteworthy reserves from higher levels.

The announcer went on to give a very brief outline of the forces involved. Some claims in this first broadcast were blatantly untrue, for instance the assertion that 'thirteen to fifteen cruisers and destroyers' had been involved. The largest warships in the naval force were the eight *Hunt*-class destroyers, and no cruisers at all were deployed. Undoubtedly, Goebbels and Hitler had imperfect information while drafting the special Wehrmacht report, but it would not have been out of character for them to exaggerate the enemy's forces for effect. Significantly, even the Germans' internal picture of events was sketchy in the hours and days immediately after the operation. The Luftwaffe initially distributed a confidential account of events which made a claim that four British cruisers were sunk in the fighting. The aftermath of combat is often murky and clouded by the infernal 'fog of war', and it was inevitable that this kind of exaggeration would make it into official documents. Consequently, the version of events heard by Germans listening to the special bulletin at home was false. The special announcement claimed that three Allied destroyers, not one, had been sunk, in addition to the 'damage' inflicted on five non-existent cruisers. Interestingly, this initial radio broadcast actually underestimated the victory gained by the Germans in the air. It claimed that the Luftwaffe had shot down 86 planes, while the RAF in fact lost 106 aircraft of all types.

However, the announcement was otherwise generally factual, save for some inevitable inaccuracies due to imperfect information. Of course, there was little need to gloss over unpleasant facts or matters which did not fit the Nazi narrative; the Dieppe fiasco played right into Goebbels' hands. For months, even years, he had been preparing the German people for such an attack against occupied France. Not only had it now happened, but the Allies' attempt had been completely and utterly crushed. The facts spoke for themselves; there was little need for political spin. Goebbels' special bulletin concluded as per the Reichsminister's own wishes with a political slant, using much the same language as he had to describe the operation when he first learned of it:

> The enemy has suffered a devastating defeat. This landing attempt only served a political end, and flew in the face of all military reason. The German Watch in the West gave this amateurish operation the rebuff that it deserved. It will face all further enemy attempts with the same calm and strength of a Wehrmacht that has pinned victory to its banners in hundreds upon hundreds of battles.[12]

Goebbels and Hitler's special radio broadcast was just one shot fired in Dieppe's propaganda war. The Reich Propaganda Minister's influence machine kicked into gear in earnest when the morning papers were published the next day. For now, though, Goebbels and Hitler went to bed in the early morning hours of 20 August immensely satisfied with their work. Goebbels was delighted that he had had the opportunity to rub salt into Churchill's wounds, and been given a chance to split the

Anglo-Canadian alliance. The Nazi propaganda message based itself on the premise that while the bulk of the Wehrmacht was fighting in the East, Germans sitting at home need not worry about the West, for the so-called 'New West Wall' was guarding their rear (this was a reference to the 'West Wall' or 'Siegfried line' on the Franco-German frontier). Getting the news of Dieppe out early served this purpose incredibly well and also helped to boost German domestic morale. Goebbels regularly dictated a diary, producing on average about twenty pages of large typescript text a day. However, he could not contain his excitement about the crushing Dieppe victory and dictated a staggering 119 pages worth of material (or 15,000 words), which his hapless secretary had the misfortune of having to type up.

At nearly 4 o'clock in the morning Goebbels finally made his way to his room. Even as he climbed into bed, his mind was in a frenzied state. He expounded excitedly on what had happened in the past 24 hours: 'It was a frenetic day, and it became a great victory. The ruin of the English invasion attempt might have even further-reaching consequences. If the English make a victory of this as they always do, you could not hold it against them.' This, of course, was what Goebbels had done when confronted with Nazi Germany's past military defeats, and he would do so many times again in the three years of war still to come. Yet his early intuition about British propaganda was spot-on. Britain's papers would do exactly as he had predicted and claim victory at Dieppe despite all evidence to the contrary. This would play right into his hands. As Goebbels observed about 19 August, 'Without substance there is no victory on the propaganda field of battle. The pen cannot compensate for what the sword is lacking.'[13] Over the coming days and weeks he would take great joy and pride in dismantling British efforts to present Dieppe as a victory.

Back in Dieppe, the Germans were hurriedly clearing the town of both men and material. As PoWs lay in fields to the south, awaiting rail transport to camps inside Germany, the beaches and promenade were cleared of debris. In this task the local French population aided the Germans; just as much as their occupiers, they wanted their home town cleared up. Some of them were in mourning, for in the inevitable confusion of battle, thirty-six French civilians had died, with another sixty-three wounded. For those French not dealing with the untimely death of loved ones, life returned to normal astoundingly quickly. All shops and services were up and running by early evening on the 19th, including the local post office. Nevertheless, the litter of war would take weeks to clear. Dieppe's front beach was a picture of devastation. Landing craft were stranded on the shore. Dead men lay on a beach which had once been a fine holiday destination. Buildings opposite the promenade smouldered, with an inescapable putrid stench of cigars emanating from the blown-up tobacco factory. Tanks and scout cars, either knocked out or simply abandoned, were scattered all over the place. Three regiments of Canadian infantry, as well as twenty-seven tanks, had attempted to land on a very small beach; Red and White combined measured less than a mile in length and only 200 or so yards in depth, depending on the tide. Such concentrated force, and such concentrated destruction, produced an awful image. The photographers of the German propaganda companies would have the easiest work of their lives in the coming days. One simply had to look at the pictures to see the scale of the Anglo-Canadian defeat. Nothing more was necessary. The German propagandists went as far as to photograph morbid scenes of dead Canadians lying on the beach. Some of these would be printed in Germany's domestic newspapers. Other images were deemed unsuitable for wider consumption. One officer climbed excitedly on a burned-out Dingo scout car, only to find the charred skeleton of the driver still inside. This was a spectacle a world away from the beautiful tourist town which had only the day before seen civilians and soldiers alike swimming merrily in the sea.[14]

Even after a great victory, as things started to return to normal, Rundstedt sat in Paris pondering a serious question: was the landing he had just defeated simply an isolated effort or part of a wider operation? Ever the cautious commander, OB West kept both Seventh and Fifteenth Army on high alert, to stand down only at 0800 the next day. This meant that every unit in northern France and their reserves – including the *Leibstandarte Adolf Hitler* – was ready in anticipation of a follow-up attack. 10th Panzer Division would also remain under command of General Kuntzen's LXXXI Corps and stay in the Dieppe area until 20 August.

Confusion dominated Rundstedt's immediate reaction to what had just happened in northern France. With his deep respect for and knowledge of air power, he could not understand why the Allies had neglected air bombardment. Not only did they fail to prepare the ground ahead of time by attacking communications, bridges, artillery emplacements and machine-gun bunkers, but the Allied effort was almost entirely devoid of tactical air support. While an admittedly strong force of fifty fighter squadrons was used to provide the air umbrella, the RAF only used eight fighter-bomber and close air support squadrons, with an additional two American Flying Fortress bomber squadrons. This was nothing like the large-scale amphibious raid or invasion that Rundstedt had envisaged in his Basic Order 13 in July. The disparity between his own imagination and the reality of the Dieppe raid worried him. He contemplated this conflict in an official appreciation late on 19 August. For him, there was only one solution to the conundrum:

> An explanation for this could only be found if the Englishman wished to save his massed bomber formation for employment in a second phase – namely the commencement of the 'Invasion' – after the capture of Dieppe. As he knew accurately where 10th Panzer Division were in position as reserve and he had to count on their coming into action, it may be that this was decisive in inducing him to refrain temporarily from the use of his bomber formations.[15]

This was not true; there was no 'massed bomber formation' waiting on the other side of the Channel. There were certainly no plans for a second wave as part of an invasion attempt. This, though, would be a common German suspicion in the days to come. Even after the captured Jubilee plan was rapidly translated just under a week later, German commanders still suspected that had Dieppe and its surrounding area been captured, a new operation on a larger scale would have been launched. Ironically, Churchill had pushed for, then reluctantly cancelled, operations like this earlier in the year (Operation Sledgehammer being the most notable). When Rundstedt read the translated Jubilee plan he was totally surprised. He had always envisioned air power as playing a key ground attack role in a divisional-scale landing attempt. To see the Allies, with all their material strength, ignore air power in this way was bewildering to say the least. The day of Dieppe was not yet over, and Rundstedt was already critical of his adversaries' undertaking. In the coming days and weeks, OB West would contribute consistently and at length to the German analysis of the Dieppe raid. After all, as nominal commander of all forces in the West, he believed he would be the one to lead the defence against a full-scale invasion of Europe in the future. Before the day was out, he took time to send a final congratulatory cable to every unit under his command: 'I express my appreciation and thanks to every officer and man', he wrote. 'Today, I was able to report: "The troops have done well".'[16] General Haase at Fifteenth Army joined in too. In an Army-wide order he exclaimed that 'under the command of General Kuntzen, 302nd Division with part of 332nd Division and outstandingly supported by the Luftwaffe, defied the enemy and destroyed or captured him!' Unfortunately, Haase neglected to mention the role played by the Kriegsmarine on land and at sea, and three days later he hastened to write a subsequent message which inserted 'and the Kriegsmarine' after 'Luftwaffe', to spare the naval service's blushes.[17]

The sheer scale of the Anglo-Canadian effort – a whole Canadian division, upwards of fifty RAF squadrons and a large protective naval force – also caused Rundstedt to pause and think. Surely such a large commitment of resources could not simply be in service of a temporary raid? As Rundstedt opined in his initial appreciation, 'In view of the forces employed … the operation at Dieppe cannot be considered a local raid. For this the expenditure in men and materials is too great.' Alas, there were no plans to 'upscale' Jubilee to a full liberation of France, but from where Rundstedt was sitting, the idea that Jubilee was 'just a raid' did not agree with him. He felt the operation was so obviously flawed that no self-respecting military force would be foolish enough to repeat it. As an old military man, he had too much professional respect for his adversaries to underestimate them. Referring to the enemy, Rundstedt confidently declared that 'he will not do it like this a second time!'[18] With these words, he neatly encapsulated the German assessment of the Dieppe raid. His criticisms would not be the last.

If the raid made little military sense, then as the German press would later repeatedly and pointedly argue, it must have had its roots in diplomacy and politics. Namely, it represented a desperate attempt by Stalin's puppet Churchill to appease his Soviet master. This line of argument was not merely propaganda; it was widely believed within the German military. Looking back with the clarity and objectivity of historical hindsight, they may well have been right.

In Berlin, a late press conference was taking place that would determine the course of the battle for minds over Dieppe. As ever, representatives from the Wehrmacht and Foreign Ministry amongst others gathered within the Propaganda Ministry to set an initial messaging strategy. Although these men had limited information available, it was clear that a landing on a scale never before seen had been crushed within several hours. They agreed that the entire German press apparatus should dedicate space to the Dieppe story, be they national or local outlets. The meeting considered one talking point to be important above all. German press outlets were called on to 'portray this operation as an attempt to pay the blood sacrifice for the Moscow negotiations' with 'the greatest possible volume and layout' in the papers, and to report that 'the English suffered an unprecedented defeat'.[19] Early the next morning, a more detailed and considered strategy would be published and distributed to the Reich's journalists, but this meeting in Berlin on the 19th set the tone for what would be an intense war of words.

Before the morning newspaper editions could appear early the next day, radio across Europe was reporting the news late on the 19th. One German news broadcast by *Deutschlandsender*, Germany's principal radio station, reported in the same vein of personal attack that the newspapers would follow: 'The amateur strategist Churchill has had his second Dunkirk … Churchill decided to go to Moscow to explain to Stalin the difficulties confronting the establishment of a second front. Stalin, however, remained adamant, and categorically demanded the immediate opening of a second front. Against the advice of his military advisers, Churchill had to give way, and the landing at Dieppe is the result.'[20] However, German radio did not enjoy a monopoly on reporting on what had occurred at Dieppe. In Italy, the columnist, writer and former schoolmate of Benito Mussolini, Rino Alessi gave his regular opinion piece on his radio show just after 7 o'clock. Predictably, this proud Italian fascist was exuberant about the Allies' humbling defeat in France, saying: 'The Axis has eliminated the word "surprise" from its vocabulary.' At the same time as Alessi was speaking, Paris radio gave an announcement in a news bulletin which once again neglected the fact that Jubilee was a Canadian-led operation: 'The Anglo-American troops, after having shown some resistance, were forced to withdraw, leaving many of their tanks behind. Many transports were sunk by German artillery and aircraft.' Two hours later, a French translation of Goebbels' *Sondermeldung* was broadcast. Just before midnight, radio in the Vichy puppet state issued a warning in another news programme: 'The failure and the heavy losses will perhaps convince British public opinion and the British High Command of the futility of setting foot on the Continent.'[21] In the Soviet Union, many Russians truly believed that the Dieppe raid was the opening of the long-awaited second front in Europe – the news was widely broadcast, only for these hopes to be snuffed out. In Archangel, survivors of PQ-17, the disastrous July supply convoy to the USSR, were brought food ranging from cabbages to yak carcasses as a sign of appreciation and gratitude. When the Soviets learned of the raid's true nature and result, they demanded that these be returned – to no avail, as their offerings had long since been devoured.[22]

In the late evening of the 19th, a large huddle of Canadian prisoners were shoved unceremoniously into boxcars and sent eastwards. The Germans transporting them told them that the wounded would be shot if anyone tried to escape. These were hardly enviable travelling conditions, but they were a world away from the treatment inflicted on Soviet soldiers who had the fatal misfortune to be captured. One group of Canadians halted at a cement factory for rest and water. After staggering out of the cramped boxcars, they were confronted by a high-ranking German officer. The secret was now out, in large part due to the captured Dieppe plan, that the Allies had planned to manacle their prisoners. This had caused outrage amongst the Germans in France, and the officer lined up his new Canadian charges and threatened to shoot one in five of the men in retribution. Thankfully for the new PoWs, this threat was never carried out.[23]

In Quiberville, west of Dieppe, 16-year-old Philippe Plantrou surveyed the scene. This excitable adolescent had been at the coast helping with the harvest, part of a civilian labour scheme implemented by the Vichy government. Although he undertook this task with his three older brothers, his parents were not with them; they remained at the family home in Rouen. From his position Philippe had seen dogfights and parachuting airmen – at one point he had rapidly taken shelter under a farm wagon laden with wheat. But now that the battle was over, all that he could sense was the stench of burning fuel in the air, which stung incessantly in the back of his throat. Going inside to try and get some sleep did not help; since the summer weather had been so pleasant over the last few days, some of the farmhouse's windows had been left wide open, allowing the oily miasma to drift inside. The defeated Canadians below him in Dieppe's valley, though, surely felt much worse.

Chapter 12

'A Picture like Dunkirk': The Day After

The day after the defeat of the raid, 20 August 1942, was almost as hectic as the day before. Propaganda companies and war correspondents flooded into the area to write their dispatches and take photographs. War artists, too, came to paint the scene. Men from the Army's *Waffenamt* came to inspect the Churchill tanks. Troops flooded in to secure the area and capture any British or Canadian stragglers still on the loose. Young Philippe Plantrou and one of his brothers set off southwards to Rouen – a trip of 35 miles – to reassure their parents that all was well. As they cycled, the Plantrous observed the mass of German men and materiel coming north. 'We passed several German military convoys coming towards Dieppe, carrying equipment large and small; tracked and wheeled self–propelled guns, trucks and the like', Philippe recalled in later life. 'We dived into the ditch two or three times when the guns were too close to us.' The boys' hours-long journey was worth it in the end – when they arrived at their home in Rouen, Philippe's parents heard the garden gate open and, with tears in their eyes, ran down the front steps to embrace their sons.[1]

Also in Rouen, but doubtless less pleased with his predicament, was Corporal Robert Prouse. After being transported hastily from Dieppe's hospital to another in Rouen, he found his lower half had become completely immobile after his long night's sleep: 'I tried to swing my legs over the side of the bed but all they did was to flop like two dead lumps of meat.' Somehow, the Canadian managed to drag himself over to the German doctor, who happily spoke perfect English, albeit with a very strong accent, and who kept Prouse busy sweeping and cleaning, with good reason: 'The doctor had told me that there were several marks of entry from small pieces of shrapnel in both legs and one foot and that the best thing I could do was to keep them moving, since some nerves could have been severed.'

Conditions were somewhat haphazard at Rouen hospital. Although Corporal Prouse and his comrades had been treated well by their captors, there were great deficiencies in the resources devoted to their care. In one curious incident, Prouse was enlisted to hold down the legs of a Canadian who had suffered a bullet wound in the thigh. As Prouse later said, 'Either there were no anaesthetics or the Germans did not want to waste them on us.' Their patient was not best pleased, calling the German doctor a 'son of a bitch of a Hun', amongst other even less printable epithets. Having finished his first day as a makeshift orderly, Prouse stumbled across the doctor with whom he had been working. The German asked him, 'What do you think of our wonderful German army? They stopped the invasion with only one division.' Prouse was at pains to stress that the Dieppe operation was in fact a raid, and not an invasion; to make his point, he pulled out a copy of the leaflet warning the French not to intervene for that very reason. The doctor crumpled up Prouse's evidence and tossed it aside, dismissing it (as many other Germans did) as mere propaganda.[2]

Early in the morning of 20 August, Field Marshal Rundstedt and his chief of staff Brigadier Kurt Zeitzler travelled north to Dieppe to interview all the key players and to survey the battlefield for themselves. At 1100, Major General Konrad Haase of 302nd Infantry Division met with Rundstedt and LXXXI Corps commander General Adolf Kuntzen. Beyond the inevitable self-congratulation, the meeting's business focussed on immediate steps that could be taken in order to improve coastal defence. The three generals concluded that the highest priority was to be the repositioning of coastal artillery into strongpoints. The concept of a strongpoint, known to the Germans as a *Stützpunkt*, was a common-sense idea. It was essentially a centre of all-round defence, in which men, material and installations could be protected. Preferably, a *Stützpunkt* would be ringed by barbed wire, trenches and the like, along with dedicated infantry protection. Consequently, so the theory went, gunners, observers, radio operators and so on could do their job without having to pick up a rifle and defend themselves as makeshift infantry. Not only this, but a *Stützpunkt* would ideally include its own organic anti-aircraft defence. With the Allies' superiority in the air, this was a significant consideration. This conclusion was motivated by the need for defence against both air and ground attack on the back of the Dieppe experience.

One place where the increased emphasis on strongpoints came too late was 813 Battery at Varengeville. Its guns had been knocked out so easily by Lord Lovat's 4 Commando because it lay in a totally isolated and exposed position. It enjoyed neither dedicated infantry support nor its own fieldwork defences, rendering it particularly vulnerable to close-quarters attack. The success of 4 Commando on 19 August was therefore entirely foreseeable, and it proved to be the impetus for 302nd Division to finally disassemble 813 Battery. In late September – after upgrading it with four 220mm guns – it was decided to relocate it five miles south-eastwards to Calmont, just inland of Dieppe. The experiences of 19 August 1942 proved to be the catalyst for many changes that the Wehrmacht had been putting off. For some time, the idea of a large-scale seaborne assault in the West had been a theoretical possibility. Dieppe had shown that it was indeed a tangible threat. This was not least the case for 10th Panzer Division, and the week afterwards was busy for its staff officers. It was fortunate that the division's tanks had not been required at all, but its sluggish reaction on the 19th had been far from ideal and prompted a comprehensive reworking of its pre-planned marching orders in case of an Allied amphibious landing. These updated plans, it was hoped, would mean that the panzers would arrive more promptly if required in future.[3]

Brigadier Zeitzler proceeded to inspect the beaches, and saw for himself the truly gruesome scene they presented. His report would become infamous amongst the German high command as a naked power grab and an attempt to appeal to Hitler in the hope of promotion. A few hours after visiting the battlefield, Zeitzler recorded his impressions and submitted them to Rundstedt's staff, starting with a phrase that became all too common in German reports on Dieppe:

High bloody English losses. Although many already buried, everywhere still dead Englishmen, especially in front of positions of heavy weapons. In front of a machine gun position covering from the flank a narrow sector of beach between the sea and the bluffs, mountains of bodies (over 100 at this point alone). Great quantities of captured enemy equipment, light and heavy infantry weapons.

These comments were all perfectly accurate, though tinged with dramatic phrases like 'mountains of bodies'. This is not the language that one would normally expect to find in an official military account, but it is exactly what later appealed to Hitler. Nevertheless, it was hard to describe the utter destruction that lay all across Dieppe's pebbled beaches. To depict it, the Germans would use their war photographers, gleefully showering the Reich's newspapers with the images that they captured.

Zeitzler's account then veered wildly from any kind of truth. In judging the fighting ability of the respective Allied nations' at Dieppe, he said that the 'English fought well. Canadians and Americans not so well, later quickly surrendered under the impression of the high bloody losses.' If Zeitzler had known the full facts, his conclusion would have been an insult. No men could have completed their mission under the conditions faced at the Canadian beaches. How he knew enough about the battle to single out the American contribution – nothing more than fifty US Army Rangers – remains a mystery. Most likely, in his ambition to write a gripping if not entirely accurate account, he embellished his limited knowledge. Interestingly, the courage displayed by the various Allied troops later became a topic of some disagreement between German commanders.

Zeitzler repeated Johannes Jörgensen's implication that there was something 'different' about the men of the Western powers. He was complimentary about the prisoners he viewed at Dieppe, as opposed to the 'Slav rabble' in the East: 'Prisoners make fairly orderly impression, are young, fresh, intelligent people.'[4] Some newly-captured PoWs, however, were hardly in a talkative mood. Paul Schmidt – Hitler's personal interpreter – was sent by his Führer to Dieppe to interrogate the British and Canadians who had washed up on French shores. He had performed a similar role a few months earlier at Saint-Nazaire. One prisoner told Schmidt with brutal crudeness that 'the men who ordered this raid and those who organized it are criminals and deserve to be shot for mass murder!'[5] The interpreter came away with a generally positive impression, though as a cultured and well-travelled man he was irked by the Canadians' ignorance of Germany. He asked one man, 'Have you ever heard of any Germans?' After a long and deep thought, the soldier replied 'Yes. General Rommel and Lilli Marlene.' After the war, and surely seeking to ingratiate himself with an English-speaking audience, Schmidt wrote despondently in his memoirs: 'I found it a melancholy experience to see these men with whose language and history I was thoroughly familiar, and whose peoples had always been so congenial to me, behind barbed wire.'[6]

302nd Division naturally had its own English-speaking interrogator, as did all German divisions in France. He was joined by a whole host of officers from across France: a lieutenant from OB West, a major and three others from the military intelligence post in Paris and a lieutenant colonel from Fifteenth Army, as well as the interpreters from 332nd and 333rd Divisions. On 19 and 20 August, Dieppe was the place to be. These interrogators did not get much out of the captured officers. Most gave only their name, rank and service number, just as they were trained to do. Some remained silent. Throughout, prisoners 'showed a smiling face, yet one of superiority', the interrogation report later noted. 'Some were cocky bordering on cheekiness', it added. The British Commandos, whether commissioned officers or not, were particularly obstinate. The Germans initially asked the prisoners what the operation's objective was – but once the Combined Operations Plan was discovered, their captors had all they needed to know in this regard. So the Germans turned to political matters. To their disappointment, many prisoners seemed indifferent to the strategic and political context in which the raid on Dieppe had been launched. The only 'juicy' material came from a few Canadians who blamed the British for sending them on what they regarded as a suicide mission. One officer remarked bitterly, 'More than anything, I want to turn my rifle on the British.'[7]

Later, the *Völkischer Beobachter* would publish some short statements made by the 'English' PoWs. No doubt carefully selected, or perhaps even fabricated, they served only to portray the German defences in France as unbeatable. One prisoner supposedly lamented, 'I think I've aged ten years. We were bombarded for ten hours straight.' Another recalled that 'my own ship got blown up. I swam for two hours and was picked up by another one; but that one got hit and sunk too.' Nowhere in the German press were the Allied soldiers or their fighting qualities criticized. Some depictions of the Allies were even unusually positive. Hans Peterson, a 10-year-old Berliner, recalled one report which described the Canadians as 'brave' and 'towering'.[8] The story that the German media wanted to convey was clear: even the best-trained troops could not overcome the invincible 'Watch in the West'.

However, the Germans did not confine themselves to publishing statements actually uttered by their prisoners. Some supposedly authentic utterances were in fact entirely fabricated. In one case, 'Colonel Douglas Allsop' said in an English-language radio broadcast from the Zeesen transmitting station south of Berlin: 'Apparently our High Command had underestimated the German strength, and had all wrong ideas about the actual military situation there. It was senseless recklessness to send our men into this murderous hell. But even more surprised than about the strong German defence force we were [*sic*] about the correct treatment our wounded men received from the German ambulance soldiers, who did their utmost to help us in every possible medical way.' The statement was full of strange and stilted language, and there was a very good explanation for this: there was no 'Colonel Alsopp'. He was nothing more than a product of the Germans' imagination. Clearly, this 'statement' had been written by a (not very fluent) English-speaking German. This broadcast went out at two o'clock in the morning (German time). At first this may seem to have been a waste, since almost no one in Britain was awake to listen. However, the fact that this fictional testimony emanated from Zeesen was significant. Zeesen was a long-wave transmitter, meaning that its signal could be received at long distances – namely across the Atlantic in America, where it would only be late evening on the east coast. 'Colonel Allsop' and his fabricated opinions about the Germans' invincibility were repeated on Norwegian radio at a more convenient hour for a British audience.[9]

Wanting to create a gripping picture, Brigadier Zeitzler used the example of another famous British defeat to illustrate his story. He said simply that 'the beach sector west of Dieppe harbour presents a picture like Dunkirk'. He went on to describe the landing craft strewn across the beach and the transports sunk at sea. One thing that particularly caught Zeitzler's eye were the funnels, masts and other such objects protruding forlornly from the various land and sea vehicles sunk just beyond the waterline. There was so much debris strewn across the battlefield that it would take five day's hard work until 302nd Division could once again begin normal operations. Georges Guibon described the scene just behind the beach, on the western side of town:

Some buildings have suffered: the bank, theatre, the Hotel de Paris, which is riddled with bullets, no wall tiles anywhere … I walk up to Villa Rachel, then to the town hall which has suffered quite a bit; the ceiling of the great hall has fallen in, the mayor's office is devastated, floor busted, doors smashed in. Upstairs, in the reception room, also badly damaged, we see the beach, a battlefield strewn with debris; a large tank is stopped in front of the garage to the casino's galleries, its barrel turned towards the pier, a caterpillar track unrolled.[10]

After reporting back to his boss Rundstedt, Zeitzler's personal impressions of the battlefield were sent straight on to Hitler at the *Führerhauptquartier* in Ukraine. They served only to heighten the already ecstatic mood around the Führer. The way in which the young brigadier had shaped his report – in particular comparing the beaches to those of Dunkirk two years earlier – struck a chord in Vinnytsia. With the bitter struggles continuing in the East, and the gargantuan battle for Stalingrad about to begin, the Führer and his headquarters staff were all too ready to receive some good news from the West. For Hitler in particular, the victory at Dieppe was welcome. He had acted personally as commander-in-chief of the Army since 1941, with General Franz Halder as his chief of staff, who performed some of the duties of a deputy and saw that Hitler's orders were implemented. The relationship between an executive commander and his chief of staff is paramount – without strong mutual understanding, military business can so easily grind to a halt. However, for some months Halder and Hitler had had a rocky relationship. In a situation conference in mid-July, Halder complained forcefully about Hitler's all too frequent tendency to refuse to allow his forces to withdraw, telling the Führer directly, 'Out there brave men and young officers are falling in [their] thousands because their commanders are not allowed to make the only reasonable decision and have their hands tied behind their backs.'

Hitler exploded. To a stunned room full of his top generals, the Führer shouted with apoplectic rage, 'How dare you use language like that to me! Do you think you can teach me what the man at the front is thinking? What do you know about what is going on at the front? Where were you in the First World War? And you try to pretend to me that I don't understand what it's like at the front. I won't stand that! It's outrageous.'

The men in the room stood in awkward silence. As the meeting broke up, it was clear that Hitler would welcome a change of personnel at his headquarters.

A few days later, Hitler remarked in passing that he wanted by his side not someone like the older Halder, but instead 'someone like this chap Zeitzler'.

Hermann Göring, ever keen to curry favour with his Führer, was all too happy to support Halder's replacement with the young Brigadier. 'Zeitzler, he is the right man for you', he told Hitler.[11]

Field Marshal Keitel, Chief of OKW, was of the same mind: 'I wanted at length to see somebody who really enjoyed the Führer's confidence occupying the controlling office in the army.'

Keitel's support for Zeitzler was at least partially selfish. The field marshal had come to blows with Hitler in the past: 'It could not be anything but a great release for me if I did not have to fight a daily battle against the Führer's distrust.'[12]

Halder was a quiet and considered professional, but Zeitzler was young and confident to the point of being abrasive. With the wider war situation seeming ever more desperate, Hitler was increasingly receptive to the optimism and energy that Zeitzler brought.

The crushing victory at Dieppe provided the perfect opportunity to make a change. A month later, in September, Hitler sacked Halder and brought in Zeitzler to be his new chief of staff. Not content with Zeitzler's lowly rank, Hitler had him promoted directly to Lieutenant General, skipping the intermediate rank of Major General. By that time, General Halder was resigned to his fate. On the date of his forced retirement he made one last diary entry, writing simply, 'My nerves are worn out.' Nor did Halder have much wish to continue working with Hitler. 'We must part', he said dejectedly.[13] Immediately after Halder had bid farewell to the Army's General Staff, Lieutenant General Zeitzler strode confidently into the room with a loud 'Heil Hitler!' He then proceeded to give a lecture on how faith in National Socialism would provide the driving force to final victory:

I demand that the General Staff officer radiates faith. Faith in our Führer, faith in our victory, faith in our work. He must radiate this faith to his colleagues, to his subordinates, to the troops with whom he comes in contact and to the troop commanders who seek him out … I demand that the General Staff officer be the truest and most reliable assistant – I emphasise the word 'assistant' – to his Führer, chief of the General Staff, branch chief or commander.[14]

Zeitzler had skilfully used Dieppe as a vehicle to achieve incredibly quick promotion, and others understandably resented his rapid rise. Geyr von Schweppenburg, one of the Wehrmacht's foremost experts on armoured manoeuvre warfare, was especially bitter. He did not mention Zeitzler by name, but it was obvious who was the target of one particular barb after the war: 'The personal ambition of a certain military personality in the West, and above all the subsequent propaganda nonsense, had changed the story of the Anglo-Saxon experimental raid on Dieppe into a fairy tale of defensive success against a major landing attempt.'[15] Walter Warlimont, who was Jodl's deputy Chief of Operations Staff at OKW, wrote likewise in hindsight that 'primarily as a result of Zeitzler's reports, [Dieppe] was greatly exaggerated' in the *Führerhauptquartier's* version of events.[16]

It was not just inside Hitler's inner circle that Dieppe was magnified into something much bigger than a simple raid. On 20 August, those Germans who had missed the radio broadcasts throughout the 19th woke up to the stunning news. Up and down Germany, people struggled to get hold of a newspaper. In many areas, the morning editions sold out almost instantly and had to be reprinted. In the streets, those who had not been fortunate enough to secure their own paper huddled around public copies stuck up on the walls of Germany's towns and cities. Throughout the day, crowds gathered to hear the great news of the Dieppe victory.

These gatherings, like all of their kind in Nazi Germany, were closely monitored by the *Sicherheitsdienst,* or SD for short. This was the feared German secret state police, formerly headed by Reinhard Heydrich, who had died in hospital just a few months earlier after being attacked in Prague by Czech Resistance fighters. Part of the SD's mandate was to monitor public opinion during the war for warning signs that the civilian population's resolve might be wavering. For this purpose, it placed plain-clothes agents in public gatherings and listened to conversations, sometimes surreptitiously asking members of the public their opinion of what was going on in the war. There were no concerns after the news from Dieppe, however. The SD's report recorded a jubilant mood. Even in internal government documents such as these, the Germans failed to accurately represent the fact that the operation had been a majority Canadian affair: 'The failed British and American landing attempt at Dieppe has impressed the entire population unlike any other events this year.'[17] In nations suffering under the Nazi jackboot, however, the SD picked up very different signals. In Oslo, its agents reported late on 19 August: 'the after-effects of the British landing attempt at Dieppe are still being felt, at least insofar as the disappointment over the British failure in this venture and the surprise at the energetic German resistance have proved to be lasting. The initial, almost unrestrained, joy as well as the lack of any realistic idea of the military import of this Allied enterprise have since given way to the generally accepted view that it was merely a "dress rehearsal" for the establishment of the Second Front. These observations, however, cannot hide the fact that British prestige has suffered another blow.'[18]

Although ammunition reserves were tight, the Germans sought to rapidly restock the munitions that 302nd Infantry Division and Air Fleet 3 had expended in the day's hard fighting. The majority of the land units' small arms and light weapons were replenished when a large supply train arrived early the following day. Another arrived two days later. It would take much longer to fully re-supply the larger weapons like the guns of the coastal artillery.[19] The Luftwaffe, too, required immediate deliveries of ammunition, for by late afternoon on the 19th all available 20mm cannon ammunition for units in the Dieppe area had been expended. There was a consequently a great re-supply effort in the days following the raid. Air Fleet 3 flew in 24,000 rounds from Germany in four Ju 52 air transports, and another 100,000 cannon shells arrived in north-western France by express goods train. Despite these measures, stockpiles were too low for routine air operations on 20 or 21 August. Additionally, the battle took a great toll on the serviceability of German airframes. By the evening of the 19th, only 70 of the roughly 230 available fighters were combat-ready, but by the following day just over 100 airframes were serviceable. The Germans did not help themselves in making good these losses. Many foreign workers in repair workshops had been temporarily detained due to the increased state of readiness throughout northern France, rendering them unable to work on damaged Luftwaffe aircraft. Aviation fuel stockpiles were not replenished until three trains arrived from Germany on the 22nd.[20]

On 20 August, the Wehrmacht press office published its *Wehrmachtbericht* press release as it did every day. It sought above all to get across to the German public how large the Allies' effort had been. Even with a day to pause and think, the German authorities still refused to recognize that the land force had been primarily Canadian. 'As announced in the *Sondermeldung*, a landing of English, American, Canadian and de Gaulle troops as well as tanks, protected by strong naval and air forces was defeated by German coastal defence forces with heavy bloody losses for the enemy. [It was launched] on a 25 kilometre-wide front against the French Channel coast of Dieppe', it began, perfectly factually. The whole communiqué was reasonably accurate considering that the fighting had only ceased less than 24 hours beforehand. It stated that 'so far 1,500 prisoners' had been counted and that 'our own losses of dead and wounded are only 400'. Figures given for air combat were surprisingly accurate considering how pilots were inclined to overestimate their own victories: 'In air battle our fighter and anti-aircraft guns shot down 112 enemy aircraft. Seventeen of our own fighters were lost.' This was all quite precise, but failed to mention the twenty-five German bombers knocked out of the sky. The only allusion to German bombers came when the follow-up attacks on Portsmouth were mentioned, of which the Wehrmacht said, 'During these [strikes], the Luftwaffe lost eighteen aircraft. Some crews were rescued.' The sole area of real inaccuracy in 20 August's *Wehrmachtbericht* lay in naval matters. It repeated the erroneous claim in the previous day's special announcement that cruiser-size forces were involved. Additionally, it boasted that four Allied destroyers had been sunk – three by coastal artillery and another by the Luftwaffe.[21] But Germany's propagandists did not have to exaggerate or put much of a spin on the pure figures and statistics of Dieppe's debacle. The facts spoke for themselves.

In Berlin, Reich Press Chief Otto Dietrich published his set of *Tagesparolen* early on 20 August; these were the 'Daily Watchwords' which dictated how the German press should report the war news. Inevitably, the attack in the West dominated Dietrich's guidelines. Unusually, the Dieppe operation was the only *Tagesparole* for the day. Dietrich felt, as did Goebbels, that the events in France were so consequential that all possible effort should be made in that direction. German newspaper editors and their staff received two pages full of excruciatingly detailed orders. As always, not only were they told what to report but also exactly how to report it.

Dietrich's instructions that day were crystal clear: 'The shining success of German arms in the West is to be utilized to the greatest possible extent. The question of the goal of the operation allows a convincing refutation of the embarrassing arguments of our enemies.'[22] That an attack on Dieppe did not offer an obvious military objective led naturally to the conclusion that it was motivated only by political factors. The German papers took this argument and ran with it. Adding to the voices influencing them was Major Sommerfeld's. He was a regular at Dietrich's press conferences, being tasked with representing the Wehrmacht's interests there. On 20 August he brought a military perspective to the discussion of Dieppe, claiming that the operation had intended to keep boots on the ground 'for at least a few weeks'. He represented the opinion of many of his colleagues in the Wehrmacht when he told the room that 'a division was landed, but even greater reserves stood in the background. These were to have been used had the first wave not been decimated.'[23]

The *Völkischer Beobachter* spoke first and foremost on 20 August with the authority that came with being the official Nazi Party organ. In large, vivid red text reserved only for the biggest and most significant events, it loudly proclaimed on its front page, 'Anglo-American Landing Failed', and it immediately sought to place the Anglo-Soviet alliance at the forefront of its coverage. In keeping with the Reich's cult of personality centred on the Führer, the *Völkischer Beobachter* placed great emphasis on the relationship between those two countries' leaders, Prime Minister Churchill and Marshal Stalin respectively. The *Völkischer Beobachter*, like all German newspapers, took this personal approach to attacking its enemies as a matter of course. In its leading article, the paper rehashed its previous criticism of Stalin's demands for a second front, once again referencing the Moscow Conference which had taken place just a week earlier. With Stalin the master and Churchill the puppet, according to the *Völkischer Beobachter*, there was only ever going to be one outcome: 'The English Prime Minister Churchill had no other option than to order a large-scale landing against the French coast, against all thoughts of military logic.' Importantly, at no point did the paper mention the fact that the operation was a raid – German readers were led to believe that this operation, at its core, had been an attempt to set up a permanent second front as per Stalin's direct orders.

Churchill was viciously and repeatedly attacked in the *Völkischer Beobachter*'s coverage on 20 August. This was a common tactic for the German press. One piece on its front page that day was entitled 'Hands Off Europe!' and read, 'Churchill's name has been connected with numerous adventurous and reckless operations that have ended in catastrophe, in both World Wars.' This was in part an allusion to the Gallipoli expedition, another ill-fated amphibious operation that had unfolded on Churchill's watch as First Lord of the Admiralty in 1915. 'Joining them is the invasion attempt at Dieppe, which collapsed after just a few hours.' The title of the front-page article was more than enough to summarize what the German press would say over the coming days: 'A New Dunkirk for the Amateur Strategist.' The idea that Dieppe was another defeat of 1940's ilk would be a common refrain in all German papers. This was not an unfair comparison; both were hasty evacuations carried out amidst a doomed military situation. It was just that in Dieppe's case an evacuation was part of the plan, though this took place much sooner than had been anticipated. For the German papers, Operation Jubilee did not demonstrate the Allies' ability to reach out and strike in Europe; instead, it was a sign that the western defences were strong enough to decisively resist any such assault.

Where the official party paper led, the others followed. The title of the *Hamburger Anzeiger*'s leading article for 20 August read simply, 'Churchill's Second Dunkirk'. The *Escher Tageblatt*, a German-language paper based in Luxembourg, splashed in massive type on its front page: 'Invasion Attempt Failed – Catastrophic Defeat'. The *Amper-Bote* published in Dachau called the Dieppe attack 'an operation flouting any military sense'. So it went, on and on. Goebbels had created a well-oiled propaganda machine that was flexible enough to respond with a concerted message the day after a significant event. Reporters located across France rapidly sent in their copy for printing in the day's papers.

Chapter 13

The Ignoble Trudge into Captivity

The Dieppe PoWs were transferred to several camps deep within Germany. Most fit non-commissioned officers and private soldiers were sent to Stalag VIII B at Lamsdorf in far eastern Germany. In a curious development that could only have occurred in Nazi Germany, those with German heritage (*Volksdeutsche* in the Nazi vocabulary) were interrogated with particular interest by SS Lieutenant Baum. He observed these Dieppe prisoners as they stepped into a truck taking them on the last leg of their journey – a trip from Oppeln to Lamsdorf. Both places were so far to the east that they are now part of Poland. Alongside the prisoners from Dieppe were some Soviet PoWs being sent to the separate satellite camp for Russians. In his report, Baum noted what happened when the Allied PoWs saw their maltreated Soviet counterparts for the first time ('filthy, scruffy and ragged ... with an obstinate facial expression' in his words). One of the Allied prisoners remarked, 'I didn't think that this is what the paradise of farmers and workers would look like!' Later, when the Soviets picked up some cigarette stubs as relief from their interminable hardship, another called his Communist allies 'uncivilized'. Like all Western prisoners, the men from Dieppe were spared the inhumane treatment meted out to their Soviet counterparts. The first Canadian letters indicated that they held their captors in high regard because they treated prisoners well, though they also complained that the Red Cross parcels were necessary to maintain a sufficiently nutritious diet – 'a small piece of bread was at times regarded as something of a godsend', in the words of one official Canadian summary.[1]

There seems to have been no deeper purpose to Baum's questioning than pure racial curiosity. Baum asked his subjects whether they spoke German or read German-language newspapers at home, whether they attended religious services and why they had joined up to fight. There was no intent to gather actionable military intelligence. The most impressive of the prisoners, Baum later wrote in his report, was Corporal Josef Wanner, a 26-year-old farmer from Saskatchewan province. Wanner made a 'very good impression', being a muscular figure 5 foot 10 inches tall with blond hair and blue eyes, and spoke with a strong South German accent.[2] What possible use this information could have had, beyond fulfilling the Nazis' morbid obsession with race theory, is impossible to know.

Another destination for Dieppe's prisoners was Stalag IX-C at Bad Sulza in Thuringia. Some Canadians found themselves brought here, including Corporal Robert Prouse of the Canadian Provost Corps. While travelling westwards through France and Belgium, Prouse had been treated rather like a public exhibit; his train made frequent stops not for fuel or rest, but instead to allow his captors to show the occupied population what had happened to those sent to establish the so-called 'second front'. Some onlookers dared to make the 'V' for victory sign as the *Dieppois* had done, but any who did so were quickly hustled away. Prouse had been wounded at Dieppe and so was placed on a hospital train. This did not mean that the conditions were good in the boxcars. Prouse recalled one horrifying incident on the very first day of his journey westwards: 'One soldier nearly bled to death when his wound opened and the paper bandage, sodden with blood, came apart.' Fortunately for this man, a German medic arrived on his usual rounds during a stop. During another stop, a German photographer arrived to take pictures of the Canadians on Prouse's train. Just as the flash went off, however, Prouse defiantly thumbed his nose at the cameraman and received a violent shove from a guard for his troubles. The Canadian did not regret his defiance, later saying that 'it was an extremely small victory, but a significant one'. It took four long days to travel from Rouen to Stalag IX-C. There, Prouse found that most of the other prisoners were British soldiers from the 51st (Highland) Division, who had been captured wholesale at Le Havre in the French campaign of 1940. In September, due to repeated escape attempts, the prisoners at Stalag IX-C were moved to Mühlhausen. Just under 200 of the most heavily wounded Dieppe prisoners were brought to Obermaßfeld-Grimmenthal, 50 miles south of Mühlhausen. Here, the prisoners benefited from an established blood transfusion set-up, which saved many lives. A visiting Red Cross team praised the hospital's work, describing the operating theatre as 'primitive but clean'. At Obermaßfeld-Grimmenthal, the British Army medical orderlies seemed to work especially well with their German counterparts, raising morale tremendously.[3]

When Dieppe's prisoners reached their respective camps, the captured Jubilee plan came back to bite them, because of its instruction that German prisoners should have their hands bound or shackled to prevent their escape. For example, the orders given to 4 Commando under Lord Lovat read: 'Prisoners will be securely tied by their thumbs with fish-line in the best Japanese tradition, after which they will be handed over the Regimental Sergeant Major and marched under escort down the cliff to Orange 1 Beach.'[4] This measure flew in the face of the 1929 Geneva Convention, which stated in its second article that prisoners of war 'shall at all times be humanely treated and protected, particularly against acts of violence, from insults and from public curiosity ... Measures of reprisal against them are forbidden.' To make matters worse, for some months tit-for-tat responses to mistreatment had been common. Earlier in the year, Germans on the prison ship SS *Pasteur* had had their belongings confiscated in response to a supposed escape attempt. This was another violation, this time of Article 6: 'All personal effects and articles in personal use ... shall remain in the possession of prisoners of war'. In retaliation, Allied officers at Oflag IX-A had their possessions confiscated. For the Germans, the inclusion of shackling in the Jubilee Combined Operations Plan was the straw that broke the camel's back, and they promptly manacled over 1,300 British and Canadians, an act which was quickly matched by the Allies. The Germans then raised the stakes further, by shackling three times that number of Allied PoWs. This meant that by early October, over 5,500 German and Allied prisoners had their hands bound. So many PoWs were being manacled that the materials used were sometimes quite makeshift. In the height of irony, Robert Prouse saw his comrades bound with the very same cord that had tied up their Red Cross parcels. When proper handcuffs eventually arrived, the prisoners managed to unlock them with a key ingeniously fashioned from a sardine can opener.[5] This situation persisted on and off until the end of 1942, when the Canadian Government, greatly concerned at the prospect of uncontrolled escalation, decided to unilaterally unshackle all German prisoners held in the country. The British soon followed suit, as did the Germans. Only then did the so-called 'shackling crisis' come to an end.

Chapter 14

'Your Success is Our Success':
The Occupier and the Occupied

An important but easy-to-ignore part of Goebbels' propaganda offensive was how the Dieppe assault was portrayed in the French media. French newspapers and the journalists who wrote for them were censored just like their German counterparts, but French coverage adopted a slightly different tone on the events of 19 August. Rather than focussing on personal attacks on Stalin and Churchill, French pressmen generally restricted themselves to reporting the facts. In stark contrast to the other side of the Franco-German border, most papers carried little aggressive political comment, nor did they seek to place the events in northern France in a wider strategic context. Undoubtedly, this was in part due to the fact that the operation had happened on French soil and was therefore of national importance. Naturally, this was a matter of nuance and focus; French reporting was still incredibly negative to the Allies. However much they might have wanted to, no French newspaper editor could have printed a positive story and avoided a German prison cell. Still, French papers were less biting in their commentary and criticism. For example, *Le Petit Marocain*'s leading article on 20 August appeared under the title: 'Total Failure Of An Attempted Anglo-American Landing In The Dieppe Region'. The case of *Le Matin*, one of Paris's most widely circulated papers, is notable. This was an unabashedly right-wing nationalist publication, whose editors had gladly collaborated with the Germans, and they duly concocted a somewhat more dramatic headline: 'The Second Front Lasted Nine Hours'. However, the article was dry and factual, and did not cover much more than half the front page. Some French newspapers did not even mention Dieppe in their 20 August editions. *La Croix*, a general interest Roman Catholic paper based in the west of France, only covered the raid the following day with a headline making a manifestly bland announcement: 'An Attempted British Landing In The Dieppe Region'.

Two Frenchmen who were delighted to see the Allies, and more specifically the British, fail at Dieppe were Philippe Pétain and Pierre Laval. These men were the dual heads of the French collaborationist government centred in Vichy, the spa and resort town located at France's heart. Officially, their titles were 'Chief of the French State' and 'Chief of the Government' respectively, and they acted rather like a President and Prime Minister. They had both been politically active during France's Third Republic, until its collapse in 1940. Laval was an out-and-out politician dressed in suit and tie, whereas Pétain was a hero of the First World War. Before 1942 both men had betrayed their country by joining the Germans, and they would plunge themselves ever deeper into a nauseating mire of collaboration after Dieppe. They were overjoyed that an Allied operation on French soil, even one aimed at aiding the country's liberation, had crashed and burned. So low had Marshal Pétain sunk that he went out of his way to congratulate the Germans occupying his country for successfully repelling the raid, immediately dispatching his ambassador to the Germans in Paris, Fernand de Brinon, to deliver his message.

Upon hearing of the raid's failure late on 19 August, Pétain set up a meeting with Roland Krug von Nidda, head of the German embassy in Vichy. This took place the very next day, so eager was he to extend his congratulations to his German masters in person. He brought along Laval and Admiral François Darlan, commander-in-chief of the rump Vichy French military. 'Yesterday was a happy day which gratified all the French people' were the words with which Pétain chose to greet the German official. He seemed to genuinely believe that the Germans were France's saviours, not her oppressors. He praised the Dieppe population's docile attitude, especially those who had chosen to aid the German defence, and lambasted de Gaulle's Free French who had taken part in the raid. He also agreed with the Nazi party line that this had been a purely politically motivated operation, set in motion on Stalin's orders. Pétain was proving his worth as the perfect German puppet. 'I despise the English – they have brought us so much trouble', he told Krug von Nidda, explaining that the greatest mistake that France had ever made was binding itself in alliance to perfidious Albion – 'The English are either crazy or arrogant.' Pétain then went on to assert that Britain could only be defeated by a similar landing on its shores, because a nation only controls the land it occupies. Incredibly, he said this as if France were not occupied by the very same German invaders to whom he was now gleefully kowtowing. Laval shared Pétain's glee, saying. 'Your success is our success.' Darlan, who always kept an eye on military affairs, was convinced, as were many Germans, that the Allies would undertake further Dieppe-style operations in 1942, possibly on an even grander scale. When Krug von Nidda cabled his account of this meeting back to Berlin he made clear that he believed the congratulations he had received were genuine. The German Foreign Office, though, prevented this meeting from being reported in the domestic papers.[1]

However, all this French congratulation was unnecessary, for the Germans already knew exactly what Laval, de Brinon, Pétain and all the others members of the Vichy government thought. Unwilling to trust their installed puppet government ministers, German intelligence agents had for some time been bugging the telephones inside the collaborationist government offices. Thus, the jubilant reaction of the Vichy ministers came as no surprise to them. On 21 August Pétain sent a letter to Hitler by special courier. It was collected by the Germans' ambassador in Paris, Otto Abetz. In it, Pétain pleaded with the Führer to allow the French a bigger role in 'defending' their country from the Allies. For this French war hero, the Allies were the enemy, not the Axis powers. In order to defeat this foe, he suggested, even greater collaboration with the German occupiers was required. 'Following the recent British attack, which took place this time on our soil, I suggest that we envisage France's own participation in its defence', he wrote effusively. 'I ask you, *Herr Reichskanzler*, to consider this a sincere expression of my will to see France contribute to the defence of Europe.'[2] Nothing came of Pétain's initiative, for the Germans were distinctly uninterested in allowing the French a role in their own defence. They were quite content to run the whole show single-handedly.

When Pétain and Laval sent their congratulations to Hitler via Ambassador Abetz in Paris, they sent the same to Field Marshal Rundstedt. He was surprised to receive this message, as he had until then had no contact whatsoever with the old French Marshal. Nevertheless, OB West replied in the best tradition of cordial diplomacy a few days later: 'The Supreme Commander in the West thanks Marshal Pétain and Chief of Government Laval for their congratulations on the swift and total defensive success against the Anglo-Saxon landing attempt at Dieppe on 19 August. The behaviour of the population deserves special recognition. Dieppe is utterly calm. As early as the afternoon on the day of the attack, it was business as usual for all the shops.'

Rundstedt was, successfully or not, trying to persuade the Frenchmen and women whose country he was occupying that the Germans were a benevolent presence, and that the Allies would not spare France in their quest to defeat the Germans. As part of this strategy, he ensured that the *Dieppois* received the 'special attention' he had mentioned to Pétain and Laval. Firstly, he secured 10 million francs to repair the battle damage in Dieppe and its surroundings. As a matter of course, this was reported widely in the French press. *Le Matin* in Paris, for instance, praised the 'perfect attitude' of the local inhabitants, and hailed the 'generous gift' from Germany's military authorities. Ambassador de Brinon conveyed a message to General Carl-Heinrich von Stülpnagel, the Military Governor of Paris (and future conspirator against Hitler in 1944's July bomb plot). He extended his grovelling, yet seemingly genuine, gratitude: 'I am instructed to convey the spirited thanks of both [Pétain and Laval] for this gesture of aid and appreciation. The [Vichy French] Government appreciates especially the honour that you have done the population of our Normandy coast, which in its discipline and calm followed the directives given by the head of state and his Government to the letter.'

Besides the diplomatic niceties exchanged at the top levels of government, the Dieppe raid had some unexpected consequences for the local population. Hitler was so overjoyed with the peaceful (and to a certain extent cooperative) attitude of Dieppe's populace that he decided to release at least 1,000 French prisoners of war who had homes in Dieppe and its surrounding area. Since their capture in 1940, these men had been held in German camps, unable to return to their homes. Some French PoWs were held as far east as Kraków in Poland. Any letters that these men sent home were censored as a matter of course, so some had taken to using German soldiers as clandestine go-betweens. The system was simple; a German soldier on leave near their camps would collect the French PoWs' letters and take them with him when he returned to duty in France, subsequently posting them through the internal French postal system. Undoubtedly, most of the Germans did well out of such arrangements, but some did fall foul of the authorities. One week before the Dieppe raid took place, a Private Zimperl of 10th Panzer Division had been court-martialled for covertly delivering correspondence of a 'subversive' nature.[3] OKW explicitly acknowledged that the French prisoners were being repatriated with a view to influencing 'the behaviour of the French population during possible future landing attempts' and because of the 'extensive and long-lasting propagandistic effect' that the repatriations would have.[4] Hitler did not make this decision out of the goodness of his heart – in essence, it was a cynical public relations move.

Ordinary men and women become caught up in great and historic events too – life in wartime, as in peacetime, is messy and complicated. For no one was this truer than one unnamed French prisoner of war from Dieppe who had fallen in love with a German war widow. The PoW and the widow had been, for want of a better term, engaged in 'intimate relations' for some time. At some point after the Dieppe raid, the man was selected as one of those to be released from his PoW camp in Germany. However, though he had been given the precious opportunity to finally return home after two years, for the sake of his German lover the Frenchman refused. What is more, he immediately signed up as a voluntary civilian worker. This meant that he could stay in Germany, and due to a quirk in the German occupation law, voluntary labour service shielded foreign workers like him from being punished for having sexual relations with German women. As if this were not enough for a best-selling romance, the Frenchman then promptly expressed his wish to marry his ladyfriend as soon as possible.[5]

Congratulations to the *Dieppois* did not come merely from German quarters. Pierre Laval, too, extended his personal congratulations to Dieppe's district chief (*sous-préfet*), Michel Sassier, citing 19 August as a 'magnificent example' of how Frenchmen and women should behave when faced with Allied landings in future.[6] Military Governor Stülpnagel asked for a list of those French PoWs who had formerly lived in and around Dieppe, and by 7 September Sassier had sent in 1,800 names. Initially, Stülpnagel chose only a thousand. When the first batch of prisoners was being sent home by train on 12 September, a small ceremony was held at Serqueux railway station – an agonisingly short distance of just 25 miles from home. German and French dignitaries were in attendance, including Sassier and Dieppe's mayor, René Levasseur, as well as Ambassador de Brinon. A French captain gave an emotional speech which concluded with the words, 'We hope, we hope with all our heart, that Chancellor Hitler's generous gesture towards us will soon be extended to all our fellow prisoners.' Before the train could leave on its last leg home to Dieppe, French officials thrust chalk into the prisoners' hands, telling them to write pro-Vichy slogans on the side of the carriages. Desperate to finally get home, the prisoners wrote whatever was asked of them. At the end of September, 302nd Division reported that the repatriations had engendered 'great gratification' amongst the local population. 'The released prisoners', it added, 'are contributing significantly to improving the image of Germany.' Generally, the returned *Dieppois* spoke well of their treatment in German camps. One German intelligence report recorded that, amongst themselves some even praised Hitler for his decision.[7] By 22 October, after some agonising pauses in the repatriations, 1,300 prisoners had been released. By mid-May 1943, a grand total of 1,581 men were back home, and this turned out to be the final total.[8] Sassier had worked admirably to secure their return, and the Germans, for their part, made good on this propaganda opportunity. The accomplished French cartoonist Pierre Fix-Masseau produced a poster showing a happy Frenchman skipping along with a briefcase, with 'DIEPPE' printed above in bold type and 'Germany is freeing more than a thousand prisoners' below.

With their cynical 'gifts' of money and these prisoner releases, the German authorities were all too happy to garner sympathy from the French population. A different sentiment existed in Germany itself, however. At an afternoon press conference in Berlin on 24 August, the gaggle of assembled journalists were told to hold off on reporting this news in the German press until a *Sprachregelung*, or official 'party line', had been decided.[9] Goebbels personally intervened and sought to prevent these concessions from being mentioned at all. His rationale was simple – if the Germans knew of them, they might become too sympathetic to the occupied French. He told his secretary that while 'the population behaved splendidly and should thus receive recognition ... I fear that the Francophilia innate in the German national character will only grow' if the news made its way into Germany's papers.[10] Goebbels could not tolerate the development of a considerate attitude towards the French in wartime. After all, at that time the Germans were the masters of France's fate. Eventually, Hitler and Goebbels came to a compromise. While news of the money and the prisoner releases would indeed be printed, it would not be very prominent and only given a very brief mention. The *Hamburger Anzeiger* duly carried a tiny item on its second page on 27 August: 'During the successful defensive battle against the British landing attempt at Dieppe, the local French authorities and population maintained an especially disciplined behaviour. Without regard for enemy fire, the French fought fires, provided German troops with food and drink, and aided airmen who were forced to make an emergency landing.' Naturally, it could not have been admitted that most of those German airmen had in fact been shot down. The *Anzeiger* then went on to list the villages whose menfolk would be released.

So low had the Vichy government sunk, so bound to the Germans had they become, that Pétain (a former Marshal of France no less) was now thanking Germany (of all nations) for releasing Frenchmen captured two years previously. It was an astonishing act of self-abasement by one of French history's greatest figures. Two years later, in a meeting with another one of his Reich's puppets – this time, Jozef Tiso of Slovakia – Hitler harked back to the events of 1942, fondly recalling the helpfulness of many *Dieppois*.[11]

Part IV

War Beyond the Beaches

Chapter 15

A Triumph for OB West

It took a few days for the gears of military bureaucracy to become engaged, but by the end of August the defeat of the Dieppe raid would be one of the Wehrmacht's most hotly discussed feats of the entire war. The Army, Kriegsmarine and Luftwaffe all produced voluminous documentation, ranging from purely narrative accounts to detailed analysis of the 'lessons learned'. They all wished desperately to tell their side of the whole Allied fiasco. English-speaking historians have asked so many times, 'What did the Allies learn?' but the Germans were asking the same question. Before this process of reflection could begin in earnest, Rundstedt and his forces in the West received a personal message from the Führer on 21 August:

To the Commander-in-Chief West, Herr Field Marshal von Rundstedt:

Thanks to the careful preparations made by command and troops, an English landing attempt on a grand scale was completely broken up in the shortest of time. I beg you, Herr Field Marshal, to express my thanks and my appreciation to all participating units of the three armed services. I know that in the future too I can rely on the commanders and the soldiers of the Wehrmacht in the West.[1]

Since he had arrived in Paris in March, Rundstedt's position of *Oberbefehlshaber West* (OB West) had been one of monotony. His fellow generals in the East were doing the 'real' fighting against the Soviet Union, as were Erwin Rommel and his Afrika Korps in North Africa. Dieppe was a welcome, if not entirely unexpected, opportunity for his men in the West to show their skill at arms, and praise from none other than the Führer was a testament to their success. Rundstedt made sure that Hitler's message was heard by all men under his command. On 22 August, OB West visited Dieppe, taking time to hand out medals to the victorious defenders, watched at every step by newsreel film cameras. Later, he visited General Haase and his staff at 302nd Division headquarters once again.[2] There was yet another surprise for the divisional commander – the same day, he was awarded a clasp to the Iron Cross 1st Class that he had won in the First World War. The whole experience had certainly raised morale within his division. Haase reported a few days later to General Kuntzen at LXXXI Corps that 302nd Infantry Division's men were eager to fight, now that they had so clearly demonstrated their superiority over the enemy.[3] But not all were so enthusiastic. After the war, Major Paul Hinz and Lieutenant Herbert Titzmann recorded in the divisional history that there was a rather more melancholy mood amongst the troops. After over a year of comfort and luxury in a beautiful region of northern France, they felt that fate had finally caught up with them: 'We survivors were happy to have escaped – but it was not a "happy day",' they wrote. 'We instead had the feeling that our division had finally been given the bill for the years living on the Channel coast.'[4]

But OB West had more to do than simply lap up the praise of his superiors. Rundstedt now oversaw a meticulous attempt to dissect the Dieppe raid and, most importantly, its lessons for the future. Nobody could be sure that such a large-scale raid would not take place again, and the Germans had to be ready to face that challenge again. The most important question appeared at first glance to be a simple one: what did the Anglo-Canadians want from Dieppe? What was their objective? All military planning stems from the objective – what is the planned operation aimed at achieving? Only once the objective is known can resources be allocated, a timeframe set and dedicated training begin. Yet Dieppe was a curious case in that the objective was not at all clear.

At 1400 on 19 August, while the Canadians were still being rounded up and taken en masse into captivity, Raeder's Naval Staff HQ received a situational update from Admiral Saalwächter's Naval Group West. It reflected the main body of German opinion in remarking that the raid had 'no particular recognizable objective. Perhaps a question of prestige.'[5] Typically in offensive land operations, but especially in raids, territory is taken in support of a greater purpose. To take two examples from the Second World War: the Commandos went ashore at Saint-Nazaire so that they could protect HMS *Campbeltown* as she rammed the dock gates, thereby preventing German pocket battleships from making port on France's Atlantic coast. And Major John Frost and his band of Paras went ashore at Bruneval in order to capture the Germans' Würzburg gun-laying radar and its technicians. To be blunt, armies do not take land for the sake of it; there must be some greater strategic purpose. Without this, one wastes time, effort, resources and men in pursuit of meaningless objectives; but to the Germans at least, this seems to have been exactly what Jubilee was about.

After the soldiers in uniform had vacated the field of battle, the spies and agents in France and Britain once again emerged to play their tricky game of bluff and deception. Britain's MI6 was tasked with gathering post-battle intelligence from their agents embedded in France, as well as from the local populace. MI6 used two primary modes of communication; covert radio messages and the rather more primitive, but nevertheless tried and tested, carrier pigeon. In the days following the raid, these trusty homing birds were dropped in small cages over the Dieppe area with small pieces of paper attached to their legs. On these a small questionnaire was printed, and British agents (or sympathetic French civilians) were asked to fill it out, re-wrap the paper and re-attach it to the pigeon's leg. The birds would then fly back to England. However, some became lost and ultimately landed in German hands. Many were turned in to the Germans by Dieppe's local population, encouraged by the promise of a bounty for each bird handed in. These little questionnaires afforded the Germans a unique chance to view the operation through the enemy's eyes – what did the Allies want to know? The questions were short yet significant: 'What military objects were destroyed or damaged? What did the Germans themselves destroy for their own protection (bridges and so on)? Did the broadcasts from English radio have any success with the population? Are similar German operations being planned against England?' These were all vital questions that the Allies still had to answer – their stay on French soil was so fleeting that they had not had time to assess what damage had been done. Ultimately, after-action aerial reconnaissance could only tell them so much, so having sources on the ground was crucial.

The carrier pigeons were only the start. On 22 August, British intelligence sent the following message via radio to their agents in the Dieppe area: 'What are the reactions of the French and Boches to the raid on Dieppe? Urgent.' Yet it was not only British agents who were listening. The Germans heard this message too. Deciding that this was the perfect opportunity to spread disinformation within British ranks, German agents decided to send a fake reply in what they called a *Funkspiel* or 'radio game'. Cleverly, they drafted this so that it came as an indirect reply to the Allies' questionnaire dropped by the carrier pigeons. Rundstedt personally approved the following message, which was sent a week later:

> It is extremely embarrassing to report truthfully about the behaviour of the Dieppe population. On the 19th and 20th the French listened to London radio with enthusiasm. After the defeat came the reaction. Generally, we are hearing that the operation failed and the prestige of the Allies has been diminished. Especially in higher quarters people are criticising the poor preparation. Great disappointment. Shameful for us is the behaviour of the population, who in multiple cases made cause with the enemy by delivering Allied soldiers to the Boches. The Boches may laugh, but he who has the last laugh, laughs best.[6]

This fake reply sent exactly the message that the Germans wanted – it implanted in Allied minds the idea that the operation had caused embarrassment to their cause, and the French population's hopes of liberation had been shaken. Crucially, the Germans' reply was based on fact – the French population did, to a significant extent, aid the German defence, and those who did not wish to collaborate were unsettled by the calamitous failure of the raid. As Goebbels knew well, propaganda is always more convincing when based on at least a kernel of truth. It is interesting to note that the fake German reply did not even attempt to answer British requests for information about military damage and similar operations being planned against the British coast. Clearly, the Germans wanted to leave the Allies guessing and undermine confidence in the cause they were fighting for. Also noteworthy was that the German reply used the term 'prestige'. Since there seemed at first glance to be no military objective, it seemed logical from a German point of view to assume that Dieppe was aimed at enhancing the Allies' reputation and not at achieving any military benefit. With Britain's relative passivity at this time in the combined Allied war effort (at least on land), this idea appeared even more logical. For Rundstedt, basing a disinformation strategy around a perceived wound to the Allied ego appeared promising.

Interestingly, the word 'prestige' was not confined merely to German assessments of Dieppe in 1942 – more than thirty years later, when the German naval historian Michael Salewski's evaluation appeared, it could have been lifted straight from a wartime propaganda script: 'If Saint-Nazaire had had a visible operational purpose – namely the destruction of the Normandy water lock – then Dieppe was an operation based solely on prestige for political reasons, and ranked amongst the most foolish of Churchill's actions during the Second World War.'[7]

The first substantial German report on the Dieppe raid came from General Kuntzen's intelligence staff at LXXXI Corps. Dieppe was the hot topic for the Germans stationed in the West, so from Rundstedt all the way down to company level there was eagerness to produce a swift account from each unit's point of view. LXXXI Corps' intelligence report, for instance, was a short piece of work. The rapidity with which it was produced showed; the Camerons, for example, are erroneously referred to throughout as the 'Cameroons'. Clearly, there had not been time for adequate fact-checking and proofreading. Regarding the details of the Jubilee operation, Kuntzen's officers could not identify a purpose other than to occupy ground while taking prisoners and capturing weapons and equipment. As far as a real military target was concerned, they correctly concluded that Jubilee was nothing more than a destructive raid with no grander strategic goal: 'The English intended to put the Dieppe Defence Zone out of action for the longest possible time. It was also their intention to immobilize, for some time to come, all military installations, coastal batteries, radio stations, airfield, ships, as well as all utilities (gas, electricity, harbour, cranes, railroads).'[8] Kuntzen's men had a unique and rare advantage in attempting to discern their enemy's intention. Since Brigadier Southam's copy of the Allies' battle plan had been captured on the beaches, the Germans could see exactly what they had planned. All subsequent analysis of the events of 19 August was informed by this precious document. It is an enviable position, the holy grail of military intelligence, to know exactly what one's enemy intends. Men like those on Kuntzen's intelligence team had made their careers piecing together the tiniest clues from scattered sources, in order to get inside their enemies' heads. With the thick Combined Operations Plan in their grateful hands, however, all the answers lay right before them. Once the plan was rapidly translated, over fifty copies were distributed to high-level commands in the Army, Kriegsmarine and Luftwaffe, including one sent to Hitler's headquarters.

It is impossible to overstate how fundamentally commanders across the Wehrmacht questioned Jubilee's objectives and methods. It made no sense to them to use a full division against a French port which held no value other than as a springboard for invasion. Dieppe was, after all, the closest port to Paris. The logical conclusion, therefore, was that the operation must have been the first stage in a larger invasion attempt. Why else would the Allies land at Dieppe and not somewhere more valuable? This was a perfectly sensible conclusion from the facts, though it was ultimately mistaken. As we have seen, Rundstedt's immediate impression was that, since the Allies seemed to hold back their ground attack aircraft, they must have been saving their effort for a larger-scale follow-up invasion. OB West's naval counterparts agreed; late on 19 August, the war diary of Erich Raeder's Naval Staff recorded a tentative preliminary observation: 'The forces employed in the operation appear too large for a mere raid, especially since more transports were standing by in the rear. It is possible that the Dieppe harbour was their first objective and that parts of the second wave were to be landed there with the purpose of establishing a real invasion bridgehead.' The Naval Staff did, however, concede that at such an early stage, all assessments that they could make were very much preliminary in nature.

One man who had no doubts was Naval Commander, Channel Coast Admiral Hermann von Fischel. By virtue of his position he had a significant interest in learning lessons from the events of 19 August. For Fischel, the fact that the port town of Dieppe was targeted provided clear evidence that the Allies had had something bigger up their sleeves. He was clear in his mind that, had the Dieppe raid succeeded, it would not have been a raid at all: 'I got the impression that behind the enemy's landing attempt lay the intention to build a bridgehead, from which further forces were to undertake an attack against Le Havre and Octeville.' Speaking from a naval and logistical perspective, Fischel put himself in the enemy's shoes: 'Taking Le Havre with the unloading capabilities of a large modern port would have fulfilled the preconditions for a successful invasion attempt on the Continent.'[9] On 20 August, with another day to consider matters, Raeder's staff changed their minds entirely, concluding that Dieppe was just an isolated divisional-scale raid – this reflected the Germans' uncertainty.

With a further day to collect information and digest the whole situation, the men of the Naval Staff wrote a scathing criticism of the whole Jubilee scheme. Even though they were sailors, they did not hesitate to criticize every conceivable aspect of the Allied operation: 'From a military standpoint such a limited operation appears even less understandable than from a political standpoint. At best, the seizure of Dieppe for a few hours would have offered the enemy facilities for quickly unloading a few more regiments with some heavy weapons, tanks and guns.' Running as a constant through German commanders' train of thought was the question of the convoy spotted by air reconnaissance before midday on the 19th. If this was the 26-ship troop transport convoy as Sperrle's planes reported, it would add credence to the view that Dieppe was simply a first step in an invasion of France that failed. Because this first phase failed, the invasion was called off – or so the reasoning went. As we know, this was an utterly misleading sighting; the 'convoy' was actually only a handful of coastal merchant ships.

In their assessment the Naval Staff poured cold water on the 'phased invasion' interpretation:

It appears dubious whether the twenty-six vessels sighted off Portsmouth were assembled there to be used as transports if the first landing had been successful. But even if the enemy had succeeded in establishing a bridgehead in the Dieppe area by landing a force estimated to have totalled 15,000 to 20,000 men, such an operation would have made sense only in conjunction with a successful attempt to tie up our reserve divisions by simultaneously landing more forces of a similar or larger size elsewhere in the West area, and especially by throwing strong airborne forces behind our line.

In view of these facts, the German Naval Staff concluded, the Allied effort at Dieppe was 'bound to end in a military setback for which no military justification can be offered'.[10] In all that was written by Germans about the Dieppe raid, this last sentence is surely the most damning; the operation was criminally under-supported and had no conceivable military objective. Even launching the undertaking in the first place was, in the considered professional view of Raeder's staff, completely and utterly indefensible. The logic employed here was simple: if the Dieppe operation had been a large-scale operation hoping to create a permanent or semi-permanent bridgehead in France, the Allies should have deployed greater forces on a much wider front – i.e. the force was too small. If Dieppe was just a small destructive raid, then the multinational, air-sea-land force with a divisional-sized land component was too large. That Jubilee fitted neither of these two models was the source of deep confusion. As one German staff officer reflected to a Canadian prisoner, the attack was too large for a raid, yet too small for an invasion.[11]

Chapter 16

'Next Time He Will Do Things Differently': Dissecting Victory and Defeat

In his final report to Hitler's headquarters a few weeks later, Rundstedt came to a balanced and nuanced position on the question as to what the scale and objectives had really been at Dieppe. This is something that any overarching joint services supreme commander with a wealth of military experience should do. Rundstedt tentatively concluded that Jubilee might not have just been a brief raid, but rather a larger-scale strategic operation. By now, Admiral Saalwächter at Naval Group West had confirmed that the phantom group of twenty-six ships in the Channel was simply a standard coastal convoy. With this went a key piece of evidence which had raised the suspicion that a second wave at Dieppe was planned. In his final analysis, OB West Rundstedt pointed to Dieppe's insignificance as a strategic objective, and the massive air-sea-land forces committed. 'One does not sacrifice twenty-nine or thirty of the most modern tanks for a raid', he declared. But Dieppe's status as a harbour town had further consequences in his line of thinking, namely that the port facilities would have been used to quickly unload further forces if the raid had proceeded according to plan: 'It is to be assumed that, by employing such considerable forces, the enemy thought to effect a rapid seizure of the Dieppe bridgehead, after elimination of its artillery defences, in order to utilize the good port facilities for bringing up and landing in succession the floating and the operational reserves.'

Even with the Combined Operations Plan to read at his leisure, the purpose of the raid still confused Rundstedt immensely. That he could see exactly what the Allies had planned, yet did not understand their overall objective, demonstrates how bewildered he was by the whole scheme. Rundstedt was so puzzled by the question of whether the attack on 19 August had just been the first stage of an intended invasion, that he could not make his mind up even with perfect information available: '[It cannot] be established without contradiction by the captured operation order whether the operation was of a local character or – in the event of success – was to be the beginning of the "Invasion" [because] the English instruction for the landing operation provides most definitely and elaborately for withdrawal or re-embarkation. It is, however, no proof of the enemy's final intention that withdrawal and re-embarkation were planned in detail.' Dieppe was not in itself an important target. It was not symbolically important to the Allied cause, and its only real strategic value lay in it being a port that could be utilized to stage longer-term and larger-scale operations. It was therefore only natural for some in German uniform to draw the conclusion that Jubilee was the failed 'stage one' of an invasion attempt – otherwise, there was no logic in attacking Dieppe.

Speaking with the authority of command as OB West, Rundstedt was also clear that any repeat operation in Dieppe's mould would be far better planned and executed.[1] He quite rightly came to the view that the Allies would learn their lesson and never repeat a landing like Dieppe with 19 August's ill-preparedness and poor planning. It cannot be stressed how much Rundstedt wished to impress upon his subordinates his belief that their enemy would learn from Dieppe just as the Germans did. OB West wisely did not concern himself merely with how the Germans could improve their system of coastal defence. He also gave thought to how the enemy would improve their conception of offensive amphibious operations against defended European coastlines. In the Allied-centric historical investigations of the raid since the war, this inescapable fact has been lost. This is strange, because the evidence is there for all to see. In his single-page covering letter to the translated Allied landing plan, Rundstedt made his concerns clear: 'It would be wrong to believe that the enemy will conduct his next operation in the same way. He will draw experience from his incorrect conception [of landings] as well as from his mistakes. Next time he will do things differently.'

With the Combined Operations plan in their hands, the Germans spent considerable time levelling criticisms at it. From the French side of the Channel, they saw the Dieppe plan as a lesson in how not to write an operational scheme, particularly because of the plan's rigidity. Once fully translated, the plan ran to 121 pages, and German commanders universally agreed that this level of detail hampered Jubilee from the outset, because it left no room for individual freedom or initiative once contact with the enemy had been made. British and Canadian junior officers had little recourse to their own decision-making ability, since the intended course of events was laid out from the very outset. The withdrawal plan, for example, contained twelve different stages, each one given an exact 'bomb line'. The bomb line was in essence a ring around Dieppe town − as the land component withdrew to its landing craft on Red and White beach, only targets outside this bomb line would be attacked by aircraft, in order to avoid friendly fire. As the force withdrew, the bomb line shrank. Yet this assumed that the operation would always be going smoothly and would not encounter any unforeseen problems that might alter the withdrawal schedule. Unfortunately, it is not the nature of war to be predictable; unexpected events can and do occur suddenly, turning plans upside-down in an instant. Therefore, it is more common in operational planning to set a fixed objective and allocate the resources to completing that objective, but leave the method by which success is to be achieved to the appropriate subordinate commanders. A battalion commander, for example, might set a hilltop as an objective and dedicate a company or two to the mission, but delegate to them the specifics such as routes and timings. No one can predict what will happen in the frenzy and confusion of war (whether on land, at sea or in the air), so expecting events to pan out exactly as hoped and planned for is a fool's game. War is not kind enough to be predictable. Not for nothing are military planners fond of remarking that 'the enemy always has a vote in the course of events'. For this reason, setting minute-precise scheduling as the Dieppe planners did should be done only with the most extreme caution. On 19 August, such precision was not justified.

The belief that the plan's prescriptive nature hindered the operation was a staple of German comment. From their perspective, it was incomprehensible how such a rigidly controlled operation could have been brought to life. As German commanders might have asked in their deliberations, 'Did nobody step back and take a moment to stop and think?' When the translated Allied Combined Operations Plan was released on 24 August, Rundstedt's brief covering note had a similar thrust: 'The plan is in German terms not a plan, it is more a position paper or the intended course of an exercise.'[2] Major General Haase in his report simply described the plan as 'mediocre', again piling on criticism that the planned withdrawal was too inflexible. Another account originating from LXXXI Corps was even more forceful, arguing that Jubilee was doomed from the start because the plan 'fixed every detail of the action for each unit. This method of planning made the failure of the whole raid inevitable in the event of unexpected difficulties.'[3] One account by 302nd Infantry Division's quartermaster summed up the German body of opinion succinctly: 'The attack was supposed to take place schematically, in precisely timed lines – as if no defence was to be expected.'[4] German reports invariably avoided the word 'raid' when describing Jubilee, using instead the more general terms 'landing attempt' or 'attack'.

Ultimately, having considered how rigidly the operation was planned, the Wehrmacht's officer corps wondered how a scheme like Jubilee could ever have expected to properly use all three services in a genuinely joint manner. Certainly, the Wehrmacht liked to think of itself as a free-thinking organization when it came to planning military operations. Rundstedt felt that the Allied plan for Dieppe went against all the principles he had absorbed in his long military career. Hence the comment in his final report, which was submitted to Hitler early in September: '[The operation] was carried out after months of almost too precise planning in accordance with so rigid a scheme.'[5] There were certainly benefits to planning some parts of an operation in minute detail. Bomb lines, for example, considerably reduced the likelihood that Allied forces would be attacked by friendly aircraft as they withdrew to the re-embarkation beaches. However, this was not how the Germans saw things; instead, they were willing to take a slightly riskier approach and keep prescriptive planning to a minimum. In his official Canadian history, Colonel Stacey tentatively addressed this question, defending his superiors and generally rejecting the German criticisms. Although he admitted that indeed 'there was much detail in the order', Stacey nevertheless came to the view that 'the action of individual units [was] not so closely prescribed as a first glance suggests'.[6]

The list of German criticisms continued. Prominent in many units' accounts of the battle is how poorly supported the Allied ground forces were. We have already seen how Rundstedt was shocked by the Allies' failure to properly employ single- or multi-engined ground attack aircraft. This led him to suggest that the RAF was saving itself for an invasion. But OB West was far from alone in censuring the Allies for poor support of their ground troops, from both the sea and the air. Indeed, in formulating the plan, fire support for the men on the ground was actually reduced to the point of impotency, leaving only eight Hunt-class destroyers, a gunboat and a handful of Hurricanes armed with cannons and small bombs. This was indefensible. The Royal Navy refused to dedicate a battleship to the naval force, because this would mean putting a precious capital ship in harm's way in the Channel. The RAF, especially Commander-in-Chief of Bomber Command Air Marshal Arthur 'Bomber' Harris, did not want to divert their precious airframes to a Combined Operations raid in France, even one as significant as Jubilee. Harris even used the word 'sideshow' in reference to the planned Dieppe raid. A large preliminary bombardment had been part of the original plan, but was eventually dropped. This move was justified by the dubious contention that a large bombardment by air and sea forces prior to the landing would only alert the defenders, and that it was in any case preferable to rely on speed and surprise. How the Canadians undertaking the frontal assault were left to their fate, unsupported by the undoubted firepower at the Allies' disposal, has occupied staff and students at military command and staff colleges across the Western world ever since.

It was this aspect of 19 August that puzzled the Germans most. How could the Allies be so reckless as to commit a massive land force in a frontal attack on French soil without commensurate air and naval gunfire support? It was the general German consensus that the Allied attack did not fail for any lack of dedication to duty on the part of the Allied troops; rather, it was the utter absence of supporting fire which dealt the death blow. LXXXI Corps summed this view up well in a short addendum to General Haase's report from 302nd Infantry Division. It is interesting to note here that while the main Canadian attack was correctly described as such, General Kuntzen's comments still labelled the whole operation as 'English':

The Officer Commanding [LXXXI Corps] is in agreement with the view of the Division that the English attack did not fail because of the bravery of the Canadian Division, but rather failed due to the total consolidated firepower of the Division, which made it impossible for the enemy to get into the town or onto the anti-tank walls in order to detonate the explosive charges they had prepared. The gunfire of the ship-borne artillery, the low-flying aircraft attacks and the bombs from British fighter-bombers were not enough to shake the defensive strength of our defences.[7]

Major General Haase agreed that British planners, and not the soldiers assigned to Jubilee, were to blame. He went so far as to praise the Canadians' 'energetic' assault. Strikingly, his words of criticism almost exactly matched Kuntzen's: 'The fact that the enemy did not gain any ground at all in Puys, and in Dieppe only captured for a brief period just sections of the beach with the exception of the western mole and the western edge, was not caused by lack of courage, but by the concentrated defensive fire of our divisional artillery and the heavy weapons of our infantry. Enemy tank crews did not lack in determination.' In all the multitude of reports that it produced, 302nd Division reserved its most intense reproach for those at the top of the British hierarchy: 'The British High Command rather seriously underestimated the quantity of weapons of all sorts required for such an attack. The strength of air and naval forces was entirely insufficient to suppress the defenders during the landings and destroy their signal communications. It is incomprehensible that the British Higher Command thought that one Canadian division would be able to overrun a German infantry regiment reinforced with artillery.'[8]

There was only one dissenting voice against the consensus that the Canadians had fought well. 302nd Infantry Division's intelligence section applied some damning words to the Canadian performance: 'The Canadians on the whole fought badly and surrendered afterwards in swarms', it declared. This judgement can surely be rejected, for with the benefit of historical hindsight it is now apparent to all students of Operation Jubilee that no soldiers could have succeeded under the infernal conditions encountered at Dieppe. Only on the British Commandos did the intelligence section feel able to bestow praise, calling these units 'well trained' and noting that they 'fought with real spirit'.[9]

That the Allies clearly underestimated the German defences at Dieppe in 1942 was all the more baffling due to the excruciatingly detailed aerial reconnaissance they had gathered. Some installations escaped detection, like the coastal gun positions dug into the side of Dieppe's cliff headlands, but on the whole the Jubilee force enjoyed an unparalleled picture of what they would face on 19 August. General Kuntzen of LXXXI Corps said simply that 'it is astonishing that the British should have underestimated our defence, as they had details of most of it from air photos.'[10] It seemed incredible to him that the Allies did not properly respect the German emplacements on the coastline. Undoubtedly, this was partly due to the fact that 302nd Division was a low-quality static division, a fact which Mountbatten and his Combined Operations staff were well aware of. On the other hand, Allied overconfidence in their own method of attack must share some of the blame. Assuming that such a large air-sea-land force could achieve tactical surprise, thereby removing the need for strong fire support, was a reckless risk to take and perhaps the central reason for Jubilee's failure. In the official British naval history *The War at Sea*, Captain Stephen Roskill struggled with the way in which the land force was in effect abandoned by air and sea power. Speaking with the authority of an official historian, Roskill ventured as far as to say that sacrificing bombardment for the vague notion of 'stealth and surprise' was 'not altogether sound', and that the failure to exploit the potential of air power 'may well have contributed to the failure of the raid'.[11] German judgements, as we have seen, were not so understated.

Another weakness that the Germans identified in the Dieppe plan was the decision not to employ airborne or air-landed troops. In his memorandum before the Dieppe raid discussing how the Allies would launch a large-scale landing, Rundstedt had clearly identified paratroops as a critical threat to the German-occupied coastline. He had felt it was nigh-on certain that the Allies would land these troops behind his lines in a divisional-scale amphibious assault. The fact that the Dieppe force excluded airborne and air-landed troops came as a tremendous surprise to all German commanders in northern France, and they considered their omission a prime reason why Jubilee had failed. In a section of their report plainly entitled 'What was the cause of the Great British Failure?' LXXXI Corps was clearly puzzled: 'Contrary to all expectations, the British did not employ parachutist and airborne troops. If they had attacked Puys simultaneously with airborne troops and from the sea, the initial position of the defenders of Puys would probably have been critical.'[12] This may have been true, but it would have been incredibly difficult to consolidate an airborne unit for a precise attack on such a small target as Puys. As the Germans knew well, airborne and air-landed infantry would take a significant amount of time to form up as a cohesive unit for an attack. Even if the Jubilee force had included paratroops, there is no guarantee they could have coordinated an attack with the amphibious force, though their presence would certainly have been of benefit. In its report, Haase's 302nd Infantry Division made the broader point that enemy infantry in the rear would have put the entire German defence at risk: 'Our position would have become ever so much more precarious if the enemy had attacked simultaneously with air-landed troops from the rear and strong tank-supported forces from the sides – at the weak points. This would have brought about an envelopment.'[13]

With a static division like the 302nd, the unit's weakness lay in its immobility. Had the Allies somehow managed to surround the German forces in Dieppe, there would have been little hope for them to withdraw to safety. Nor would the reserves have had the speed to prevent such an envelopment. Unbeknownst to the Germans, for Jubilee's predecessor, Operation Rutter, there had indeed been provision for the use of airborne forces. However, this was cancelled when Mountbatten remounted Rutter as Jubilee after the former operation was cancelled in July. There was some foundation for the removal of the parachute troops; Colonel Stacey highlighted the fact that air drops needed almost perfect conditions, and it had always been uncertain whether these would be present in August. Furthermore, the Canadian official historian noted that paratroops required considerable briefing time before being deployed, primarily because of the complexity of airborne operations.[14] Ultimately, the paratroops were replaced with 3 and 4 Commandos' flank attacks for the Jubilee plan as launched. Despite all the legitimate reasons why Combined Operations Headquarters omitted the paratroops, and the perfectly justifiable grounds both for and against their inclusion, the Germans were of one mind – they were incredulous that such a large-scale operation was not supported by an attack by airborne infantry. They had planned their coastal defence on this basis, and indoctrinated their troops with the assumption that airborne troops would be a vital part of Allied amphibious strategy. Not only would such an attack have avoided the Germans' strong frontal defence line, but it would also have allowed assaults from multiple directions. Fundamentally, the Germans regarded the benefits of including an airborne element in an operation in Jubilee's style as far outweighing the risks, to the point that the decision to omit it was almost inconceivable to them.

Besides the movements, timings and general scheme of the operation, the Germans also condemned the equipment that the Anglo-Canadians brought to Dieppe. From armour to aircraft, they conducted a thorough technical assessment of Allied kit. A few days after the raid, at his Wehrwolf Headquarters in Ukraine, Hitler ruminated on the events in France to a small group of friends and advisers. This was a not uncommon event; he regularly talked for hours in these select and informal gatherings. Normally, these were wide-ranging conversations and often had nothing to do with the war. As the Führer, Hitler was free to speak his mind for as long as he wanted, and his entourage had to listen to his thoughts on every topic under the sun, from the papacy during the Renaissance to his dog Blondi's decidedly uncarnivorous penchant for herbs. Hitler's remarks, his 'table talk' as they have come to be known, were officially transcribed from July 1941 onwards on the orders of Martin Bormann, head of the Nazi Party Chancellery. On the evening of 26 August 1942 the Führer turned to the war situation and spoke at length about the Dieppe raid. Erich Raeder was a special guest in Vinnytsia that day. As ever, Hitler was fascinated by machines, engineering and technical detail, so the capture of so much Allied equipment gave him great joy. After expressing delight in the boost to German morale that a victory in the West had provided, the Führer added: 'Less important, perhaps, but equally pleasing, is the gift the British have given us of a first-class collection of their latest weapons; never before, I think, has anyone taken the trouble to cross the seas in order to present his adversary with samples of his most modern arms! It is always so much easier to decide on the specifications of a new tank, for example, when one knows beforehand the weapons it will be called upon to face.'[15]

Of all the technical evaluations conducted by the Germans in the wake of the Dieppe raid, the most significant and well-documented was the evaluation of the Canadian Calgary Regiment's Churchill tanks. Almost as soon as the shooting had stopped, men from the *Waffenamt* hurried to the northern French coast to inspect the Canadian armour. As 19 August was the first time that the Churchill had been used in combat, it was a unique opportunity for the Germans to assess and understand the tank that they would have to confront in the future. The Churchill was what the British called an 'infantry tank' – a heavily armoured vehicle intended to support infantry on foot. Its main strength was its thick, but unsloped,

102mm of frontal armour. This was essentially the same as the armour possessed by the famed German Tiger, which would make its combat debut in the battle for Stalingrad in September 1942. Due to this weight, however, the Churchill was quite slow, only capable of a maximum speed of 15 mph.

When the *Waffenamt* got their grateful hands on this new armoured gift, they were extremely disappointed. After a few weeks of testing and analysis that took place just outside Dieppe, the *Waffenamt's* engineers released their findings. The report struck an unmistakably negative tone. It was very matter-of-fact, and would surely have made painful reading for the tank's designers at Vauxhall had they been given the chance to see it: 'The vehicle offers the experts nothing remarkable; neither in terms of construction nor in terms of metallurgy, nor in terms of firepower does it bring anything new to the table.' The German armour experts then proceeded to give a lengthy list of its deficiencies; the machine guns were 'bad and outdated', and the 40mm main armament on the Mk. I and II was 'outdated in construction and in effectiveness'. The improved 57mm on the Churchill III fared no better in the German technicians' eyes. According to their assessment, it did 'not match the Russian gun of equivalent calibre'. Even the tank's supposed greatest strength, its armour, was not up to snuff on account of its constituent metal: 'The armour of the vehicle is indeed strong, but the material is to be considered poor and not to be compared with the equivalent materials on German or Russian vehicles.' All these assessments were based primarily on live firing conducted on a test range. To do this, the *Waffenamt* assembled a whole host of weapons. This smorgasbord of firepower ranged from a small *Karabiner 98* bolt-action rifle (the Wehrmacht's standard individual infantry weapon) to a monumental 150mm field howitzer.

The results of these firing tests in and around Dieppe supported the belief that the Churchill's armour was poorly constructed. At a range of 100m, the standard German 37mm anti-tank gun effected some penetration through the frontal armour at a flat 90° angle. More modern and capable anti-tank guns like the 50mm Pak 38 achieved clean penetration at as much as 200 metres. At three times that distance, it still managed occasional damaging hits. For even larger weapons like the 88mm Flak 18 anti-aircraft/anti-tank gun (a version of which equipped the brand-new Tiger heavy tank), the results were even clearer.

At an astonishing range of a full kilometre, the Flak 18 achieved clear and consistent penetration. With this in mind, it might not have been necessary to test even more powerful weapons. But for good measure, the *Waffenamt* fired a massive 150mm field howitzer at one of the captured Churchills from 400 and 600 metres. Needless to say, the outcome was 'devastating' according to the *Waffenamt*'s meticulous data table produced after the tests had concluded. In their experiments, only the *Karabiner* rifle with armour-piercing munitions and a 20mm anti-aircraft gun failed to have an effect on the Churchills. The standard German heavy anti-tank rifle, the 28mm *Schwere Panzerbüchse*, was only effective on the side armour at a 90° angle at 100 metres.

So the probing and testing continued. German tests confirmed that the tank's tracks were made of 'very brittle' material and were 'clumsily constructed', which explained why so many of them had been ripped off on the stony Dieppe beach. When they engaged the Canadian tanks in a road test, the Germans found that the tracks made such a loud noise that it was almost impossible to communicate inside the vehicle. Mostly, the tank had to be stationary in order to send and receive radio messages. If all this was not scathing enough, the final sentence of the *Waffenamt*'s assessment would have been most painful for the Allies to hear: 'In summary, it can be said that the Churchill in its current form is easy to combat.'[16]

All this experimentation on the gifts left to the Germans by the Calgary Regiment served a long-term purpose. The Wehrmacht readily understood that if and when the Allies tried another raid on Dieppe's scale (a possibility they considered entirely likely), or even mounted a full-scale invasion somewhere in Europe, the Germans would almost certainly have to contend with tanks landed in the first waves via LCTs. The Wehrmacht's leadership recognized, as did the leaders of the Allied armies, that if tanks could be adapted to reliably operate in the first waves of a seaborne assault, the attackers might gain the upper hand. Perhaps the most important aspect of such an operation is transferring the assaulting forces from sea to land. This is hard enough for the infantry, who have to huddle in cramped landing craft and then disembark when their forward ramp comes crashing down. Tanks, however, weigh in at tens of tons and can struggle to gain traction on the pebbly ground commonly found on beaches. No more clearly was this demonstrated than by the events of 19

August 1942, but despite all these challenges, armoured vehicles provide not only heavy-weapons capability in the form of their main gun, but also protection for the boots on the ground. If the Allies could crack that nut and put tanks on the beach reliably in the first wave, the German defence would face serious problems.

Operation Jubilee revealed to the Germans their enemies' ability to disembark armour during an amphibious landing. Prior to August 1942, German commanders imagined that their enemies probably possessed this capability, but the Dieppe raid confirmed their suspicions. The revelation provoked a rapid response from the Wehrmacht, despite the fact that the Churchills had totally failed – only twenty-seven of the fifty Calgary Regiment tanks actually landed and very few of these made any progress past their initial disembarkation points. Although they had roundly dismissed the Combined Operation Plan, German commanders had too much respect for the Allies to ignore the mortal threat that armour posed to their defensive plans; after all, the Allied powers were professional military organizations and would learn from their failure. The Wehrmacht knew that although the armour landed by LCTs had failed in this single instance, this fact was immaterial. Dieppe Port Commandant Wahn encapsulated German thought: 'We must now as ever reckon with tanks. The enemy will take steps to overcome terrain unsuited for landings with armour.'[17] On 20 August, Major General Haase ordered a round of anti-tank training for his 570th, 571st and 572nd Infantry Regiments in a series of training courses run by his divisional engineers. This meant that every single one of his infantrymen would soon receive updated training in anti-tank tactics.

Field Marshal Rundstedt shared these assessments, but as OB West he had much more scope to act than a mere divisional commander like Haase. Since many of the Churchills' tracks got stuck in the fine shingle on Dieppe's beaches, Rundstedt ordered a raft of tests using the Germans' own armoured vehicles on the very Dieppe beach which the Canadian Churchills had attempted to cross. In contrast to the Churchills, the German tanks had very few problems navigating Dieppe's beaches. Even on a gradient of 20°, the Germans did not experience the difficulties faced by their adversaries. Only when the gradient rose to 30°–40° did problems arise – although the Germans' tracks did not become stuck, the vehicles simply could not climb at steep angles on such unstable ground. Only by rocking back and forth could they flatten the ground sufficiently to allow the tanks to move off. Noticing this, Rundstedt devised an ingenious method to further restrict the movement of enemy tracked vehicles. He suggested that the beach's natural angle should be artificially increased by moving gravel and sand in such a way to make tracked movement impossible. If this worked, any Allied tanks would spend so much time negotiating the terrain that they would make easy targets for German anti-tank guns. Alternatively, they might get this debris stuck in their drive wheels, as happened at Dieppe, immobilizing them completely. Rundstedt hoped that this measure, though crude, would be effective.[18]

OB West was a grizzled veteran of countless campaigns and was not prone to being caught by surprise, even by an operation of Jubilee's rapidity. By 1942 he had served in the various forms of the German armed forces for an astounding fifty years. What could surprise a man who had seen so much in two separate centuries? Rundstedt's half-century in uniform had imbued him with a calm and collected character. He was not given to wild outbursts like his subordinate General Curt Haase at Fifteenth Army, and his temperament had served him well in high command, with his responsibility for all of France, Belgium and the Netherlands. Unlike flashier German field marshals such as Erwin Rommel or Erich von Manstein, who were both outstanding exponents of armoured warfare, Rundstedt does not enjoy a sizeable reputation in western historiography. This is undeserved. His sober consideration of what Dieppe meant for the Germans under his command was a perfect example of his abilities. He ordered practical – and most importantly cheap – anti-tank measures to reinforce his defence against armour. Rundstedt did not have the resources of his fellow generals in the East, but he knew well enough that Allied armour would have to be defeated anyway. In case the Allies came back to Europe in a repeat operation, perhaps even before the end of the year, he worked tirelessly to ensure that his men were ready.

Facing this potential threat, the Germans sought almost immediately to beef up their anti-armour capability. Everything was on the table: from infantry man-portable weapons like the *Panzerbüchse* anti-tank rifle or simple satchel charges, to heavier equipment like the 50mm or 88mm Pak anti-tank guns, German coastal commanders grabbed anything they could get. So neglected was the Western Front at this midpoint in the war that Rundstedt was faced with a paucity of anti-armour weapons.

Neither he nor his commanders on the front line could expect to hold an Allied assault which had successfully deployed armour en masse in its first waves. Consequently, German commanders in coastal commands cried out for help in the wake of Operation Jubilee. Major General Haase almost instantly requested more weapons for his men, to support the engineer-led training that he had ordered. His corps commander General Kuntzen understood that since the frontal attack on the Dieppe port had failed so badly, the Allies were unlikely to try to repeat this in any subsequent operation. Therefore, he emphasized to his superiors that he needed mobility in his anti-tank units – since the Germans could not be sure that the Allies would land at a port, German coastal forces needed to be flexible enough to respond to any threat, wherever it might appear. Furthermore, General Kuntzen threw his weight behind his subordinate Major General Haase's request for anti-tank guns. Subsequently, 302nd Division was promised thirty 50mm guns. Additionally, LXXXI Corps' neighbouring Corps-level command swiftly moved to itemize all its anti-tank rifles, grenade rifles, Bangalore torpedoes and anti-tank mines so that the scale of the shortage could be assessed.[19] These calls did not just emanate from the Army. Even Admiral Otto Schulze as Commanding Admiral of France demanded more anti-tank weapons along France's coastline. Dieppe Port Commandant Commander Wahn said firmly that 'troops that have to combat tanks must immediately be equipped with armour-piercing weapons of the most modern type.'[20] Notwithstanding this plethora of requests for anti-tank aid, it would prove almost impossible to fit out the German units in the West with all the kit that they needed. Simply put, the West was too far down the priority list for a significant volume of Germany's precious industrial capacity to be devoted to its defence. For a long time to come, Rundstedt and his subordinate commanders would just have to make do.

As OB West, Rundstedt was understandably pleased and proud that his men had stood the test of battle. For all the trials and tribulations of higher theatre command – vicious inter-service rivalries, inevitable want of men, material and machines – he had overseen a stunning German victory. Rundstedt had had very little to do with preparing the Dieppe sector, and nothing to do with the battle itself, yet he could claim rightly to have carried out the task delegated to him. In remarks sent in mid-September, OB West circulated his final conclusions on the whole

Dieppe episode. He first praised those under his command, especially his officers, making sure not to confine his commendations purely to those who had fought on 19 August: 'The months-long preparatory work carried out in every area by officers and men with great diligence and vigilance have paid off. The officers and men have been ready for months. On 19 August the officer corps led well and with confidence, the men did well. This is the main experience from Dieppe.' Conveniently, but not surprisingly for a high-level commander, Rundstedt exulted in his success and decided not to mention the sluggish response of many of his men to the sounds of the convoy battle out at sea. This was a time to commend his men, not distribute blame. Nonetheless, OB West assured them that this was no time to let up: '[This experience] compels us to lie in wait, weapons made ready, and be ready every second to destroy enemy landing attempts. It compels us to never abate, not for a minute, our exertion and stamina. Because that minute may bring us the fruits of our labour.'

It was not just in material ways that the Germans sought to improve their conduct of coastal defence. During the battle, the naval communication system had collapsed; this was not due to Allied interference such as the destruction of telephone cables, but because of the Germans' own incompetence. Convoy 2437, the small group of merchantmen which stumbled upon the Allied landing force, was wrongly thought to have been entirely destroyed, despite it being seen at Le Tréport at 1000 and the accompanying sighting report being passed through normal naval traffic channels. Furthermore, it had taken too long for observers at Dieppe to realize that the attack on the coastal convoy was not just a customary attack by a few British patrol craft. Accordingly, the German defenders were somewhat less prepared than they would otherwise have been, though this did not in the end prevent them from inflicting a crushing defeat on the Anglo-Canadians. Two British ships were seen by a coastal battery but were not fired upon because it was assumed that they were friendly. Had units along the coast been properly warned to watch for a seaborne assault, this battery would have engaged the ships and raised the alarm earlier. Understandably, Field Marshal Rundstedt was particularly frustrated by this error. Had the true nature of the conflagration at sea been recognized, Operation Jubilee could have been annihilated before it had even begun in earnest. In his frustration, he urged vigilance above all:

Officers and men – down to the individual guard post – cannot be blunted by the normality of waiting. Every message, whether from agents, whether from the local population, whether from [radar or radio] detection, must be taken seriously and verified. Every irregularity at sea, every single one must be constantly monitored – even if it is a sea battle some distance away. It might be the origin of a landing attempt. Every minute that it is detected earlier can be decisive. Every officer and soldier who is tasked with sentry, observation, identification or analysis duties must be imbued with this [idea]. He cannot take his mission and responsibility seriously enough.

It was a tough ask to demand that men on occupation duty in France be more vigilant. There comes a point when every soldier simply ignores repeated calls for increased watchfulness. Amid the rare comforts and luxuries of wartime France, most men learned simply to tune them out.

During debriefing, some German soldiers admitted that they had been unaware of the general alarm issued at 302nd Infantry Division at 6 o'clock. Rundstedt, as a vastly experienced campaigner, knew that he had to do more than simply issue the vague demand that his men be more alert when carrying out their duties. More practical, tangible measures were required. So, OB West ordered that throughout Europe's Western coastline, 'Every leader commanding an independent unit must have a sheet at his battle station detailing whom he is to alert during an alarm when it is triggered. Every company must have a nominated NCO or officer to act as "Alarm NCO" or "Alarm Officer", who is responsible for this. This is necessary because the commanding officer will have no time. He has other things to do.' Rundstedt's new alarm system was to be practised every single week.[21]

The failure of the Germans' communications infrastructure on 19 August did not end there. Admiral Raeder's Naval Staff headquarters was not even aware that an attack was taking place until signals intelligence personnel intercepted the British broadcasts to the French population late in the afternoon. Only at 1400 did Admiral Saalwächter, Raeder's overall naval commander in the West, dispatch a message to inform his superiors that Convoy 2437, despite colliding with the Allied raiding force, was mostly intact. This brief report seems, however, to have become lost somewhere in transmission. Raeder and his chief of staff Vice Admiral Kurt Fricke were enraged that their Kriegsmarine could have failed so miserably on a defining day for the Wehrmacht in the West. Compounding this embarrassment was the ever-present rivalry between the three services. It was humiliating to watch Kriegsmarine personnel fail in such a basic task while the soldiers of the Army and the airmen of the Luftwaffe were winning such an astonishing victory.

Raeder laid the blame for these failures squarely at Admiral Saalwächter's door. As commander of Naval Group West, Saalwächter had responsibility for all naval affairs from the French Atlantic Coast right up to the Jutland Peninsula. This made his position analogous to that of Field Marshal Hugo Sperrle of the Luftwaffe, who controlled air forces over the same area. In a sternly-worded message to every naval theatre command throughout the entire Kriegsmarine, written under Fricke's name on 26 August, the Kriegsmarine's leadership demonstrated their fury at failures both past and present. Although it carried his chief of staff's signature, the message was signed off by commander-in-chief Raeder, and its references to Dieppe made it clear that Saalwächter was the main object of criticism. It began in a thinly veiled passive-aggressive tone by quoting a German doctrinal manual: 'Intelligence and reports on the enemy form an important foundation for decision-making and giving orders in wartime. They are of decisive significance for properly assessing the situation.' Fricke then stated the reason for his message: 'These fundamental requirements for reporting have often not been met by the reports reaching the Naval Staff Headquarters.' This was a strange and unconventional message for a professional military document. In the interest of clarity, internal communications are normally purely factual and quite dry in nature. But Raeder and Fricke were so appalled by how they were being misinformed or simply cut out of events on the ground, that they felt the normal courtesies and conventions need no longer apply. Their fury was justified. A breakdown of communications had not only military consequences, since any Kriegsmarine failure was a gift to their rivals in the Army and Luftwaffe. As top-level commanders, Raeder and Fricke always had one eye on public affairs and inter-service politics: 'During the enemy landing at Dieppe, the alarm raised by the naval forces out at sea represented a significant contribution by the Kriegsmarine to raising the battle readiness of the defence. Since this fact was not reported to the Naval Staff, it was impossible to include it in the first official statements about the fighting.' Fricke concluded, 'The examples from recent experience are proliferating at will.' He promised that new regulations would be forced through to stamp out communications breakdowns like those experienced at Dieppe. It is striking that the blow to the Kriegsmarine's reputation and its loss of face at Dieppe played such a large part in Raeder and Fricke's desire to reform naval communications. Such was the bitterness between them and the heads of the other two services that made up Hitler's Wehrmacht.

Having been personally attacked by his commander-in-chief, Admiral Saalwächter tried to deflect blame for the errors committed on his watch. In a direct response to Fricke's letter written in the first days of September, the commander of Naval Group West took issue with the criticism levelled against him and his command: 'That the Naval Staff first heard of the landing of enemy forces at Dieppe through English radio can be explained by the fact that the English revealed the operation with a call to the French population at the time of the landing.' Saalwächter insisted that it was unclear to German commanders in France, including OB West Field Marshal Rundstedt, what the nature of the Dieppe operation was. This uncertainty lasted until as late as 0700. For this reason, he argued, Naval Group West's earlier reports attempting to give a definitive answer would have been purely speculative. He was at pains to stress that afterwards, communication between him in France and Raeder in Germany was adequate. As to the question of Convoy 2437, Saalwächter was dumbfounded: 'I cannot understand why the Naval Staff still had the impression well into the late afternoon that the convoy was totally lost. The sighting report from the coast timed at about 1000 about parts of the convoy being at Le Tréport … was immediately forwarded on to the Naval Staff's situation room after being received by the duty officer.' He posited that destroyed communications wires were to blame for this and most of the issues that the Kriegsmarine faced when trying to share information on 19 August. Moreover, Rundstedt had introduced a system whereby Army, Kriegsmarine and Luftwaffe commanders had to check with him before sending reports to service headquarters in Germany like the Naval Staff or OKW. This was to avoid messages containing the same information being sent multiple times by different services. However, it introduced something of a delay before reports were sent 'upstairs'. Although Saalwächter agreed with this principle, he submitted that it had slowed down communications on 19 August. Saalwächter was due to give up his command of western naval forces later in September, and he wished desperately to deal with the issues that he faced before then: 'I ask that as soon as possible the cases be given to me where the briefing by Naval Group West did not satisfy the Naval Staff, so that I can deal with them before I give up my command.'

Saalwächter was indeed replaced by Vice Admiral Krancke (formerly naval liaison officer to Hitler's *Führerhauptquartier*) later that month. In late November he retired from the Kriegsmarine after more than forty years' service, but this gave him just enough time to witness many of the fundamental changes which the Kriegsmarine made in order to better respond to another Dieppe. One of the most significant was to update the standard operating procedures for reporting enemy landings in the first place. In late October, a new codeword system was introduced; whenever an Allied landing was detected, special words could be immediately telegraphed to higher command to describe its strength, time and place. A table sent to all German coastal commands laid out the new codewords to be used from October 1942 onwards. Firstly, the kinds of ships in an Allied force would be represented by types of trees. For example, if an Allied landing contained battleships, the word *'Eiche'* (oak) would be inserted. A cruiser would be reported with *'Erle'* (alder), and destroyers with *'Fichte'* (spruce). This list continued for all kinds of vessels. A landing's location was designated by numbers. Each represented a section of coastline along the northern and western coasts of Western Europe. A German personal name indicated how long it was assumed the enemy operation would last. If it had not yet begun, a German boy's name would be given; if the landing was ongoing, a girl's name was used. For example, if the Allies landed at Brest on France's Atlantic coast with destroyers, and the Germans believed it to be only a short operation requiring no deployment of strategic reserves, the following message might be sent: 'Spruce Nine Dora'. Likewise, 'Oak Two Anton' would be sent if the Germans somehow got wind of a three-day-long raid on Belgium with battleships that was to take place the day after next.[22] This new system was much faster than a long official report in writing or by voice. Considering that time was of the essence, and it took some time to decode a message, using short codewords was a notable step-up in German coastal communications. That the Germans came up with this new way of operating was a direct result of the Dieppe raid and the Kriegsmarine's failures there. One thing was sure: they did not want to be caught out a second time.

The Army and Luftwaffe also took a great deal from their experiences at Dieppe. These two services contributed by far the most to the crushing German victory. It would be easy to think that, because the Germans were victorious on 19 August, they simply rested on their laurels and expected any future landing to turn out the same way – and that the Allies were the only ones who learned from their mistakes. As we have established, this was not the mindset of German commanders, especially Field Marshal Rundstedt, who was almost pathological in his insistence that the Germans must learn from success: 'Just as we have drawn the most valuable of experiences from the day of Dieppe, so has the enemy. Just as we evaluate these for the future, so will the enemy, perhaps to an even greater extent because he has paid so dearly for his lessons.' This was a particularly astute point. It made sense that, in the face of complete failure, the defeated Allies would do everything within their power to ensure that they would never endure another such humiliation. After all, necessity is the mother of invention. Rundstedt continued assertively: 'We must therefore be prepared that next time [the enemy] will do it with more skill and greater means. He will certainly make greater use of air power. He will bring large warships as fire support and land paratroops to attack strongpoints from behind and to draw off reserves. He will also make use of sabotage in every respect.'[23]

The Germans' thirst to learn from Dieppe extended into the aerial domain, too. One area in which the Luftwaffe gained greatly from 19 August was in bomber escort tactics. While Sperrle's airmen had been fighting the RAF's incursions into France on and off for many months, Dieppe represented the first occasion that fighters and bombers were called upon to cooperate against a seaborne assault. This presented some serious issues. First and foremost was the dual role expected of fighter-interceptors like the Bf 109 or FW 190. Not only were they employed to wrest air superiority from the Allies, they also found themselves committed to stick by bomber formations as protective cover. This created a serious issue in the light of the precious few fighters that Sperrle had to hand, since an aircraft could not be in two places at once. Either they waited for the bombers to arrive over the fighter airfields, and then proceed on to Dieppe, or they flew to Dieppe regardless, leaving the bombers defenceless while they transited to the battle area. On 19 August, the Luftwaffe's fighters were overwhelmingly deployed in the latter manner; if the RAF had been less defensive about providing its aerial umbrella and flown inland it could have inflicted serious casualties on the unprotected formations of Junkers, Dorniers and Heinkels. Air Fleet 3's officers racked their brains trying to find an answer to this thorny problem. Of course, the simple answer would have been to have more fighters delivered to the West, but this was out of the question. Germany's war economy was stretched enough as it was, and the situation was not about to improve, with the cataclysmic battle for Stalingrad beginning in August. The solution that Sperrle's men came up with was an intelligent compromise. The bomber headquarters would first send a request for escort to the fighter headquarters, as was indeed common beforehand. However, instead of waiting over their own airfields, the fighters would now 'pick up' their bombers as close to the bombers' target as possible. If all went well, the fighters could simultaneously contest air superiority and provide escort when the bombers were at their most vulnerable.

Another grave difficulty of fighter/bomber cooperation dominated Sperrle's mind after the Dieppe raid. Since there was very little motorized transport available in the West (even space on rail transport was precious), bomber and fighter crews had never been able to travel to meet each other in a social setting. The first time that many crews interacted with each other was when they were flying in battle over Dieppe. The basic principles of teamwork dictate that those who cooperate with one another on the battlefield (such as tank crews and their infantry escort or bomber crews and their fighter escort) must build personal relationships and, most importantly, trust. It is incredibly hard to put one's life in the hands of somebody one has never even spoken to. The complete absence of friendship, or even acquaintance, between bomber and fighter crews was a serious headache for Air Fleet 3's commander Field Marshal Sperrle. With his authority as commander-in-chief of all Western air forces, he put this issue at the very top of his priority list. Travel by rail was often unavailable, so Sperrle reassigned some of his valuable cars, trucks and other vehicles so that his airmen could travel to meet one another once in a while. He even dedicated some aircraft to this task. This may at first glance seem to have been a waste of scarce resources, but the fact remained that bomber and fighter crews needed to get together before they could work together. Despite all the equipment and technology involved, war is ultimately a human activity, and it is people who fight, not machines.

In the final analysis, from strategic bombardment to close air support, all air power operates in support of ground forces. Air-ground collaboration, or the lack of it, drew some attention in the Germans' post-battle analysis. Although the Luftwaffe had thrown itself almost exclusively at the Allied naval forces out at sea on 19 August, there were a few instances of ground strafing by German planes, particularly around Pourville. While German foot soldiers were generally appreciative of the help provided by air support, German pilots had a nasty habit of misidentifying friend as foe. As any combat veteran unfortunate enough to experience it would testify, 'friendly fire' is anything but friendly. Predominantly, this was caused by the ground forces' failure to adequately mark out their positions. Consequently, there were no clear visual indicators of German ground positions by which Luftwaffe ground attack aircraft could operate. In one instance, a Union flag laid out by Allied forces had not been removed once the area was recaptured, causing German aircraft to strafe their helpless comrades below. Throughout the day, visual signals were not used at all by 302nd Infantry Division, and Air Fleet 3's final appreciation of the Dieppe battle demanded that ground forces be more attentive to this in future.[24] Unlike their counterparts flying in the East, those Germans serving in the West had had little or no experience of operating smoothly with ground forces. Interestingly, the experiences of the Western Desert Air Force in North Africa offer a close parallel to this facet of Dieppe's air engagement. There, the British were constantly operating in a combined arms environment in which air power mattered just as much as land operations. The RAF had consistently encountered such issues of misidentification and had successfully begun implementing visual signalling – amongst other measures – as a remedy. However, there was comparatively little direct air-ground cooperation at Dieppe, since bomber and fighter-bomber forces were overwhelmingly directed against naval targets. Therefore, Dieppe did not offer a significant learning experience in this regard. Other than isolated instances like the strafing at Pourville, German ground forces had little to do with their comrades in the air.

In spite of all the criticism that came the Allies' way, there was one constant aspect of Operation Jubilee that never failed to impress the Germans: artificial smoke. While it did indeed hamper visibility for both sides, this was very much in the attackers' favour – without it, the Allies could not have approached the coast in the face of such strong German artillery. Since it had been so successful on 19 August, German commanders from all services knew that it would play a key role in any future Allied landing. Whether this came next month or next year, they knew that it would be accompanied by a generous helping of this impenetrable white mist. With this in mind, how to respond was the next question. For each service operating its own weapons systems, the answer would be different. For the coastal artillery, manned and controlled by both Army and Kriegsmarine personnel, the Allies' artificial smoke was blinding. At some points during the battle, visibility dropped to only a few metres, making accurate shooting utterly impossible and increasing the expenditure of ammunition tremendously. Rundstedt was so concerned that he suggested to OKW in the days following Dieppe that Germany's scientists should be charged with concocting with some kind of chemical that could be sprayed into the smoke in order to disperse or condense it.[25] One solution that was immediately practical was the setting up of observation posts away from the smoke. If these could relay bearings and ranges to coastal batteries, they did not need even to see the target they were firing at. Although this had been part of German artillery doctrine before Dieppe, it gained a new importance after 19 August. The Artillery Commander (*Artillerie-Kommandeur*, or simply *ArKo*) 117, a colonel-level position with responsibility for all artillery in LXXXI Corps, noted on 20 September that his 'main successes came from shooting under observation. This could only be achieved when the battery observation posts for each battery were directly next to the coast, so that their observation was not obscured by fog or artificial smoke.' ArKo 117 now suggested that one battery observation post placed near the coast could direct the fire of multiple batteries if visibility was down to a minimum.

ArKo 117 also recognized in his after-action report that, in part due to poor visibility, it was difficult to observe the fall of shot when firing at naval targets. If multiple guns were firing at a single Allied ship, how could one tell whose shots were hitting and whose were missing? To combat this problem, he introduced a system whereby the coastline was split into different sections. A battery was assigned to each of these sections, so that it was clear where each shot was coming from, and corrections could be made smoothly and without confusion. Then each battery and 'section' was assigned a codeword, much as the Kriegsmarine did with their new communications system. Thus, a set of batteries could concentrate fire all at one section of coastline. ArKo 117 used fruits, vegetables and animals as codes to demonstrate his idea: 'All Animals, observed fire on section Anton!' or 'All Animals: Apple. All Vegetables: Pear. All Trees: Plum!' This was just an example; the details were yet to be decided.[26]

The Luftwaffe, too, had felt the effects of artificial smoke. Even though planes operated above it, the low-lying smoke was still a source of great frustration on 19 August. Aircraft at low altitudes, both German and British, were particularly difficult to observe from German fighters operating at higher altitudes. In order to preserve the efficacy of Luftwaffe air power in such low visibility, a new emphasis was put on forward-placed direction. At Dieppe, an officer was sent with a radio to the coastline from inland in order to observe and report on enemy aircraft flying in the area; this gave higher headquarters a detailed and up-to-the-minute picture of what was occurring in the air engagement. As Air Fleet 3 said in its report, this officer was incredibly useful but would have been even more so had he been directing aircraft instead of merely observing them – becoming in essence a forward air controller. Air Fleet 3 now massively expanded the use of fighter controllers/observers, mandating that they should all have access to a radio and their own motorized transport. Bearing in mind the scarcity of the latter in the Western theatre, it was another significant commitment from Field Marshal Sperrle as Air Fleet 3's commander-in-chief.[27] The controllers would have the authority to independently direct friendly air forces within their area of operations. The goal here was simple: to maintain proper command and control during the chaos of battle, especially in conditions of poor visibility like those of 19 August 1942. The importance of forward-situated direction, as opposed to mere forward observation, was a key German lesson from Dieppe – both for the Luftwaffe and defensive coastal artillery on the ground. Interestingly, this was a lesson for the British too – with their forward air controllers based on ships, the RAF also experienced first-hand the benefits of centralized control with decentralized execution.

Throughout the Second World War, the Axis 'alliance' was hardly worthy of the name; the Axis powers were more akin to a loose collection of aligned states. Germany, Italy, Japan and their allies were joined only in their opposition to the Allied powers, and failed to collaborate as good allies should. Washington, London and Moscow understood the importance of an alliance to grand strategy far better than Berlin, Rome and Tokyo. Nevertheless, in the case of the Dieppe raid there was some sharing of information and experiences. For Mussolini's Italy, resisting amphibious attacks was a particular concern because of its extensive Mediterranean coastline. Italy drew its own conclusions from 19 August, and these closely mirrored those of its German ally. The need for unity of coastal command, air superiority and mobile reserves were three lessons that the Italians took from Dieppe.[28] Bulgaria, too, had a vulnerable coastline. With the Soviet Union facing them on the other side of the Black Sea, the Bulgarians also had to contend with the possibility of large-scale amphibious invasions striking their shores. One article in a Bulgarian military journal noted the utility of artificial smoke and coastal artillery. Amongst other things, it concluded as the Kriegsmarine had done that early warning was vital – the earlier an amphibious effort was detected, the earlier it could be annihilated.[29] In Asia, the Japanese also saw the Germans' success as an opportunity to learn. An Imperial Japanese Navy manual printed in 1943 took Dieppe as an example of how an amphibious landing could be defeated at the water's edge.[30]

Chapter 17

A War of Words, not Bullets and Bombs

After the initial flurry of press activity, Goebbels and his propaganda machine settled into a rhythm of almost continuous coverage of Dieppe until the end of August. The Propaganda Minister had a long-term strategy. Not only was he going to simply report the Dieppe news – though the raw facts were damning enough. Goebbels wanted to present this to the German population as a turning point and he decided that, instead of ending Dieppe coverage after a few days, he would unleash a bombardment of words upon the German people. Newsreels in cinemas, radio broadcasts and newspaper articles were all to play their part. Early on 21 August, German journalists gathered as usual for Otto Dietrich's press conference. By his ministry's own judgement, the Dieppe story had been a great success. 'The press coverage of the Dieppe events has so far been good', the journalists' press packets read. 'Political analysis … continues to be at the front of the newspapers.' But Germany's reporters and editors were told not to let up: 'Churchill's dependence on Moscow and his catastrophic policies are to be pointed out as firmly as possible.' Churchill's character continued to be the target of German propaganda in the week or so following the raid. Specifically, the media were instructed by the Propaganda Ministry to unleash a new and very personal line of attack on the British Prime Minister: 'Dunkirk followed his desperate visit to France, Hong Kong followed his first visit to Washington, Tobruk his second, and finally after his Moscow excursion came Dieppe.'[1] It was unfortunate for Churchill that these events had coincided, but the coincidences nonetheless represented a neat and effective way to undermine his war leadership as a whole. The Germans' main 'talking points' continued to be seen throughout: Churchill was Stalin's puppet; Churchill was an 'amateur strategist'; Dieppe may well have been an invasion attempt; and last but not least, the German 'Watch in the West' was invincible. That Jubilee was primarily a Canadian operation was hardly mentioned – this was a Churchill-Stalin affair. All these themes were conveniently crammed into two compact sentences on the *Völkischer Beobachter*'s front page on 21 August, in an article entitled 'Planned Defeat': 'The entire world stands under the impression of the withering rebuff encountered by Churchill's attempted invasion undertaken on Stalin's orders. The whole horrific episode was over in nine hours.' The idea that the Allies had been thrown back in just 'nine hours' became intimately associated with the Dieppe raid thanks to Goebbels' ruthlessly repetitive propaganda campaign. Helmut Schneiss was serving elsewhere in France when his father wrote to him. Clearly, the elder Schneiss had readily absorbed all of Goebbels' lines of attack: 'In about nine hours the whole spat was done. We laid on a warm reception for the amateur strategist Churchill and gave him a serious disappointment.' He quipped that, had his son been there, the battle would have been over even more rapidly.[2]

As Hitler's Propaganda chief, Reichsminister Joseph Goebbels was not merely standing by and dictating the course of events. He was so eager to twist the knife that he could not resist intervening personally. It was not enough to view the work of others from afar. In fact, he was so involved in the Dieppe story that he personally penned a lengthy polemic entitled 'The Kremlin's Prisoner' (*Der Gefangene des Kremlins*) in the form of an attack on Churchill. This was perfectly in line with his own direction for German propaganda. His piece was due for publication in the national paper *Das Reich* on 28 August, but in order to keep up the pressure on the British – to 'keep the discussion bubbling' in Goebbels' words – he decided that his contribution should appear earlier than planned, on the 24th. Not only would 'The Kremlin's Prisoner' appear much earlier, but it was also moved to the all-important *Völkischer Beobachter*, where Goebbels' views would receive as much exposure as possible. It was rare, but certainly not unprecedented, for Goebbels to write his own piece for one of the German papers; as Propaganda Minister, he ultimately controlled their entire output, but he reserved the right to publish his own writing at moments of crucial importance. Dieppe was one of these occasions.

Goebbels' piece hit every single one of the targets that his propaganda effort had already been aiming at over the previous few days. Still referring to the Prime Minister somewhat sarcastically as 'Mr Churchill', Goebbels launched a piercing personal attack marked by his characteristic use of idiomatic language, in an attempt to appeal to as wide an audience as possible. This was not a boring, bland political tract. He set the scene with a ferocious strike against Churchill's political character. Having been an arch-anti-communist his whole public career, it seemed odd that Britain's leader, who in 1920 had characterized the Soviet government as a 'criminal regime', was now teaming up with 'Uncle Joe'. 'True, with the entry of the Soviet Union into the war against the Axis powers [Churchill] became as pious as a lamb', Goebbels opined, 'burning everything he had previously worshipped and worshipping everything he had previously burnt, but what does a man of his calibre care! He is not one of those politicians who have the luxury of a firm character, and when it comes down to it, he changes colour like a chameleon.'

For Goebbels, the coincidence between Stalin's continuous demand for a second front and the recent reversal at Dieppe was ripe for exploitation. Indeed, as Germans were reading Goebbels' article on 24 August, Churchill had not yet got back to Britain from Moscow, since his schedule called for visits to Tehran and Cairo. Picturing Churchill landing at Moscow for his conference with Stalin, Goebbels wrote:

He now had to walk down the front of a detachment of the Red Army to the sound of the Internationale, only to be 'taken to the works' for four days by Stalin and his henchmen. One did not have to be a fly on the wall to know what it meant to him. His initial intention was to make it clear to the Soviets that a Second Front could not be established at the moment. Instead, however, it was made clear to him that such a front was indispensable and was categorically demanded by the Kremlin. All his powers of persuasion and his tortuous explanations obviously did him no good. He was put under pressure to keep his promise, which he had made under quite different conditions during Molotov's visit to London, and to make good on it as soon as possible. Stalin is certainly not a man to be trifled with, and for the rest the Soviets are in such a catastrophic situation that they have no choice but to demand relief from England, whatever the cost may be.

The Reichsminister lampooned the British for claiming victory at Dieppe: 'If a fool claims it is raining when the sun is shining and continues to insist that he is right, one does well not to come at him with logical proofs. The sun is self-evident. When the English, after a harrowing defeat, speak of victory and mindlessly repeat it, let them be. Victories are self-evident.' Goebbels' parting message for his readers was simple. 'Mr Churchill must carry out Stalin's orders. He is trying to give himself an alibi before the British people. We are not concerned … He who feeds off Bolshevism perishes from it. Dieppe was simply more evidence of that fact.' Naturally, Goebbels conveniently neglected to mention Germany's own previous pact with the Soviet Union, signed in September 1939.

As the propaganda battle played out in newspapers and on radio, on 26 August yet another medium joined the fray – newsreels. On that day, the new edition of *Die Deutsche Wochenschau* (The German Weekly Review) was released. This was the official Nazi Party-endorsed version of events shown in cinemas throughout Hitler's Reich, and it was yet another powerful weapon in Goebbels' rhetorical armoury. As the old saying goes, a picture paints a thousand words. Articles in newspapers or announcements in radio broadcasts could only take Goebbels' messages so far – he knew he needed images too. Each *Wochenschau* edition was narrated by the 39-year-old former Berlin theatre actor Harry Giese, whose shrill yet boastful tones filled German cinemas with each weekly edition. Giese's voice became a very well-known one in Germany; he had also provided narration for other propaganda such as the infamous film *The Eternal Jew*. Footage for each *Wochenschau* came from film companies sent to the front line and, as with the daily *Wehrmachtbericht*, it was a great privilege for one's unit to be named or shown. The Germans had no shortage of material when it came to producing film on Dieppe for 26 August. Goebbels again partook in creating the newsreel for Dieppe, working right up until the evening before its release. He also hoped that it could be sold to foreign neutral countries – for Goebbels, this had always been the clearest measure of success.[3]

Announced as usual by the title shot of an eagle accompanied by a grand fanfare and drum roll, the week's *Wochenschau* opened with a map of Dieppe. Harry Giese announced the 'catastrophic failure' of a 'large-scale landing' on the Channel coast. Silhouettes of fighters and ships filled the screen in order to convey the magnitude of the Allies' effort. Giese repeated the initial German claim, known to be false, that a floating reserve stood ready to make this a fully-fledged invasion of France. 'The strength of the enemy force proves that this landing was one of the Anglo-Americans' long-since-planned invasion attempts', he told viewers. In much more excited tones, Giese then proceeded to give a sports-style play-by-play description of the events on screen. As British Spitfires raced in at terrifyingly low altitudes, with Dieppe's cliffs providing a background, he exclaimed, 'British fighters and bombers attack Dieppe's port – in the face of our anti-aircraft guns they are forced to turn away time and again!' Eagle-eyed cinemagoers would have noticed that some of the footage used was recycled stock film, but there was enough original material there to keep them interested. German fighters soon appeared on the screen in neat, tight formation. Then wispy white contrails could be seen high above the camera position as Giesel exclaimed, 'Another one shot down!' As Giese described the aftermath of the operation, viewers saw nothing but destruction: dead bodies lying prostrate on French beaches, as well as tanks and landing craft burning; it was as if these heartless metal machines, too, were humiliated by their defeat. Fast patrol boats coursing through the waves and massed formations of Junkers bombers impressed upon Germans at home that this was a tri-service victory. All this action lasted an unusually long ten minutes on screen – half the week's *Wochenschau*. Even more significantly, the Dieppe story pushed the Eastern Front news to the newsreel's end. The film was an impressive piece of work. With light-touch narration, the black-and-white images of abandoned tanks, boats, helmets and bodies were allowed to speak for themselves. Seeing these, no reasonable person could fail to agree that Jubilee had been a debacle for the Allies. Hitler certainly agreed. Having been given a sneak preview the day before the film's release, he telephoned Goebbels from Ukraine to congratulate him on his fine work. To a man who adored and admired his Führer, no higher praise was possible. The *Wochenschau*'s coverage did not end there. Next week's edition, in the same triumphant tone, showed OB West Rundstedt inspecting the still-ruined beach. Flourishing his field marshal's baton in salute, he awarded Iron Crosses to one hundred proud infantrymen. Without doubt, the two Dieppe newsreels made an impression on public opinion. Hitler's secret state police, the SD, noted in one of its reports that the images from France had 'reinforced the [public's] impression that, because of the strong German defence, any future enemy landing attempt is doomed to failure.'[14]

Affirmation came not only from Hitler. Dieppe's *Wochenschau* was translated into several languages, including French, Italian and Dutch, for foreign audiences. The French version cut out most shots showing the German defenders and was much shorter than the original edition; instead, it focussed on the prisoners of war and the material damage caused to the battlefield. There was demand for the film not only from occupied territories, but also from neutral states. While the British continued to claim that the raid had been some kind of a victory, their propaganda output was not popular with unaligned countries. Goebbels was ecstatic. The German newsreel's factual nature and relative objectivity appealed to overseas governments not wishing to involve themselves in the war. Neutral but Axis-friendly Francoist Spain printed a lengthy account of Jubilee in its armed forces' monthly publication. The Germans' Japanese allies seemingly did not devote much press attention to Dieppe, and one of the few mentions in Japanese media expounded the view that if such large-scale operations were to be repeated, Germany would have to move greater forces westwards. In neutral Sweden, an American correspondent told his listeners in the United States that 'the Swedish press has been flooded by stories of the impossibility of an Allied landing on the French coast, and that as there was no evidence to dispute this claim, a portion of the German propaganda had taken root in common Swedish conceptions.' In Turkey, domestic press outlets provided a balanced view of events, repeating the British claim that this had been a dress rehearsal in which casualties on both sides were high.[5]

In Germany, the SD reported that newspaper articles, especially those written by war reporters present in Dieppe, had been consumed 'voraciously and devoured word for word'. Agents embedded amongst the population noted 'admiration of the strength and speed' with which the operation was beaten back. 'The population's faith in the German defence measures on the Channel coast has been fortified so much', they recounted, 'that some are convinced that the British and Americans will "get beaten up" again and finally realize the futility of a military confrontation with the Wehrmacht.'[6] Others were more relieved than overjoyed. Gustav Roos was a 21-year-old fighting in the East when the Dieppe raid occurred. He wrote to his father Anton in Saint-Malo, the rather elderly soldier who had been sheltering in an inn on 19 August guarding one and a half million Reichsmarks of unit funds: 'Thank

God the whole affair at Dieppe went well.' Just over a week later, he wrote again: 'Hopefully it will always turn out that way; it would be awkward if we were to get another active front!'[7] Lieutenant Kaltcis, who had intercepted many of the Allies' wireless messages from his listening station in The Hague, wrote to his friend Otto Wessel (also a lieutenant, serving in Libya): 'Now I'm hoping that Tommy will be kind enough to pay us a visit here so that we can give them "what for".'[8] This cheerful and optimistic response was exactly what Goebbels wanted to hear. In the Propaganda Minister's mind, he had won this small battle in the war of words and pictures. He was probably right, and the success was a great boost to his confidence. Goebbels recorded gleefully in his diary on 27 August that 'the German people are once again filled with great enthusiasm by the smashing of the English at Dieppe'.[9]

Another figure who contributed to Goebbels' propaganda offensive was Rear Admiral Friedrich Lützow. Like his contemporaries, he had experienced a lifetime of military service in Wilhelmine, Weimar and Nazi Germany. Like Rundstedt, Lützow had retired from service but been recalled to active duty. Unlike Field Marshal Rundstedt, however, he was not destined to hold a combatant command in this new war. Instead, he was to be the Kriegsmarine's public face as its official spokesman. As part of his wartime job he gave regular radio lectures and commentaries on military events. Like Harry Giese, Lützow's voice became a popular one in Nazi Germany, and he remained the foremost speaker about naval affairs on German radio throughout hostilities. Surprisingly, he garnered applause from his enemies as well. In their meticulous study of contemporary German radio published in 1944, the American academics Ernst Kris and Hans Speier gave the German admiral a backhanded compliment by describing him as 'certainly the most dignified liar on the German radio'.[10] The Dieppe raid was the perfect opportunity for Lützow to flex his rhetorical muscles. On 26 August, the same day that the week's *Wochenschau* appeared, he once again took to the microphone. 'Neither in the current nor in the First World War have the British had luck with landings on enemy coasts', he began imperiously. Gallipoli, Narvik and now Dieppe were one and the same, Lützow told his loyal listeners. He explained how the British had chosen to arrive on the French coast at about 6 o'clock in order to travel in darkness, yet also benefit from daylight once the land battle began. Moreover, they had not landed at Calais because the tides there ran as fast as eight knots, whereas those around Dieppe were at most three knots. This sort of granular detail was what his audience tuned in for each week. He moved on to question the operation's intentions, considering Dieppe's insignificance as a strategic target. Inevitably, he concluded: 'Examining all circumstances of the landing attempt leaves no other conclusion than that it was the fulfilment of a promise to Stalin.' Lützow ended with a comforting message, declaring that 'we know that our Führer has so far known how to preserve his freedom of decision on all theatres of war, and that he wields it with inspired certainty, and that the results of this assuredness strengthen our resolve to be victorious on all fronts.'[11]

However, by the time of the flurry of activity on 26 August, exactly one week after the raid, a distinct shift of public focus had taken place. No longer were Germans at home so concerned by or interested in the Dieppe battle, if they ever had been; instead, they wanted to return to the bread and butter of German war news – the Eastern Front. This was where most of their sons, brothers and fathers were fighting, and the Wehrmacht was closing in on the River Volga, on which Stalingrad lay. In fact, after only a few days, press chief Otto Dietrich had noted a shift in attention eastwards. As early as the morning of 22 August, he wrote in a brief to his pressmen that 'it is self-evident that the public's shift in attention to the fighting on the southern part of the Eastern Front should not mean that public discussion of the Anglo-American invasion catastrophe should be stopped immediately.' Rather, Dieppe should be addressed, but the military events on the Eastern Front were to slowly come to the fore.[12]

There existed a clear logic in pushing the Dieppe story, despite the tendency of Germans at home to focus on the fighting on the Soviet front. Goebbels, Dietrich and the others within Germany's war propaganda establishment felt it was irrelevant what their audiences wanted to hear. What was important was the message, and how this influenced public opinion. Although listeners and readers quickly lost their appetite for bold headlines like 'Churchill's Second Dunkirk' and 'Churchill's Invasion Catastrophe', those within the Reich propaganda ministry felt the message was too important to be ignored just because of the wishes of the public at large. By highlighting Dieppe as a great German victory of all three Wehrmacht services, Goebbels sought to convince

Germans that they need not worry about the West. In his table talk at the *Führerhauptquartier*, Hitler mused to his attentive guests: 'As I see it, the most important result of the Dieppe raid from our point of view is the immense [boost] it has given to our sense of defensive security; it has shown us, above all, that the danger exists, but that we are in a position to counter it.'[13] This is exactly what Goebbels wanted the rest of Germany to believe. While the German population had been impressed by the Wehrmacht's victory, they had wondered how safe they might be when confronted with further landing attempts. The SD had surreptitiously observed that many civilians were worried by the fact that the Allies had been able to land large numbers of tanks on German-held shores.[14] Goebbels' propaganda campaign was directed at countering this concern. *Die Wehrmacht* magazine, the vast majority of whose subscribers were not military servicemen, labelled the western defences the 'Steely Rear'. This phrase perfectly epitomized the propaganda strategy implemented after Dieppe; even while the bulk of the Wehrmacht fought Stalin, his hopeless lackey Churchill could not hope to win a victory in the West. Another article in the same magazine asked if the rebuff at Dieppe had 'healed' the 'psychosis' of the second front concept. In September 1942, Reich Press Chief Dietrich laid out his philosophy in no uncertain terms during a speech to a gathering of journalists in Berlin. He told them:

How newspapers position themselves is very important in today's situation. Papers used to adapt to the readers' wishes. Their wishes defined each paper's style and content. In peaceful and calm times that may be right. In war, the task of newspapers is governed by different laws. Today it is like this: papers align themselves not according to the public's wishes, but instead the public is aligned by the papers according to national requirements ... We cannot today align ourselves according to what will be approved by the public. The press has the task simply of helping to win the war.[15]

In the week following Operation Jubilee, the French papers continued to discuss the raid in a more vigorous and prolonged manner than their German counterparts. The physical effects of battle on the town were highlighted. In its main story for 25 August, *Le Matin* dedicated two pages to a report by one of its war correspondents who had visited the town. The word 'battlefield' in its title was encased in quotation marks, as if Dieppe was not a battle at all. They were not far from the truth.

After a few days of intense discussion on German (and French) front pages, the Dieppe story fell into obscurity. After a week, it had essentially disappeared as a topic of conversation, as Dietrich's press ministry recognized. As early as 24 August, OKW's representative at Dietrich's conferences complained that the Wehrmacht's propaganda companies were producing reports that were not being picked up and published. This was a remarkably swift change of focus. Normally, such a significant event would have been hammered home to audiences in Germany and its occupied territories for much longer, especially considering its incredible propaganda value; a total Anglo-Canadian disaster following in the footsteps of an Anglo-Soviet conference was a gift. However, other events overtook the Dieppe story. The Wehrmacht's advance on the Volga and bitter fighting in the Caucasus Mountains dwarfed anything that could ever have happened in France. This summer's campaign would decide the Second World War's outcome in Europe, and German newspaper readers knew it. Their interest in a failed Anglo-Canadian raid, which was minuscule by comparison, soon flagged. It was but a blip in their almost constant focus on the East. The SD reported as much on 27 August, reporting in a matter-of-fact fashion that 'after the successful defence against the attempted Anglo-American landing at Dieppe, the public's interest has once again shifted to the military events in the East.'[16]

At the end of August there was one small flurry of activity in the papers which interrupted the Germans' attention on the Soviet Union. On 30 August, OKW released an unclassified report on the Dieppe raid to the German news agency. This was in no sense a typical military report; in fact it was a very general outline of events with an extreme political slant. This had been in the works for some days when the German Propaganda Ministry told its journalists across the Reich: 'With these documents the Dieppe operation will be stripped of its last secrets. Churchill's catastrophic policies will be exposed to the world … The unalterable facts speak a common language.' Although the Dieppe story had run its course, Press Chief Dietrich was determined to exploit it as long as humanly possible. The new OKW take on events provided a perfect opportunity for one last hurrah. 'The presentation of, and commentary on, this large factual OKW report should be something special', one brief said confidently.

The official *Völkischer Beobachter*, as ever, led the way for all others with the front-page headline in striking red type: 'Churchill's Attempted Invasion Exposed'. Its subtitle left little to the imagination: 'Dieppe bridgehead was to be a springboard for ambitious strategic targets'. The *Hamburger Anzeiger* led with a commanding headline, 'The Operational Order Confirms: Invasion'. Likewise, the *Westfälische Tageszeitung* led with 'Dieppe Was Supposed To Be The Second Front'. Germany's chief propagandists were delighted with how the morning German papers treated OKW's report on 30 August, praising their performance as 'excellent' at an afternoon press conference. But they still wanted more. British papers had been claiming Dieppe as a learning experience, a useful 'test run' for a future liberation of occupied Europe. This 'lessons learned' argument was made in 1942 just as later historians have put it forward. Indeed, the papers had been directed to do so by Canadian Military Headquarters in Britain (CMHQ). CMHQ was ever-positive and almost congratulatory, stating that the raid had been 'experimental' and had brought 'vital experience in the employment of troops in large numbers in an attack as well as an experience in the transport of their heavy equipment during combined operations'. Allied papers followed suit. The Canadian French-language paper *Le Canada* claimed that the attack was 'a dress rehearsal for the day when British forces throw aside Nazi fortifications'. To back up its arguments with foreign voices, the *Daily Express* in Britain reported various Canadian and American commentators who agreed that the operation had been a successful 'test'.

The Germans were keen to counter the 'dress rehearsal' narrative head-on. Dutifully, the *Aachener Anzeiger* argued on the very last day of August: 'When the English talk about having gained valuable experience during the operation, we can reassure them that the experience we have gathered by testing out their newest weapons and studying their military staff documents day after day – these are priceless, and the impact that they will have cannot be ignored.' That paper's journalists could not help but end their front-page story with an acidic put-down: 'We believe that after us, the Canadian and British prisoners are the ones who have gained the most experience from this invasion attempt, for they know exactly how sharp and well-organized the German defence is.'

While both sides published newspaper articles and issued radio broadcasts aimed at a general audience, there was yet another front to the Dieppe propaganda war: air-dropped leaflets. At least two significant leaflets appeared as a result of Operation Jubilee, one German and one Soviet. In early September, the Germans dropped a four-page booklet over Sussex and Hampshire, where many Canadian units were stationed. It was a simple piece of propaganda: pictures laying bare the utter destruction on Dieppe's main beach, with images of wounded 'Tommies' all around. Some photographs showed them receiving aid and cigarettes from their German counterparts. It quoted *The Times'* 20 August issue: 'If then this is not in any sense the opening of a "second front", what may it be taken to mean?'[17] Some of these leaflets fell into Hampshire resident A. C. Hayward's garden and, somewhat perturbed by this, he wrote to the editor of *The Times* enquiring after their provenance. The paper replied to Hayward that the leaflets were nothing more than 'a characteristic example of the dishonesty of German propaganda', pointing out that the article quoted had actually described the attempt to magnify the raid into an abortive invasion as a 'clumsy pretence' which 'will deceive no one but Germans'.

Naturally, the Germans also created propaganda leaflets for their own soldiers' consumption. *Mitteilungen für die Truppe* ('Messages for the Troops') was a single-page double-sided leaflet distributed widely amongst the non-commissioned men of all three services in the Wehrmacht. It appeared throughout the war roughly seven times a month and was partly indoctrinating, partly informative. Two copies were given to each company-level unit. It was a useful communication tool, giving the German leadership a regular opportunity to speak directly to the men on the ground. This, too, had something to say about Dieppe. Addressing the readers directly, one September edition told them not to worry about what the media was saying, for the results achieved on 19 August were self-evident: 'We know as soldiers: neither the headlines in newspapers nor the exuberant words of enemy broadcasters and politicians matter. Rather, in war military facts have the last word. As so often, the Wehrmacht had the last word at Dieppe: Victory.'

A few thousand miles away from south-east England, and in a very different climate, other leaflets were dropping in the Soviet Union. These were not in English like those over Hampshire and Sussex; rather, they were in German. Produced by the Soviets' psychological operations department, they were aimed at the Wehrmacht's soldiers in the East. Another version was aimed at civilians behind the lines. These flyers did not just stretch the truth like the German effort; rather, they were a complete bag of lies. The claims made were absurd. If this Soviet-produced effort were to be believed, then 15,000 Englishmen and Americans had landed with artillery and armour at Dieppe, successfully withdrawing in good order after nine hours. Not only this, but the Germans had supposedly lost 'over 200 aircraft, a third of the entire Luftwaffe stationed in the West'. Anyone seeing photos or newsreels from Dieppe would surely have seen through this, but Stalin's propagandists had clearly not heard the maxim of all propaganda that 'a kernel of truth goes far'. They obviously did not want to pass up the chance to exploit the opportunity that Dieppe provided – even if that meant totally mischaracterizing the operation as an unqualified success and making claims that were not worth the paper they were printed on. The Soviet leaflet then went on to list three things that this 'exploration' had shown: firstly, the 'absolute Anglo-American air superiority'; secondly, the 'excellent' training of their amphibious troops; and lastly, the 'readiness of civilians in occupied countries to aid the Allies'. 'So the operation of Dieppe showed Hitler's weakness and the Allies' strength', concluded its boastful yet utterly fictitious list of claims. On their respective back pages, the civilian and military versions diverged. The variety dropped at the fighting front read: 'SOLDIERS! Very soon you will be facing war on two fronts! For you that means sure death and inescapable defeat for your armies. END THE WAR BY YOURSELVES! Hurry, before it is too late! Refuse to fight! FLEE TO YOUR HOMES! OR GIVE YOURSELVES UP!' The shorter civilian version repeated some of this language, but ended with one blunt command: 'DEPOSE HITLER!'[18]

Looking back at the war of words following Dieppe, one can see that the repelling of the raid represented a short but sweet propaganda coup for the Germans. While public interest quickly turned to events on the Eastern Front, the successful German defence of Dieppe was happy and uplifting news for Germans at home, as well as servicemen in the field. For the first time, the 'Watch in the West' had proved itself capable of defeating a concerted, large-scale attempt at amphibious invasion. Above all, this was comforting for the Reich's domestic population, which was greatly concerned at the possibility of a second front in the West. Although media coverage of Dieppe was short-lived, it had a lasting impact. Memory of the operation remained strong in German public consciousness for a considerable time afterwards. At the end of September, more than a month later, Hitler spoke at Berlin's grand Sportpalast indoor arena, the same location at which Goebbels would give his infamous 'Total War' speech five months hence. In a long and meandering address, the Führer covered the entire course of hostilities up to that point, assuring his enraptured audience that Stalingrad would be taken, even with the difficulties which the upcoming winter would pose. At one point he lambasted his opponents in Britain and America by attacking the mendacity of Allied propaganda. With intense sarcasm, he compared Dunkirk and Dieppe as two defeats that his adversaries had claimed as victories:

> We cannot reach common ground with these people over the concept of 'belief'. Whoever believes, for example, that … Dunkirk was the greatest victory in world history, or who believes that any expedition that lasts nine hours is an amazing and encouraging sign of a victorious nation – of course, we cannot compare our modest successes with these! For what are our accomplishments compared to these? If we advance a thousand kilometres, that is nothing – an absolute failure![19]

The phrase 'nine hours' had been repeated so often in German propaganda that Hitler's audience knew intuitively that the Führer was referring to the events of Dieppe. Another reassuring voice was that of the insatiable SS propagandist Toni Winkelnkemper. This experienced orator turned to prose in response to the RAF's first 1,000-bomber raid on Cologne in May 1942, producing a book which covered the whole span of the war and explained why Germany would emerge victorious in the end. Winkelnkemper was fortunate that his book was published by the Nazi Party's central publishing house in Berlin and thus enjoyed the seal of official authority. 'During the campaign in the east', he told his readers, 'the western front is once again defensive, but it is resilient enough to resist any enemy attack, as the Dieppe adventure demonstrated. Due to its concentration of forces, Germany will win the deciding battle in the east, and with it the war.'[20] The correspondence between two friends soon after 19 August demonstrated the effect that such arguments had. Otto Richter and Hugo Kreutzer had become closely acquainted just before the outbreak of war. Even after they had both been called up to the Wehrmacht in 1940 – Otto to the Army and Hugo to a Luftwaffe signals detachment – they exchanged frequent letters. A week after the assault on Dieppe, Otto wrote to Hugo expressing his wish for an end to the war in the East: 'Russia will fall with Stalingrad … and I'm telling you, Stalingrad will fall in the next few days', he noted confidently. 'I have this hope that the war in the East will then be over. And even if Stalin doesn't get his Second Front, he's finished. Dieppe has shown that the Englishman, wherever he lands, will take a good beating.'[21] This message above all is what Goebbels wanted Germans to believe in the aftermath of Dieppe. To drive it home, he employed all the methods at his disposal; newsreel, newspapers, radio, books and leaflets.

Dieppe Through a Strategic Lens

The German experience at Dieppe had far-reaching consequences which extended well beyond the beaches of northern France. Any competent German observer realized that another Dieppe-style operation was on the cards, perhaps even before the close of 1942. As a result, at Hitler's headquarters, Army, Kriegsmarine and Luftwaffe officers assigned to OKW collectively racked their brains. How could the Germans defeat land-sea-air operations in future, be they large or small? With the benefit of the many lessons learned throughout the war, OKW initiated a new project with the ultimate goal of producing new operating procedures and guidelines for front-line units. They would report their findings in late September.

The planners at OKW relied heavily on historical precedent. Three main examples came to mind. First were the ultimately unsuccessful attempts by British and French forces to evict the Germans from Norway in 1940. While the Germans had indeed prevailed in this case, the Kriegsmarine had suffered heavy losses. Secondly, there was the Saint-Nazaire raid, still something of a sore point, even months after the fact. Although the Allied raiding force had effectively been destroyed, it had nevertheless accomplished its goal. HMS *Campbeltown* had somehow managed to come so far inshore that she could ram the port's dry-dock gates. This was a humiliation, especially for Admiral Raeder's Kriegsmarine, which was supposed to uphold coastal security. The third case study that OKW investigated in their review of German coastal defence policy was the Dieppe raid. Unlike Saint-Nazaire just a few months earlier, this was a successful defensive operation, but by September 1942 the Germans had already identified many ways in which coastal defence doctrine could be improved. They hoped to codify these in a new official strategy from OKW. Not to be ignored either were the various small Commando-style raids executed against occupied Europe under Britain's Combined Operations Headquarters, headed by Mountbatten. There was a wealth of experience of such small-scale defensive operations, too numerous to count, but Operation Claymore against the Norwegian Lofoten Islands in 1941 and Operation Biting were two of the most significant. Using all of this experience of facing large- and small-scale raids, the German officers at OKW hoped to produce a new, durable coastal defence doctrine that would operate for years to come.

When OKW finished its work and published its final memorandum on 23 September, it was signed by none other than Wilhelm Keitel, Chief of OKW. The OKW staff gave the fruits of their labour a rather anodyne bureaucratic title: 'Memorandum on Experiences in Coastal Defence: Composed after the Enemy Landing Attempts in Norway and France'. This innocuous description belied the document's real significance; in eighteen pages it provided a developed understanding of what the Germans expected to face in an amphibious landing, and how they would go about defeating it. Many of its ideas were already well known to German officers in the field, but the memorandum finally provided an official document in which these were all laid down. Crucially, OKW's analysis was split into two parts. Their memorandum differentiated between small-scale Commando raids by a handful of men and larger ones like those at Dieppe or Saint-Nazaire, which involved thousands. So impressive had the Commandos been that the Germans had adopted the word 'Commando' in official documentation.

In its memorandum, OKW pointed out from the very start that Clausewitzian fog of war would play its part in coastal operations as in any other. Feigned attacks and uncertainty over the attacking enemy's true intentions would be expected. Thus, vigilance in defence was required. After some preamble, OKW went to the very heart of the German conclusions from Dieppe: 'The enemy learns just as we do from every operation.' With these words, OKW was faithfully echoing Rundstedt's worries about the prospect of Allied 'lessons learned'. Hitler was in agreement too. In a secret speech to his commanders in the West in September 1942, he delivered the following words of warning: 'We must realize that we are not alone in learning a lesson from Dieppe. The British have also learned. We must reckon with a totally different mode of attack – and at quite a different place … If nothing happens in the west next year, we have won the war.'[1] Hitler's perceptiveness in this matter was impressive; it is a grave mistake for any military force to underestimate its enemy. With such a view coming from the very heart of the Führer HQ, it is unsurprising that it was well represented in Field Marshal Keitel's new memorandum on coastal defence strategy.

In an admirably realistic manner, the memorandum further recognized that the Allies enjoyed some immutable advantages over the German defenders. It noted that 'the lively activities of his agents and his aerial reconnaissance will always provide him with the newest information about our methods and dispositions. The enemy can land at any time, anywhere and by exploiting all conceivable possibilities and methods; he will commonly use ruses of every possible type (e.g. scouts and saboteurs in civilian dress or foreign uniforms, flying false flags and displaying false insignia).' For this reason, OKW posited that 'camouflage has the same value as the protection offered by armour and concrete. Great use is to be made of dummy positions.' Whether a poor infantryman hidden under a flimsy roof of foliage saw things that way is questionable – the 'man on the ground' is always grateful for extra physical protection whatever the higher-ups might say – but with the Allies' preponderance of reconnaissance aircraft, using camouflage and fake installations was a useful strategy. The German concern over Allied reconnaissance was justified. At Dieppe, the planners at COHQ had been able to produce an incredibly thorough and accurate picture of the German defences. The only major error was their assured belief that 110th Infantry Division was stationed there, not the 302nd. OB West quite correctly wrote that the Allies had enjoyed accuracy 'right up to the very smallest detail'.[2]

OKW's study began in earnest by describing the 'expected enemy behaviour' – what the Germans thought they would come up against in future. Only once this was established could they then decide how they should lay out their own coastal defence system. OKW noted how cliffs were no longer such a hindrance to attackers as once thought. As Operation Jubilee had demonstrated in August, Allied infantry (especially the feared Commandos) could scale parts of the coast previously dismissed as unclimbable. What was most striking about this new memorandum was how perceptive its contents were; the returns on OKW's intellectual labours were remarkable. For instance, even though at this point in the war Allied infantry had not yet been dropped by parachute during a seaborne assault, OKW still considered air landings to be of grave danger to any coastal defender. So threatening were attacks from the rear in German eyes that OKW mandated that coastal strongpoints be capable of an all-round defence. 'Since, in coastal areas, an attack is to be reckoned with not just from the sea, but also from the land', it declared, 'the land fronts of [defensive positions] are to be built up in the same way.' Earlier that month, Keitel had signed an OKW order from Hitler which decreed that any and all male German citizens in a war zone, whether in the inner German Reich or occupied territory, could be called up for temporary 'short-term conscription' during an unexpected attack. These men would not be given uniforms; instead they would be identified as combatants merely by wearing a German helmet. This measure was partly justified by the speed with which an airborne assault could surprise a coastal area.[3]

Continuing the theme of air power, OKW further concluded that counter-air operations aimed against Luftwaffe installations would form a central part of large-scale landings. This was despite the fact that this had never been a part of Allied doctrine. Indeed, even at Dieppe the ground-attack air squadrons were vastly outnumbered by fighter interceptor squadrons. 'The preparation of a landing can occur using consolidated air attacks above all against our own airfields – with the objective of knocking out our own air force, especially fighters. These attacks will be directed against our own defence installations, especially the anti-naval batteries, the lodging and assembly points of our reserves as well as the significant transport routes necessary to bring them up.' OKW concluded the same about naval bombardment and fire support: '[The enemy's] ships will often exploit the element of surprise at daybreak, in concert with air forces, but will mainly stay outside the range of our own anti-ship batteries.' Even though large preparatory naval bombardment had never (up to that point) been a significant part of Allied operational doctrine when it came to amphibious operations, the Germans still had the foresight to consider this a possibility. With the benefit of hindsight, this may now seem obvious, but large-scale amphibious operations were a new art in 1942 and much was unknown and theoretical. Only from 1943 would the Allies begin massed operations against German-held European coastlines.

After considering how a large Allied landing might be prepared for with air and naval bombardment, Keitel's analysis then moved on to how the landing force would approach. Above all, air power was highlighted:

'Strong fighter protection is necessary during this period of an attack.' The OKW's operations staff correctly identified that fighters – with their relatively short range – would not always have the endurance required to cover an amphibious landing comprehensively. They believed that the Allies might have to rely on naval aviation, surmising that fighter cover 'might not be adequately assured, as long as the enemy is reliant on aircraft carriers'. With later actions in mind, this was something of a forlorn hope; in Italy and France in 1943 and 1944 respectively, the Allies always had adequate land-based fighter cover for their ground movements. One more accurate prediction related to Allied artificial smoke. With the experience of Dieppe fresh in German minds, it was natural that this reassessment of German strategy would include a reference to it: 'Artificial smoke is an effective shield when approaching the coast and landing; however, it does reduce the effectiveness of both sides' weapons. It is also expected to be used during any re-embarkation.' OKW's assessment was fully justified, as this was exactly what the Allies had surmised. A year later, the US War Department would write in a briefing that, thanks in no small part to the Dieppe experience, smoke had been proved 'invaluable' to landing operations.[4] From 1942 onwards, screening smoke would be a cornerstone of Allied landing technique.

Keitel's memorandum concluded its first section with a general overview of the land forces they expected to face. For smaller-scale raids, this was simple: small teams of Commando-trained infantry carried in small boats. For larger operations, this was more complicated. OKW predicted 'infantry with heavy weapons and engineers brought via landing craft' from the very first wave, not excluding the very real possibility of heavy armour. Particularly in this section of OKW's survey, Operation Jubilee's shadow is clear to see. 'Dropped at the main landing points, "Commandos" may be tasked with neutralizing strongpoints (batteries), which flank the landing points', it suggested. 'The engineers in the first wave have the task of freeing a path for the armour, as important carriers of offensive strength (by clearing barbed wire and mines).' This closely mirrors how the Dieppe battle was supposed to have unfolded, according to the plan which the Germans had captured. There was no clearer evidence that the Germans were concerned about another, improved, Jubilee-style attack.

Keitel and his OKW also wished to lay down some fundamentals of coastal defence upon which commanders in the field could build their defensive plans. The memorandum defined the moment of weakness for an attacking force as 'the approach to the coast, unloading and delay on the beach'. The centre of gravity of coastal defence was sensibly established as being 'around ports and landing areas suitable for the enemy'. Importantly, at no point did OKW expound the view that only ports would be targeted by Allied landings. Although the Germans recognized the logistical significance of ports in sustaining forces ashore, this idea was not all-consuming. If anything, the Dieppe experience taught them that next time, the Allies might choose to land at a place other than a port. Roskill's official history states: 'The Germans decided that the Dieppe raid indicated that, when the time came for the Allies to invade the European continent in earnest, their initial thrust would be aimed at capturing a large port.'[5] As the architect of a disastrous operation, Mountbatten found convenient retroactive justification for Jubilee with this argument. In a speech to Dieppe veterans in 1973 he argued like Roskill that 'the Germans learnt the wrong lessons from the operation. They were certain we would have to go for ports.'[6] Such a bold claim is not supported by the evidence. Although ports self-evidently had to be defended, the Wehrmacht did not believe a landing there was certain. Among Hitler, Keitel and Jodl at OKW, and Rundstedt in France, none advanced the view that only a landing directed at a port could be successful. One Luftwaffe assessment, quoting an unidentified agent, made the opposite point that the gravity of the defeat at Dieppe might well dissuade the Allies from attacking a port: 'The experiences of Dieppe have shown the English that the German defence of points that are suitable for a sustained landing (most significantly areas near ports viable for the unloading of supplies for tanks and guns) is so strong that an extraordinary force is needed to overcome the defences.'[7] OKW's report released to the German press in late August explicitly made the point that a fresh landing would be 'better and more robust and not necessarily at a port'.[8] The myth that Dieppe was a great 'deception operation' (as Mountbatten put it), in that Jubilee brought about a German over-emphasis on port defence, is one of Dieppe's many legends that should have been discarded long ago. It emerged from a public 'spin' campaign by Mountbatten and his supporters, and has no basis in fact.

In Keitel's new guidelines, the concept of tri-service 'strongpoints' also gained new importance: 'The elements of all three services in the Wehrmacht are to be integrated into enclosed resistance nests and strongpoints.' While 'resistance nests' (*Widerstandsneste*) were small self-contained defence works with only a handful of men, the 'strongpoints' (*Stützpunkte*) were larger and contained many individual resistance nests. Heavy weapons like mortars and heavy machine guns were normally to be found in the larger strongpoints. This new drive to integrate all elements of German defence included specialist technical equipment like radar stations and communications hubs. OKW stressed that the men forced together into newly created resistance nests and strongpoints must constantly train and drill. 'Every soldier must be a "multi–purpose fighter" (*Mehrkämpfer*)', the memorandum explained, 'and be able to operate every weapon within his strongpoint.' This was not much of an issue, considering that the West was such a relatively quiet sector. There was ample time for repetitive training, and training is an age-old way to keep otherwise bored soldiers, like those guarding the inactive West, active and content – a busy soldier is a happy soldier. These strongpoints were so important to German defence doctrine that they were expected to hold out independently for many days, with no outside support. The guidelines continued: 'All strongpoints and resistance nests must be stockpiled with ammunition, food and drinking water to such an extent that they are capable of multi-day, independent combat operations without a stream of supplies.'

Artillery was integral to the German system of defence in France, Belgium, the Netherlands, Denmark and Norway. In many divisions, including Haase's 302nd Infantry Division, artillery represented a substitute for strength in numbers. OKW's memorandum devoted an entire section to how artillery should be employed. As in previous German doctrine, it divided artillery batteries into two types: for land or for naval defence. The former would concentrate on hitting the enemy after he had landed, while the latter would focus on sinking ships at sea. Most batteries were better suited to one of these tasks, either due to their location or rate of fire, but some could operate in a dual-purpose role. Guns with higher firing rates, for instance, were much preferred for the anti-shipping role. Consistent with standard operating procedures, these too would be integrated into strongpoints so that they could defend themselves more easily against air or close-quarters infantry attack.

Reserves, too, formed part of OKW's remit. Since so few motorized vehicles were available, other methods to increase the speed with which reserves were brought up had to be considered. An obvious factor was how far the reserves were placed behind the lines: 'Local reserves have to be held close, otherwise they will arrive too late.' Moving tactical reserves closer to the coast was a crude measure – it somewhat reduced their scope for manoeuvre laterally (i.e. up and down the coast), but it meant that they could arrive in time, even without fast motorized transport. Another practical measure that OKW prescribed was the use of a single codeword, in place of longer radio or telephone messages, to bring reserves up to full readiness. Staying with the theme of rear-area operations, Keitel's memorandum also briefly mentioned sabotage: 'In order to defeat sabotage attempts, the entire interior is to be split into districts each commanded by a responsible officer. Surveillance is to be secured inside these districts, alongside the constant securing of important objects (staff headquarters, communications lines etc.).'

In crafting their new coastal defence strategy, OKW had to make one critical tactical call: should the German defenders try to defeat an Allied landing force close to the landing beaches (if possible while still at sea), or adopt a more flexible strategy centred on surrounding and crushing an already established beachhead? There were arguments on both sides of this debate, and it would not be the last time that the Germans faced the question – before the landing in Normandy in 1944, Erwin Rommel favoured a forward-based strategy aimed at defeating the enemy at the water's edge, while Geyr von Schweppenberg favoured a mobile defence with heavy reliance on armoured manoeuvre. In 1942 this question was not nearly as important as it became two years later, nor was there the ill-tempered wrangling within OKW that would take place between Rommel and Schweppenberg before D-Day. Most vocal on this issue was Rundstedt. As OB West, he spoke with the authority of a theatre commander who had wiped out an enemy landing in just nine hours. In a message to his Army-level commanders six days after Dieppe, he wrote that 'It must be the aim of our operations to destroy the enemy on the very day of his landing. To that effect, and further to the measures that have been taken by the Army and Corps commanders in respect of their own reserves, I have disposed my motorized Army Group reserves in such a manner that, on most of the coastal front, one motorized formation at least will be able to intervene on the first day.'[9]

Nevertheless, whether or not to forward-deploy forces in the hope of a quick victory was still an issue for debate, for the Germans did not know when another large-scale amphibious operation might arrive. In their memorandum, OKW ultimately came to a clear decision in favour of a forward, coast-facing strategy. Based on their conclusion that the enemy was weakest while at sea, approaching the coast or unloading men and materiel, it was logical to prevent a stable beachhead being established at all. Destruction at sea or shortly after landing was the key, so placing defensive strength as close to the coast as possible was the name of the game. As we have seen, placing reserves forward was part of this strategy. Artillery, too, would play its role: 'In order to annihilate an enemy in the process of landing as early as on the water, in addition to anti-naval batteries, individual land defence guns and armour-piercing infantry weapons must also be built facing out to sea.' It was clear where the inspiration for this idea came from. 'According to the latest experiences at Dieppe, flanking fire from anti-tank and machine guns on beaches and coastal cliffs are particularly suited to annihilating the enemy when they make landfall.' Bearing in mind that they expected the Allies to bring heavy fire support in future, OKW then gave guidelines as to how such positions should actually be built: 'For this purpose, weapons are to be deployed in embrasures or caverns which can only provide enfilading fire, and built in such a way that their embrasures cannot be taken under fire from seawards.'[10] The embrasure is an ancient piece of military engineering, simple yet effective and used since the age of bows and arrows. A small firing port, perhaps a tiny slit no bigger than a gun barrel, is made in a pillbox. The firing gap in the pillbox is then widened to provide a full field of fire, but only a small firing port. This design allows freedom of fire for the defender, yet provides only a small target to the attacker.

What the Germans feared most about the Allies was their tanks. Operation Jubilee had unequivocally reinforced their concern that, even in the first wave, a large-scale landing could bring heavy armour down on them. The new OKW memorandum classified Allied armour as 'the greatest danger for coastal defence, both on the sea-facing and on the land-facing fronts'. Radical measures were thus in order. Sections of the coast suitable for landing were to be made 'artificially tank-safe' with 'bottlenecks and bogs, artificially created slopes, anti-tank walls made of reinforced concrete, anti-tank ditches, humps, rail obstacles and tank traps. At Dieppe, gravel and the anti-tank wall greatly inhibited the movement of tanks.' Helpfully, OKW provided an appendix full of engineers' designs for such obstacles.

In its last section, Keitel's OKW memorandum discussed how the local population could be used to aid the defence. It envisaged a surprisingly close relationship between the occupied and occupiers in relation to coastal defence. At one point, OKW suggested that reliable elements of the local population could be used to observe friendly convoy movements and installations, if there was a lack of available German manpower. In construction, too, OKW foresaw a substantial role for the local populace: 'The population is to be used to the widest extent possible in all construction matters. Earthworks, laying of barbed wire and similar work can be carried out even by untrained labourers.' Harsh measures were prescribed for those who attempted to aid the enemy during an actual battle: 'Participation by the civil population in battle for the enemy must be prevented by hostage-taking and the threat of draconian punishments.' Espionage was to be punished in the same manner. If what OKW termed 'internal disturbances' caused by civilians arose during battle, then military reserves held in the rear would 'nip incipient revolts in the bud'.

This lengthy document represented a significant intervention in German coastal defence planning. OKW lay at the very top of the Wehrmacht's organizational hierarchy. Although it was supposed to be a joint services organization to unite the Army, Kriegsmarine and Luftwaffe in one structure, after years of war it had essentially become Hitler's mouthpiece. Although it did not carry the Führer's signature as 'Commander-in-Chief of the Wehrmacht', it can safely be assumed that Hitler was a driving force behind OKW's new initiative. His and Rundstedt's insistence that the Allies would also learn from Dieppe was a wise one. If one accepted this premise, then the Wehrmacht needed to anticipate and pre-empt the changes that the Allies would make in their landing technique. One significant aspect in which the Germans were convinced that Allied landing technique would change was the prioritization of ground communications as a target for air attack. In this crucial aspect, the Germans did not merely stand still and expect their enemies to repeat what they had done at Dieppe by failing to properly realize the value of communications infrastructure to coastal defence.

Dieppe showed physical telephone-wire communications to be particularly vulnerable to air attack, even though there was no concerted attempt by the joint Allied force to disrupt their adversaries' communications. This weakness in the Allied plan brought great relief. LXXXI Corps noted that connections between it and its subordinate 302nd Division had only held because the Allies did not attempt to destroy them. One lucky hit from the B-17 Fortress attack on Abbeville airfield had rendered all telephone lines responsible for reporting aircraft contacts completely inoperable, but Luftwaffe commanders were surely thankful that the Allies had made no intentional attacks on their communications infrastructure. The Germans knew that their opponents would not make the same foolish mistake again. Change was clearly in order, and LXXXI Corps thus urged its subordinate units to employ wireless radio communications as well as wired, as a back-up in case the latter were somehow knocked out. It also suggested the establishment of so-called 'message centres', every ten or so kilometres along the coast at strategic road junctions which could reliably relay messages to reserves approaching from the rear or flanks.[11]

Just after OKW had released its study on coastal defence, German commanders in France were implementing their own plans. General Wilhelm Wimmer, in charge of the Belgium/Northern France Air District, ordered a new training regime for his ground troops. Like all commanders of an Air District, Wimmer was a Luftwaffe officer responsible for land affairs. Included in this remit was guarding Luftwaffe installations such as airfields against Allied attack, for which purpose he had infantry assigned to him. Wimmer was a perfect candidate to lead such an effort; in addition to being a trained pilot, he also had extensive previous experience as an infantry officer in the inter-war period. For German generals with coastal commands like Wimmer, the Dieppe raid had been a wake-up call. Although they had well understood that a Dieppe-style operation was possible, and had prepared for it, Operation Jubilee made clear how real the danger truly was.

General Wimmer elected to act decisively. First, he mandated a new standing order throughout his command: no man, however or wherever he was deployed, was to be permanently stationed outside a designated 'strongpoint'. Wimmer considered the risk of surprise attack too great to allow anything else. His plan was not a new one, however – he based it on ideas laid out by Lieutenant Colonel Kusserow, a Luftwaffe officer based at OKW. Kusserow had completed his work at the beginning of August, but his lengthy memorandum was somewhat ignored by operational commanders. The raid on Dieppe, and the startling success of 4 Commando there, gave the Germans the impetus to finally act on Kusserow's anti-Commando concept, which emphasized individual initiative and night-time tactics.

'Every leader of men must adjust to the fact that even more and even larger aggressive enemy operations, including the employment of parachute and glider forces in concert with Commando (Gangster) operations, will occur', wrote Wimmer by way of introduction. Undoubtedly, the Commandos would have taken great pleasure in being referred to as 'gangsters' – it proved that they were having an effect on the enemy. In line with what Kusserow's study at OKW had suggested a month earlier, Wimmer now ordered a six-week intensive night-time training programme for all infantrymen under his command. The first two weeks were dedicated to listening, observation and silent movement at night. During weeks three and four, the students would learn how to react during an unexpected close contact with the enemy – including the very same throat-and-stomach techniques or hand-to-hand combat that Kusserow at OKW had suggested. Up to this point, all the training was related to individual skills. The last fortnight, however, was devoted to group activities. Giving orders at night and rapidly creating a tactical formation in the dark were just two of the exercises on the menu. Throughout the month and a half, the men were supposed to undergo vigorous physical training and night shooting, as well as hand grenade practice. All of this was designed to make the individual and the group more accustomed to operating in darkness, conditions in which the Commandos had time and again proved themselves superior to their German counterparts.

Every 'Air District', like General Wimmer's in Northern France and Belgium, was necessarily a very large command. For organizational purposes, these were split into various airfield 'sectors', or *Flughafenbereiche*. Each sector comprised one or more individual airbases. As a consequence, the *Flughafenbereich* commander was much more intimately involved with planning for the defence of individual airfields than his superior 'Air District Commander'. He knew that blame for any breach of security, however it came about, would be placed squarely on his head. One such sector commander, and a man particularly eager to implement Wimmer's programme, was Brigadier Erhard Krüger. He commanded an airfield sector in Picardy which included the Beauvais-Tillé airfield, a major hub used by both bomber and fighter units, with satellite sites in its vicinity. Only a few days after he had received General Wimmer's orders, Krüger passed down the following message to his men: 'The systematic training in small-scale warfare is to begin immediately.' Understandably, given the track record of Commando attacks, not least in Crete, Krüger shared the fears of his fellow officers about sabotage: 'The prerequisite for the successful completion of training is that everyone knows the threat of sabotage, which is constant, and is in a position to defeat it at any time.' He continued by saying that in all exercises the 'purpose and significance of sabotage defence is to be discussed with urgency'.

Others, however, did not see any rush. After more than a week, despite Brigadier Krüger's insistence that the new training regime begin 'immediately', those under his command did not seem to have got the message, since no extra training had begun. Krüger was told that immediate action was simply impossible due to the bureaucracy involved; apparently, the paperwork was just too complex. Krüger was not best pleased. Hence his frustrated and exasperated follow-up order early in September: 'The full and intensive training of this entire command in small-scale warfare has still not been implemented, despite the order to this effect around ten days ago.' Krüger's comments read like a distinctly unfavourable headmaster's report: 'I see to my dismay that the importance of the [force protection troops] in the current situation, in all its magnitude, is not recognized everywhere. So much so that measures are still being neglected that are absolutely necessary for the personal safety of every individual and for the protection of the aerodromes.' Krüger could not tolerate this behaviour, which he considered tantamount to insubordination, and he had a nasty punishment up his sleeve: 'From this moment onwards, every single soldier, civil servant and relative of a serviceman will, until further notice, gather daily for at least 40 minutes [of instruction] – in addition to the ongoing night training. There will be no exceptions (other than due to illness).'[12] It was highly irregular to involve civilians in military training like this, but the order demonstrated Krüger's worries. He would not have acted so radically had he not been concerned. He was not alone; there was general concern amongst German commanders that each would be the next to fall victim to the Commandos. With the authority that came with being OB West, Field Marshal Rundstedt had the following message for every German in the West after Dieppe:

> The 'Commandos' have conducted themselves with skill and have fought well. They are well-selected raw material with good specialist training and good equipment. They look for particularly challenging terrain such as cliffs for their mission. Our own troops must know that the 'Commando Man' is a skilled adversary, who will work with any means possible – including subterfuge. However, our troops must know that they are totally superior to [the 'Commando Man'] in their well-built defensive positions with their many heavy weapons, if their exertion and attention does not abate and they stay calm and fight doggedly to the last. This toughness is necessary because the 'Commando Man' is tough too.[13]

Later, in October 1942, the fear that German commanders shared would manifest itself in Hitler's infamous 'Commando Order', which stated that all Commandos captured during raids were to be executed, even if they were dressed in proper military uniform or tried to surrender.

General Wimmer expected attention from his men even late in the year when conditions were not conducive to large-scale military operations, especially something as complicated as an amphibious landing. At the beginning of October he ordered a unit-wide period of increased readiness. The paper on which his order was issued carried a thick bold red outline: 'I have stressed it often enough and order it once again: Every soldier under my command, regardless of where he is stationed, must keep his eyes and ears open more than ever!' Wimmer told his men that they must not let their guard down. Paratroops, he explained, were a great danger even when dropped at night. 'The dark time of the year has begun, and soon the cold will follow. Nevertheless, the Führer expects increased readiness from us in the West in order to secure the campaign in the East.' He assured his men that he would be touring the area to see that these orders were carried out.[14]

Historians have often speculated about what effect Operation Jubilee had on the numbers of German forces deployed in the West, though it is a question that can be misleading to pose. There were several factors utterly unrelated to the Dieppe raid that had affected the number of units stationed in the West. One was that the Germans were preparing for *Fall Anton* ('Case Anton'), the occupation of the southern Vichy-administered region of metropolitan France. For some time, Hitler had suspected that his Vichy puppet regime was neither willing nor able to defend its French or African territory. Indeed, on 8 November, when the Allies landed in French North Africa (Operation Torch), they met little resistance. This apparently provided the spark for Hitler to order the occupation. On 10 November, Case Anton was finally put into action, and so two German armies and one Italian advanced into Vichy France. By the end of November all of European France was under direct German military control. Now, OB West was duty-bound to defend France's Mediterranean coastline as well. As a result, the number of divisions given to Rundstedt increased. Another important reason for transferring some divisions westwards was for refit and recuperation. With the fighting in the Soviet Union so intense, it was necessary in 1942 for some units which had suffered particularly serious attrition to spend time in the West, where the chance of combat was slim. On 13 September Hitler signed an order to this effect, stating in its preamble that 'in order to restore the fighting strength of the armies in the East, it is necessary to remove the units most degraded by combat'. The order duly prescribed that fifteen infantry divisions were to be removed from service in the East. These were partly to be replaced for the campaigns of 1942 by the West's 'static' divisions, including 302nd Infantry Division. Hitler's order precipitated a flow of units back and forth between West and East well into 1943.[15]

All this had a noticeable effect on the number of German land divisions in France, Belgium and the Netherlands. On 12 August 1942, Rundstedt had thirty-five divisions of all types under his command. The rest of the year saw a significant increase in divisions stationed west of Germany. By mid-October the figure had increased by thirteen, and by mid-November another six had been transferred westwards, bringing the total number of divisions that Rundstedt commanded to fifty-two. This would ultimately represent the new standard level of commitment to Western Europe. With a few fluctuations, the German land forces would remain at this level until 1944, when the numbers increased again in anticipation of 'the Invasion'.[16]

There is no reason to believe, therefore, that the Dieppe raid had any appreciable effect on the balance of forces allocated between West and East. There were far more important and wide-reaching factors in play at the turn of 1942/43. Nor was there by any stretch of the imagination a direct and immediate shift of German forces to the West in response to the raid. As we have seen, this division had been transferred to France from the east well in advance of Dieppe as part of its conversion to motorized status. Indeed, the 1:1,000,000 scale maps of France that Rundstedt reviewed on 19 August and 4 November were remarkably similar, save for some extra divisions awaiting Case Anton; but all these additions were in central and western France, some distance away from any threatened coastline. In short, the Dieppe raid was so insignificant in strategic terms that the Germans saw no need to relocate any air, land or sea forces westwards.

The same is true of static coastal defences. Dieppe did not cause Hitler or his generals to expedite the creation of the so-called 'Atlantic Wall' in the West. Plans for its expansion had been in place for some time; indeed, the Führer had informed his inner circle of his ambitions in a secret speech on 14 August. As per Hitler's wishes, this monumental plan called for a network of 15,000 coastal fortifications all along the Atlantic coast of occupied Europe, to be implemented through a so-called 'winter construction programme' in the winter of 1942/43.[17] Not only would these defences make an initial Allied landing more challenging, they would also provide hard 'shoulders' to guard the flanks of defensive operations. But the reality was, fortunately for the Allies, very different. At the end of September, the Führer gave another three-hour oration to nine of his senior officers in the Cabinet room in Berlin's Reich Chancellery. His audience included Göring, Rundstedt and his new chief of staff Blumentritt, as well as Albert Speer, Reich Minister of Armaments and War Production. He told them candidly: 'You know that I have never surrendered, but I must say quite openly that a major landing by the enemy in Western Europe would put us in a critical situation.' He went on: 'Above all I am grateful to the British for having confirmed my views by their various landing operations, and for saving me from appearing as a visionary before those who are forever saying, "Where then are the British going to appear? Here on the coast there is definitely nothing wrong; we go swimming every day and we have never seen one yet".' The Führer was quick to stress that the Allies had considered how the Dieppe experience would influence future large-scale landing operations, expounding the opinion that though 19 August was 'highly instructive', both sides should avoid misguided conclusions. Hitler believed that 'the British should not consider such operations hopeless, nor can we underestimate the danger'. As a parallel, the Führer examined the tank battle at Cambrai in the First World War in some detail: 'After the failure of this operation, both sides drew misguided conclusions. The British, for example, placed all the blame on the shortcomings in technical and fighting qualities of the recently invented tanks.' Hitler continued in a similar vein:

> The erroneous conclusion reached [in Germany] after Cambrai was: 'The tank is nothing but a bogeyman to frighten children with!' … In this war, a novelty like the tanks at Cambrai during the World War is the first large-scale but failed landing operation at Dieppe. Just as it should never be assumed that the enemy will draw wrong conclusions from it, so we too should avoid the mistake of thinking that the British have now realized they cannot do anything against our coastal defences. The enemy will not give up the idea of forming a Second Front, because he knows that it is without doubt his only remaining chance of achieving victory.

Hitler had a clear strategic motive for expanding his static defences west of Germany. However, this imperative had existed well before Dieppe; the events of 19 August served merely to reinforce it. Hitler wanted to create a new Siegfried Line stretching along Europe's occupied coastline, yet demands on men and resources meant that this ambition could never be fulfilled. The very next day after Hitler's speech, and only six miles east of the Reich Chancellery, Inspector of Western Land Fortifications Major General Rudolf Schmetzer was addressing his own attentive listeners, a class of engineering cadets at the engineers' college in Karlshorst. Schmetzer told the students that Hitler's plans would be 'much more challenging' than building the Siegfried Line on the Franco-

German border: while in that case there had been one worker for every one kilometre of front, there would be seven kilometres of front for every worker in the West, including Norway.[18] To compound the problems, many of these would be forcibly conscripted foreign workers. Only a few weeks previously, Hitler had signed an order allowing for an expansion in the role of foreign labour in building the Atlantic Wall. This order made receiving a ration book dependent on doing war work, and forbade foreign workers from switching jobs or leaving the regions in which they were working without the express permission of the military authorities.[19] From his office in Paris, Field Marshal Rundstedt hoped not just to build more fortifications, but to reorganize those already in place. Many of his artillery batteries, for example, had been built when Germany was on the strategic offensive against Britain in 1940–41. They were placed in forward but exposed positions to support a seaborne assault against British shores, by engaging either Channel traffic or targets on the British mainland; 813 Battery at Dieppe was a fitting example. Now that the strategic picture was reversed, these batteries needed to be relocated to more defensive positions. This was another key goal in the 1942/43 building programme. However, it was never to be completed. With fighting on so many different fronts, on land, at sea and in the air, the industrial and financial resources to implement Hitler's winter construction programme simply did not exist. In the end, only a third of the 15,000 planned fortifications were built by mid-1943.

Chapter 19

The Enemy Within: Inter-Service Rivalry and the Response to Dieppe

In launching Operation Jubilee, the British and Canadians opened a wound that had festered at the very heart of the Wehrmacht's being. Tensions between the German Army, Kriegsmarine and Luftwaffe, as we have seen, had been simmering for some time. The Germans' adversaries had managed to put in place structures that more often than not managed to smooth over the differences between their various services. The British, for instance, had their Chiefs of Staff Committee, while in 1942 the United States created the Joint Chiefs of Staff. Hitler's Germany, on the other hand, had never made an attempt to unite its armed forces into a true joint services organization, and never would. For one thing, Hitler was too devoted to the principle of divide and rule, even under the stresses of wartime. For another, the system of personal fiefdoms and empires was too strong. Neither of Hitler's two other service commanders-in-chief – Göring at the Luftwaffe and Raeder at the Kriegsmarine – would ever have tolerated being subordinate to an overarching high command. Hitler, of course, headed the Army himself. Furthermore, OKW was a High Command of the Armed Forces in name only. It did not have the power to compel action from anyone. In essence, it was merely a vehicle for Hitler to issue orders to the Wehrmacht. It was, for example, the organization that drafted his 'Führer Directives' (*Führerweisungen*). These overrode any and all other military directives, orders and civilian laws.

Dieppe exposed this fundamental weakness. By its very nature, coastal defence was a joint services effort requiring input from the Army, Kriegsmarine and Luftwaffe collaboratively. Indeed, German doctrine (as written in Rundstedt's Basic Order 13 in July and Keitel's OKW memorandum in late September) readily recognized this reality, but the Wehrmacht's three consistent parts – Army, Kriegsmarine and Luftwaffe

– were not set up to act harmoniously with one other. Even before the Dieppe raid, these tensions had revealed themselves in the wrangling over the control of coastal artillery. The Army and Kriegsmarine had been forced to accept an uneasy solution in Hitler's Directive 40 from March 1942. Under this regime, sea targets were prioritized, and the Army only gained tactical control of coastal batteries when land targets were being engaged. Even training was split – naval personnel trained the gun crews for naval engagements, while Army personnel did the same for land battles. Naturally, Hitler's generals wished to rid themselves of this unfavourable system as soon as possible, and the Dieppe raid gave them the perfect opportunity to do so. Indeed, in his final report to his superiors, Major General Haase of 302nd Infantry Division had argued that the Dieppe experience should be a catalyst for change: 'One of the lessons gained in this attack is the abandonment of subordination of Army coastal artillery to the Kriegsmarine. The Army coastal artillery is naturally being placed by the Navy ... from the perspective of the necessity of engaging mobile sea targets. Thus the Army coastal artillery troops will not be able to cope with the task of repelling a landing or landed enemy.' This sentence summarized the view that most Army commanders had held for some time – that the Kriegsmarine's primacy was endangering the battle on land, and that only by making the Kriegsmarine relinquish their favoured position could balance be restored. Haase's report, though, made one startlingly bold declaration: 'The strength with which the artillery will conduct its defensive fire should the enemy navy at some time or other fire at our coast has no bearing on the course of the war, but the effectiveness of the defence against an enemy penetration on land may well decide its outcome.'[1] This showed how strongly Haase felt, having personally defended the coast against a divisional-scale landing. Indeed, in 1942 he was the only divisional commander to have done so anywhere in Europe. The only logical conclusion, according to his argument, was to end the Kriegsmarine's primacy at the coastline and place more artillery batteries to the rear, where they would win the battle after invading troops had made landfall.

In October the Army made its move, initiating discussions at OKW about changing the organizational set-up of coastal artillery. For all its weaknesses, OKW did at least provide a formal environment in which the different services could meet and present their ideas to one another. Naturally, the Kriegsmarine was given a right to respond, which precipitated a whirlwind of position papers and memoranda that flew across German admirals' and generals' desks. As their opening gambit, the Army submitted that the current system was not fit for purpose, and that coastal artillery should be split – one set that would concern itself with land targets, and another that would do the same for naval targets. No longer would all batteries be in one 'basket', constantly having to switch their attention from sea to land. Once this split had occurred, land and sea batteries would receive separate training from the Army and Kriegsmarine respectively. The Army presented its many complaints against the system laid out by Directive 40 in a position paper on 13 October. This was a somewhat precarious move, because Directive 40 had been implemented over Hitler's own signature. Fundamentally, according to the Army staff at OKW, the whole naval emphasis of coastal batteries was wrong. In fact, they argued rather unsurprisingly that the really decisive point lay on land: 'The main task of coastal artillery is not correctly recognized. According to all available documentation and the experiences of Dieppe, it lies not in fighting ships, but in the fight for the coastline.' Next, they went further by attacking a central tenet of all previous defence planning: 'The assumption that we might be able to destroy the enemy during a large-scale attack before they have even reached the coast is not justified. [This is due to] the enemy's expected superiority, his advanced technology and tactics as well as the relative weakness in manning of our coastline.' This statement represented a first. The Army was now directly challenging a prime principle of German coastal defence: that if enough men and materiel were placed forward, even a divisional-scale assault could be wiped out before any enemy set foot on shore. This change was a long time coming. It was a dubious notion to begin with, but Dieppe had shown beyond doubt that even a weakly supported force could get ashore in spite of strong, determined resistance. Indeed, when Keitel's memorandum raised this point, it seemed only to be a faint ambition to wipe out the enemy at sea, rather than a concrete strategy. An enemy could well be weakened before reaching land, but it was highly unlikely that every landing craft could be stopped, especially in the face of a naval and air bombardment designed to suppress defensive firepower. On 19 August, the Canadians and British Commandos were only defeated after they had made landfall – and in that case, there had been very little fire support for the ground force, either from the air or sea. The Army now sought to use this fact against the Kriegsmarine and thereby upend the way in which the whole Wehrmacht went about planning the defence of Germany's occupied coastlines.

The events of 19 August also supported another point made by the Army. Due to the preference given tackling an enemy at sea, most coastal batteries were placed far forward and were therefore vulnerable to infantry attack. If one accepted the Army's claim that a determined enemy would always be able to make landfall, then placing batteries forward did not make sense. To validate their point, the Army used the example of 813 Battery: 'The danger is therefore that these batteries, like 813 Battery at Dieppe, will be overrun by the enemy before they can have any effect at all.' This was a reasonable argument. Moving coastal guns rearwards would make life easier for approaching enemy ships, yet this was immaterial if one assumed, as the Army did, that the true decisive point lay on land.

Of course, the Kriegsmarine were not going to meekly accept these claims, since they threatened the dominance that the naval service had achieved under Directive 40. They were not about to give up that influence without a fight. Two days after they received the Army's position paper, the naval staff at OKW responded in kind: 'From the outset it is to be established that from the time that Directive 40 was issued, nothing has changed which would give rise to altering the directive, which was extensively considered at the time.' With this mission statement of sorts, the Kriegsmarine was making it clear that no previous experience, not even that gained at Dieppe, was reason to reduce the emphasis given to the battle at sea. Point by point, the Kriegsmarine's riposte proceeded to challenge the claims made by those wearing army uniforms. This included the contention that, in favouring targets at sea, batteries were being placed too close to shore. At Dieppe, the guns at Berneval were temporarily silenced by only a handful of Commandos from Yellow Beach. This would seem to support the Army's viewpoint, yet the Kriegsmarine rejected it out of hand: 'The battery at Berneval cannot be used as an example, because its position was considered unsuitable by both Army and Kriegsmarine, with a view to relocation that had not yet taken place.' This was indeed true; with Germany's Organization Todt workers stretched incredibly thinly all over the Reich's occupied territories, there had been no one to carry out this work. Moreover, those wearing naval uniform argued that littoral trade was too important to ignore; ships carrying chromium, aluminium and molybdenum from Norway were vital to Germany's war effort, for example.[2] Iron ore from nominally neutral Sweden, too, fed Hitler's industry with a crucial resource for modern warfare. In taking this standpoint, the Kriegsmarine were thinking on a broader strategic level – what were the resources needed to power the German military machine at large? The Army, however, were concentrating on the lower, tactical level of thought – how could a battle against an approaching amphibious force be won? Both were reasonable and justifiable arguments to make. The only sticking point was that inter-service rivalries between the Army and Kriegsmarine ran so deep that they were unlikely to reach a compromise on their own, and certainly neither would agree to back down. Nor was there a powerful overarching tri-service organization which could compel them to reach a decision, or even make one for them.

Another objection raised by the Kriegsmarine was a simple practical one. The Army's proposals would take operational control of many coastal guns away from the Kriegsmarine, and it was the Kriegsmarine which had the best knowledge of coastal matters and maritime operations. Coastal traffic, both military and civilian, was managed by the appropriate naval area commander anyway, so the Kriegsmarine argued that it made sense for coastal artillery to remain under naval control. The Army simply did not have the nautical nous to manage this, and 'the result would be confusion between friendly and enemy forces'. The Kriegsmarine's objections were partly aimed at protecting their 'patch', since the ground forces dominated Hitler's inner circle – at OKW, for example, there were about five times as many Army officials as there were from the Kriegsmarine.[3] Retaining every last shred of representation in high office, each possible opportunity to exert naval influence, was Raeder's utmost priority.

An important figure in this debate was Field Marshal Rundstedt. As head of all German forces in the West, his area of command would most likely be the target of the Allies' next large-scale amphibious strike, whenever and wherever that might occur. He brought the experience of Saint-Nazaire and Dieppe with him, so his word carried significant weight. Influenced partly by that recent experience, and partly no doubt by loyalty to his uniform, he came down on the Army's side. He agreed with the Army's position that no determined Allied thrust could be stopped before it reached the coast, and that the battle on land should necessarily take priority.[4] He wrote directly to Jodl's Operations Staff at OKW: 'After thorough examination and consulting many practitioners, as well as four months experience – especially those of Dieppe – OB West considers a profound organizational and technical change necessary.' Rundstedt suggested that a small but well-equipped Kriegsmarine-controlled coastal artillery force be kept for targeting ships. Keeping a relatively low number in exposed forward positions meant they could be protected by strong infantry support. The vast majority of batteries, however, would be placed safely inland under Army control in order to primarily engage the enemy on land. Rundstedt wished the question of coastal artillery to be cleared up before the winter construction programme began, so that his solution could be integrated into the building plans.[5]

At OKW, the Army put their ideas on paper and drafted a Führer order with the intention of gaining Hitler's signature. Its very first sentence was a frank statement of intent: 'The fundamentals of the organization, deployment and training of coastal artillery have not proved entirely successful, especially on the basis of the experiences of landings in Norway and France.' It laid down two tasks for coastal artillery: engaging land targets and engaging sea targets. These would be fulfilled separately by Army-controlled guns and Kriegsmarine-controlled guns respectively. No longer would ships at sea take priority as targets over infantry and vehicles that had already landed. The draft Führer order envisaged that each theatre commander – OB West in France's case – would agree with his naval counterpart which batteries were to be allocated to the Army, and which to the Kriegsmarine. If no agreement could be settled by mid-November, the matter would be sent upstairs to OKW's Operations Staff.[6] Alas, none of this would ever come to pass. Either because it was shown to Hitler and he rejected it, or (more likely) because the Army and Kriegsmarine could never come to an agreement, the Army's draft proposal never reached Hitler's desk. The matter was unceremoniously dropped for several months until early December, when the head of OKW's Operations Staff, effectively Wilhelm Keitel's deputy, Alfred Jodl, gathered the courage to raise it again at a daily Führer conference on 2 December. His efforts were fruitless, however, and Hitler merely confirmed the plan already in place: the battle at sea took priority over that on land, and all Army batteries situated inland which were suitable for sea gunnery were to be placed under naval control.[7] Hitler did agree, though, that coastal artillery should be split into anti-land and anti-ship batteries. Three days later, a circular telegram was issued which confirmed this. 'Based on the Führer's oral statements … the basic principles of Directive 40 will stay in force', the sailors of Raeder's Kriegsmarine were glad to read. 'Batteries suitable for engaging both targets at sea and an enemy ashore' were to be determined 'in joint agreement' between theatre and naval commanders. This implemented the Army's wish, yet it came at a price: 'the mission of combating targets at sea will have priority' was not what they wanted to read. The Army still hoped that at a later date the Führer's opinion could be swayed further in their favour. The circular telegram made mention of a 'detailed directive that is expected in the near future regarding the questions of utilization and command of coastal artillery'. But for the time being, the Army had to admit that the war on land had lost out. They would never realize their wish for another, more favourable Führer directive.[8] The Naval Staff's war diary, on the other hand, recorded a rather more cheerful reaction: 'This directive, which correctly takes into account the necessities [of the situation], is commensurate with the Führer's decision in response to the Army's proposal which was considerably less favourable to the Kriegsmarine.'[9]

Arguments between the services were not solely restricted to questions of high strategy and the organization of coastal defences; sometimes they could become downright petty. 571st Infantry Regiment of General Konrad Haase's 302nd Division, having borne the brunt of the Canadians' main frontal assault, had expected to reap the rewards of success in the battle's aftermath. Watches, trinkets and other paraphernalia looted from both dead and living were the expected spoils of war, but since Dieppe was an amphibious battle, there were also all manner of valuable objects floating about in the water. The considerable quantities of food and tobacco that the Canadians had brought with them were particularly prized. These captured luxuries belonged to them, the soldiers of 571st Regiment believed. Not so, according to the naval personnel stationed in Dieppe's harbour, who had other ideas. On the logic that all flotsam at sea was naval property, it was all happily fished out and distributed amongst the sailors. Wounded by this affront, the soldiers complained and, after a few weeks, the matter reached the ear of Albert Speer. At a conference on 7 September, Speer presented these claims to Hitler, who awarded 571st Infantry Regiment a special bounty in lieu of the war booty that they believed they deserved.[10] Yet this was not the end of the matter. In December, the case went before a military tribunal in Rouen overseen by Naval Commander, Channel Coast, Admiral Hermann von Fischel. This hearing eventually cleared Dieppe's naval servicemen of any wrongdoing, meaning that no further disciplinary action was taken.[11] The end of these military-legal proceedings at 1942's close put a neat seal on the Wehrmacht's Dieppe experience.

Chapter 20

Dieppe in Review

If Germany had collectively reflected on its experience at Dieppe, its reflections would surely have been positive. While the mass of Germany's military might was committed in the East, a great victory had been achieved in the West. It was a particularly meaningful victory for the men of 302nd Division, who had been at the rock bottom of the Wehrmacht's priority list yet had pulled off an astonishing success. The divisional emblem was changed from a generic crossed-swords image to a ship set within a large 'D', in recognition of the formation's performance at Dieppe.[1] In December, as the unit was pulled out of the line, re-equipped and upgraded to become a mobile infantry division for deployment in the East in 1943, they carried the nickname 'the Dieppe Division'. Major General Konrad Haase, their triumphant general, did not go with them, however. Although he had performed well at Dieppe, he was not considered suitable for a divisional combat command on the Eastern Front – he was overweight and suffered from heart problems. A personal review signed by Rundstedt judged Haase to be 'mentally fresh' and 'reliable', but noted that his 'physical capability does not suffice for more demanding endeavours'.[2] Consequently, Haase lost his divisional command and was placed in Hitler's reserve pool of inactive commanders. In his farewell address to 302nd Division he expressed his thanks to the men for their service during his two years in command: 'Working together, in this time we have mastered all tasks given to us. We look back on the day of Dieppe with pride, where the division stood the test.'[3] This was by no means the end of Haase's military career, though he was never again found suitable for promotion. After five months without a job, he worked as a staff officer in the Soviet Union, France and finally Italy. In April 1945 he was awarded the German Cross in Silver for his war service, and at the end of hostilities he was taken prisoner, then released in 1947.[4]

In its post-battle analysis, the Wehrmacht showed it had learned a great deal about coastal defence. From new bomber escort tactics to revamped communications procedures, their doctrine had been tested and modified. The British had even been kind enough to leave behind its brand-new Churchill tanks for the weapons engineering experts at the *Waffenamt* to test. Although Jubilee had exposed some weaknesses in how the Wehrmacht operated – or more accurately failed to operate – as a truly united tri-service force, this fact seemed insignificant. In the battle of words, Goebbels had surely brought off a notable propaganda coup. While the Allied newspapers and radio, especially those in Britain, had claimed victory or at least their own 'lessons learned', Hitler's Propaganda Ministry had responded in the simplest but most effective way; by merely describing the course of the battle and enumerating the Allied losses, with liberal use of images captured by war photographers, Goebbels had demonstrated that no objective observer could claim the Allies had come off successfully on 19 August. Every year, the Propaganda Ministry released a large picture book – *Grossdeutschland im Weltgeschehen* or 'Greater Germany in World Events' – which was packed full of photos taken by propaganda organizations. The events at Dieppe on 19 August featured prominently, as if a message to the Canadians intended to add insult to injury.

Proper consideration of how the Germans viewed the Dieppe raid reveals a fascinating picture, vastly different to the one previously given by historians. For too long, the literature on Dieppe has consisted of books and articles which exclude the German perspective, as if only the Allies were present on 19 August 1942. Ultimately, without two opposed armies, there is no battle. The first issue investigated in this work was the German state of readiness before the day in question. No document, statement or other piece of evidence proves directly or indirectly that the Germans knew the British and Canadians were coming specifically to Dieppe. In fact, multiple German reports explicitly stated in the battle's aftermath that there was no such intelligence, only a more general concern about possible landings somewhere in occupied Europe in mid- to late 1942. There were no large troop movements in the Dieppe region, nor an increased state of readiness beyond those regularly ordered as a result of wind, moon and tide conditions favourable to an invader. Indeed, there had been so many repeated warnings of an Allied attack that many soldiers disregarded them outright; this was a constant source of frustration to their officers. As in the story of the boy who cried wolf, a warning meant nothing if there had been several false alarms in the recent past. Hitler and his generals were supremely aware that, because of the savage fighting on the Eastern Front, Churchill might well increase the intensity of his raiding programme, or even attempt to create the so-called 'second front'; Stalin's demands for the latter had been made repeatedly and in public. Hitler issued a circular telegram in mid-July to warn against this exact possibility. Even before conducting an in-depth investigation of German sources, it was clear that there was no such thing as German foreknowledge, as some historians and veterans from both sides claimed after the event. As regards the former group, it was reckless of them to claim that the Germans had actionable intelligence that led to the raid's failure. For one thing, there exists no evidence to support that view. For another, such claims of German foreknowledge fuelled Canadian veterans' understandable anger and frustration over being sent into an unwinnable battle in which a thousand men died. They yearned to know the 'true' purpose behind their horrifying experiences, and historians writing books and articles or speaking on television programmes have given academic legitimacy to these heartfelt yet inaccurate views.

While the merits of the 'Allied lessons learned' question have been fervently debated by historians, with special reference to the later landings in Normandy on 6 June 1944, there has been no consideration of the German lessons learned. This book has considered that very question, and the verdict is clear: the Dieppe raid constituted as great a learning experience for the Germans as for the Allies, if not more so. The Luftwaffe learned much, for example, about the technical performance of its FW 190 as a multi-role aircraft during intensive operations. Moreover, the Germans – like their Anglo-Canadian adversaries – noted the benefits of forward air control and made immediate steps to introduce this as a means of controlling air combat on a tactical level. The Luftwaffe took a considerable amount from the air battle regarding close escort of bombers and the importance of their immediate maintenance after flying, even following night operations. The prevailing German conclusion after Operation Jubilee was that any Allied joint operation on a divisional scale would come with far greater air and naval fire support for the land troops. The absence of such support on 19 August was scarcely believable to German commanders, chiefly because this ran contrary to the fundamental principle of all fire in war: the enemy's ability to engage friendly forces should be eliminated or at least ruthlessly suppressed. What the Wehrmacht expected from Allied landing tactics did not radically change, but the Germans predicted that the Allies would alter some aspects of their technique. Although there was no attempt to disrupt German ground-based communications networks during the Dieppe raid, some German commanders were convinced that disrupting these connections would form a vital part of future Allied strategy. Therefore, the Army enhanced its protection of its communications networks from air attack by digging them in or covering them with concrete and stone. In addition, the Luftwaffe was acutely aware of the potential for counter-air attacks against its own airfields, despite the RAF's failure to conduct these as part of a wider and coherent local air superiority effort. Those on the German side of the Channel harboured no illusions as to the Allied capacity for change – they saw the raid as an aberration. They believed that they had to change too, and proved capable of shrewd and penetrating introspection. Although they had won the battle decisively, the Germans still found much to disapprove of on their own side, for example 10th Panzer Division's sluggish response to the morning alarm and orders to move. The Kriegsmarine's failure to keep commander-in-chief Erich Raeder abreast of developments was another point of censure.

In his seminal study of organizations, *The Nerves of Government*, the Czech political scientist Karl Deutsch memorably defined power as 'the ability to afford not to learn'.[5] The Wehrmacht in the West readily recognized that they did not enjoy power as Deutsch would later describe it – its senior officers knew that they could not afford to sit back and enjoy their victory. They had to learn. They were sure that the Allies would be back. Mountbatten's Combined Operations Headquarters had demonstrated the Allies' ability to land a divisional-sized force on a contested beach under even the most testing of battle conditions. That heavy armour could come ashore in the first wave was worrying to military men and civilians alike. Hitler, Rundstedt and the other generals firmly believed that the Allies would learn their own lessons. At a Führer conference at the Wolf's Lair in mid-December 1942, even while the titanic Battle of Stalingrad was being fought, former captain of the pocket battleship *Admiral Scheer* Vice Admiral Theodor Krancke voiced concerns about continued large- and small-scale raids against continental Europe in the coming year. To remind them of that threat, British radio continued to broadcast warnings to the French coastal population, urging them to leave their homes.[6] Just as Winston Churchill had told Britons after the fall of France that 'Hitler knows that he will have to break us in this island or lose the war', so did Hitler know that the Allies would have to break his armies in Continental Europe to win it. Hitler understood that the only way that the Allies were going to achieve this in the west was through a series of large-scale seaborne assaults. These would surely be cast in Operation Jubilee's mould and assuredly on an even larger scale. In December 1943, Hitler told his staff during a daily situation conference that 'if they attack in the West, then this attack will decide the war … If this attack is driven back, the whole affair will be over.'[7] In March 1944, he briefed his western commanders, giving them another stark message: 'The enemy's entire landing operation must under no circumstances be allowed to last longer than a matter of hours or, at the most, days, with the Dieppe attempt as a model.'[8] Given this state of mind, learning the lessons of Dieppe was imperative, and the Wehrmacht ultimately proved itself to be an organization capable of considered self-criticism.

In hindsight, any lessons the Germans might have learned at Dieppe may seem at first glance to have been worthless, because ultimately they lost the war. This is not how we should view historical events. In several amphibious landings in France and Italy, the Wehrmacht was comprehensively defeated. But this was not attributable to any lack of tactical insights gained at Dieppe in 1942. Rather, Germany's failure to defend the beaches at Salerno or in Normandy was down to wider strategic-level factors of resource allocation and industrial capacity. Had the Axis powers enjoyed industrial might resembling that of their adversaries, Hitler would have been able to give his generals a fighting chance against the various landings that followed Operation Jubilee. Armies around the world in their military academies and staff colleges invariably teach a version of the phrase, 'The enemy always has a vote in your plans'. Its meaning is simple: when planning and conducting military operations, one must always take into account what the enemy might do. He may well do something unexpected, and almost certainly will not do what one wishes. War is an interaction between two opposing sides, and events do not always play out as intended. As the great strategist Helmut von Moltke the Elder of Prussia and Wilhelmine Germany opined: 'No plan of operations extends with certainty beyond the first encounter with the enemy's main strength.' Or, in its simpler modern form, 'No plan survives first contact with the enemy'. Just as we can say, 'the enemy always has a vote' during the battle, we can also say that he has a vote afterwards. The Dieppe case proves this to be true. One can always expect the enemy to 'use their vote' to learn from their experiences, which will affect how battles are fought in the future. While the Allies used Operation Jubilee's failure as a learning experience for the future (a point argued forcefully by Mountbatten after the war), so did the Germans. English-speaking historians have debated time and again the merits of the view that Dieppe was an Allied learning experience, yet have not paused to consider that this may have been true of the Wehrmacht too.

While Hitler's military men were busy evaluating their battle experience, the propaganda battle was hectic. No sooner had the Allied fleet set course for home than Goebbels was crafting a media attack strategy from the Führer's headquarters in Vinnytsia. In the corridors of Berlin's Reich Press Ministry, Otto Dietrich oversaw the intimate details of a ruthless war of words. For several days, every one of his 'Confidential Information' press guidelines issued from the Propaganda Ministry offered a new line of attack. Radio, newspapers and newsreels sought to convince Germans at home that the Wehrmacht's 'Watch in the West' had stood the test thrust upon it; civilians and military personnel alike could now rest assured that they need not worry about the vaunted 'second front'. In other words, they could now focus all their efforts on supporting the decisive offensives in the East. An 'amateurish buffoon' like Prime Minister Winston Churchill, a mere lackey to his master Stalin, could never pose a serious threat to Germany's position in Continental Europe. Or so they thought. German journalists made these arguments with great rhetorical force, and the German domestic population generally responded well. Ordinary Germans viewing the war's events from afar wanted the West to be secure just as much as their Führer did. The SD secret state police noted as much in one of their reports, recording a confident mood amongst the civilian population, who surmised that any similar operation would not be launched against Continental Europe, but in Norway or the Iberian Peninsula instead.[9] Goebbels' propaganda campaign was given a helping hand by the Allies' forlorn efforts to portray the raid as a success. Mountbatten at COHQ released communiqués describing the operation as a learning experience, and journalists were directed to follow this line religiously. German papers pounced on these claims, publishing photo upon photo of Canadian bodies, tanks and landing craft strewn forlornly across the beaches. Moreover, Churchill later described Jubilee as a 'reconnaissance in force'. If either side won Dieppe's propaganda battle, it was Goebbels' Propaganda Ministry. German newsreels, for instance, were picked up even by neutral countries for their comparative accuracy and objectivity. Notably, Dieppe had a lasting legacy well beyond August 1942. When a 700-man raid on Axis-held Tobruk failed in September, the German press dubbed this a 'Second Dieppe' and a 'Dieppe on African soil'. Indeed, when Hitler gave his New Year's address on 1 January 1943, he made sure to mention the great success achieved in France the previous year, hoping that his words might inspire confidence in final victory.

In France itself, Goebbels ensured that the newspapers carried his message almost as fervently as the German media had. However, here the German experience of the battle was minimized, and French publications put more emphasis on the damage done on French soil – the Allies were not potential liberators; rather, they were crazed incompetents who cared nothing for the damage done to France. Furthermore, French papers presented the Dieppe battle as a British defeat much more than a German victory. Many French reporters completely omitted the word 'German' or 'Germany' from their stories. Doubtless, this was to spare French insecurities about the occupation. The Vichy puppet government, on the other hand, was not shy about its complicity with the occupiers. Marshal Philippe Pétain and Pierre Laval heartily congratulated the Germans for 'defending' French territory. At first glance, it is conceivable that this was an artful ploy to gain concessions from their occupiers, such as came in the form of ten million francs and prisoner releases for the *Dieppois*. This view seems misguided. The Vichy government's stance represented a sincere policy, and indeed represented a step deeper into wretched collaboration. Antipathy towards Britain made this course of action ever more likely. In particular, Pétain nurtured a definite hatred of anything Anglophone. Vichy propaganda was rabidly anti-English, using the myth of Joan of Arc amongst others as an inspiring example of France's historical struggle against the eternal enemy across the Channel.

Considered as a whole, Dieppe in August 1942 was a significant victory in military and political/propaganda terms. This truth notwithstanding, we should not delude ourselves by exaggerating its importance to Nazi

Germany's military and its domestic population. The victory was a welcome surprise, especially for Hitler, while the tough battles in the southern Soviet Union were taking place on a far grander scale than anything in the West or North Africa. Hitler believed, correctly, that the Eastern Front was the decisive theatre of war on land. If Stalin could be defeated, then there was nothing to fear from the Western Allies. In this sense, the Dieppe raid was a less-than-relevant sideshow in deciding who would win the war. A strategically insignificant victory like that achieved on 19 August was not going to boost the Germans' military fortunes significantly, nor would it do the opposite for their enemies. Although the men of 302nd Infantry Division were understandably proud of their achievement, far greater trials lay ahead of them.

We should see the German response to the Dieppe raid as a neat microcosm of the Wehrmacht's character in 1942, and one which spoke to many of its essential weaknesses. Many of the 'German' defenders in 302nd Infantry Division were not Germans at all, being instead Poles or Czechs, or men with some other decidedly non-Teutonic heritage. This was because the Wehrmacht was so overstretched that forced conscripts like these had to make up the numbers in low-priority theatres. For the same reason, much of 302nd Division's weaponry consisted of captured French or Czech models, or materiel of First World War vintage. Even then, there were critical shortages, especially in heavy weapons. Likewise, 813 Battery was in its exposed position at Varengeville, despite general consensus that its location was unsuitable, because moving it was not considered a high engineering priority. The Luftwaffe was greatly outnumbered, yet performed respectably. After the shooting had stopped, the Dieppe experience revealed the discord between the three services that made up the Wehrmacht. The Army and Kriegsmarine went at each other's throats over coastal artillery, each arguing that 19 August proved that they deserved control. This spat resulted in the Army drafting a replacement to Hitler's Directive 40, against the Kriegsmarine's furious objections. If it had gained Hitler's signature, this would have completely reversed the precedence given to engaging naval targets in German coastal defence doctrine (as Directive 40 had set out in March). However, despite much haggling and a personal appeal by Jodl to Hitler in December, the Führer refused to countenance any changes to his Directive. Inter-service tensions extended beyond the purely military realm. The Kriegsmarine fought a public relations campaign to tout its involvement in defeating the Allies at Dieppe – not necessarily to boost its own institutional self-confidence, but to increase its profile at the expense of the Army and Luftwaffe. The Wehrmacht's three services were not happy bedfellows. Importantly, one crucial aspect of the Wehrmacht's way of war was the power held by Hitler as overall commander-in-chief. After the raid, the Führer was so impressed by Brigadier Zeitzler's work with Rundstedt at OB West – justifiably or not – that he promoted the young officer to Lieutenant General and made him his chief of staff at Army headquarters. Obviously, this rapid rise came much to the chagrin of the Wehrmacht's officer corps. Zeitzler's rise signalled that rational military thought had begun to break down in favour of faith in National Socialist conviction and loyalist zeal.

Despite the Wehrmacht's obvious frailties, the Germans pulled off a remarkable victory. How was this possible? Firstly, it is important to note that they did not have any tactical genius or flair to thank for their triumph. None whatsoever was needed. Major General Haase followed the broadest and simplest tenets of military tactics – he pushed his reserves forward to where they were needed, but did not over-commit himself in case of an unexpected breakthrough. Instead, the Allies were to blame for their own defeat – not the individual soldiers, one should hasten to add, many of whom fought with distinct skill and bravery. General Curt Haase of Fifteenth Army noted in the raid's aftermath that 'the large number of English prisoners might create an impression that the fighting value of the deployed English and Canadian units should not be rated highly. This is not the case. The enemy ... fought well and with courage – so far as he was able to fight at all.'[10]

Rather, the plan as laid out by COHQ was far too reliant on surprise, to the point of recklessness. Accordingly, too little fire support was given, a point that all German generals made in their reports. All military plans benefit from surprising the enemy, but Operation Jubilee was totally dependent on it for success. Without surprise, there could be no success; so it turned out to be, and 2nd Canadian Division and 3 Commando paid the price. Some elements of the Jubilee force did achieve surprise. Orange beach, where 4 Commando landed, was not fired upon at all, and the South Saskatchewan Regiment initially made landfall at Green at Pourville without incident, although they were taken under fire shortly after landing. The closer one got to the convoy battle north-east of Dieppe, the more prepared the defenders were. Those few men from 3 Commando who landed at Yellow beach on the far eastern flank came across stiff resistance, yet somehow managed to distract the enemy and withdraw without loss. The Royal Regiment of Canada at Blue beach was annihilated in front of Puys' barbed wire and narrow, booby-trapped gorges. The main Red and White beach was almost as terrible a sight for Canadian eyes. All this happened despite the fact that until very late, most Germans on land believed that the convoy engagement was just another naval skirmish between fast boats and coastal merchantmen. What is more, the widespread communications failure in General Haase's area of responsibility meant that messages could not travel back and forth between units. Undoubtedly, this contributed to 302nd Division's sluggishness in response. Nevertheless, most individual unit commanders took it upon themselves to make ready for battle when they heard the sounds of naval or small-arms gunfire, regardless of whether or not they had received specific orders from higher headquarters. Even in low-quality units like 302nd Division, there was evidently some personal initiative on display. As a partial solution to the communications problems, officers were strongly encouraged to use radio rather than fragile wired telephone lines.

A fatal flaw in the plan for Operation Jubilee was the utterly inadequate fire support for the men on land. The Royal Navy did not dare put battleships in the Channel, while the Royal Air Force's Bomber Command refused to divert heavy bombers from the strategic campaign over Germany. This last omission seemed obviously wrong to the Germans. From Haase at 302nd Infantry Division to Rundstedt in Paris, German commanders justifiably questioned why an operation on Jubilee's scale was launched without proper consideration for neutralizing German defences either by air or sea. Overall, the German defence system was not so strong that it could not be overcome with an adequately resourced and well-considered plan. In both manpower and material terms, the defenders could easily have been found wanting. But sadly for 2nd Canadian Division, the Royal Marines and Commandos, Operation Jubilee was anything but adequately resourced and well-considered.

This work should close with a comment on any practical benefit that the Germans gained from their lessons learned at Dieppe, with reference to the later large-scale amphibious assaults against Sicily, mainland Italy and Normandy. In essence, though the Dieppe raid was a useful learning experience on a small-scale tactical level, the Germans were unable to exploit these lessons due to broader, strategic-level concerns. If they had possessed a functioning joint-services command system and been blessed with the materiel abundance enjoyed by the Western Allies, the lessons gained at Dieppe would surely have made a far greater impact on the future conduct of German coastal defence during the Second World War. One can certainly conclude that, at least on a tactical level, the Germans learned as much as if not more than the Allies. In every aspect of coastal defence, from fighter escort tactics to command and control of artillery, or from anti-tank strategies to communications security, the Wehrmacht profited immensely from their victory at Dieppe on 19 August 1942. The crucial point was, however, that the German war effort could not afford to expend the resources and manpower needed to exploit these new ideas. Strategically, Hitler was such a deficient war leader that he willingly brought the combined forces of the United States, the Soviet Union, Britain and its Empire together against him, deluded by the belief that he could win a mammoth battle for world dominance. In short, the same ultra-nationalist ideology which brought Hitler to power in 1933 ultimately deprived him of the clear and rational thought necessary to win the Second World War.

Engaging in counterfactual history is fraught with dangers, but it is sufficient to note one inescapable fact: the Allies were fortunate that the Axis powers were unable to exploit the lessons of Dieppe with the same means that they themselves possessed. The air power picture after 1942 illustrates this point particularly well. With obligations in the skies all over occupied Europe, only a paltry Luftwaffe force could come together to face Allied amphibious landings after 1942. When the Allies invaded Sicily, Field Marshal Wolfram von Richthofen commanding Air Fleet 2 recognized that, in the face of overwhelming Allied air strength, competing for air superiority as practised at Dieppe would be counterproductive. Instead, he concentrated his attacks on the Allied fleet and ordered his pilots to avoid Allied fighters. Even then, the successes against shipping – 80,000 tons of merchant shipping and two small warships sunk – came early in the campaign while the Allies did not possess airfields on Sicily. When this position changed, Allied fighter cover was total and precluded daylight Axis operations. A year later, on 6 June 1944 (D-Day), the Allied Expeditionary Air Force flew more than 14,000 sorties, while the Luftwaffe managed fewer than a hundred. German air power never posed a serious threat to Overlord – German aircraft flew one tenth the number of Allied sorties from 6 June until the month's end.[11] In the face of such overwhelming air supremacy, the lessons of Dieppe were not applicable two years later. The utility of mobile units is a striking example of this change. At Dieppe, the Germans found that mobile reserves were extremely helpful to coastal defence. 302nd Infantry Division was a poor-quality 'static' division with few mobile assets, but the little mobile capability that it did possess was extremely useful in repelling the Jubilee landings. Thus, mobility was held to be the key counter to the improved landing operations that the Germans universally believed would come at some point later in the war. To give one example, LXXXI Corps reported immediately after Dieppe:

> If the British attack us again on the same scale, or on a broader front, it is to be expected that they will attempt to penetrate weak spots and try to encircle the harbours. They are not likely to repeat a massed frontal attack against a strongly fortified area, as in the Dieppe attack of August 19, 1942. It is therefore most important that we have mobile reserves ready for a counter-attack. Those mobile reserves must be equipped with many motorised anti-tank weapons.[12]

Analyses such as these were based on one central premise – that the Luftwaffe's presence would be strong enough to prevent Allied close air support from destroying motorized and armoured German formations, which would be incredibly vulnerable to air attack while manoeuvring over open ground. At Dieppe this premise held true. In 1943 and 1944, though, total Allied air supremacy precluded outright any defensive plan relying on large mobile land reserves, rendering the 'lesson' of mobility useless. In any case, the Wehrmacht would never possess the means needed to create such a resource-intensive force.

This was true for all three domains – on land, at sea and in the air, the battle space in amphibious landings later in the war bore little resemblance to that of 19 August 1942. The distinct material imbalance rendered null and void any advantage in tactics the Germans might have accrued via the Dieppe experience, not to mention in the assaults on Sicily and mainland Italy. To have adequately developed Dieppe's lessons into a viable concept, and sufficiently supplied that new mode of defence with men and materiel, Hitler would have required an inordinately greater industrial and strategic resource base.

Large-scale amphibious assaults, both in attack and defence, require a close working relationship between land, air and naval forces, and the Allies achieved this to great effect. However, the Wehrmacht never rid itself of the inter-service rivalries epitomized by the debate over controlling coastal artillery in 1942. In October 1943, for instance, Fifteenth Army commander Hans von Salmuth referred to Kriegsmarine officers as 'prima donnas'.[13] Not to be outdone, a year later Admiral Dönitz (then Kriegsmarine commander-in-chief) argued in a paper presented to Jodl and Hitler that the Army had an 'instinctive dislike' of water: 'The infantry soldier trained on land ... dislikes having the water in front of his positions and wants to get away from the coast.' This was simply pettiness. He said this months after Operation Overlord, or 'The Invasion' as the Germans called it, had taken place. Continuing to argue about coastal control beyond this point was fruitless, as it was clear that there would be no further large-scale seaborne landings in Europe.[14] It can only be explained by the fact that the Wehrmacht's rivalries and personal animosities were inherent in its way of war. It is no wonder, then, that one historical study has concluded forcefully that the three services 'opposed each other almost as much as they opposed the idea of a united command structure imposing its will upon them from above. Even when we remove Hitler from these considerations, the fact remains that [jointery] was foreign to the German tradition and could not have existed in the 1930s and 1940s.'[15] For all these reasons, the three services either could not, or did not want to, work together in a harmonious partnership to collectively improve the way in which the Wehrmacht conducted coastal defence operations. As a consequence, they were never able to implement the lessons from their Dieppe experiences with one voice. Even after Dieppe had proved the need for unified command, OB West never gained overall control of Army, Luftwaffe and Kriegsmarine forces. For the rest of hostilities, these reported solely to their own individual service commanders.

Compounding these structural issues were personal ones. When the Allies launched Operation Overlord, Field Marshal Rundstedt still held his OB West command – at first glance, a useful continuity. However, Field Marshal Erwin Rommel, newly arrived in France as commander of all land forces along the Channel coast, consistently went over Rundstedt's head to Hitler when the former did not give him what he wanted. War had aged Rundstedt, and by 1944 he was consuming alcohol and nicotine in prodigious quantities. Sperrle, still commanding Air Fleet 3, was lethargic and disillusioned and had no appetite to fix the structural problems in the West.[16] At the fighting front, many miles from the generals' headquarters, the Wehrmacht became dependent on unreliable forced foreign conscripts as German manpower became ever scarcer. Private Aloysius Damski was a 21-year-old Pole forcibly recruited into the Wehrmacht in early 1943. Assigned to the Channel coast, and asked by his commanding lieutenant how German he felt, the young Pole responded bluntly, 'I will tell you the truth. I was born in Poland, I was educated in Poland, both my parents are Polish and still live in Poland. How can I feel anything but Polish?'[17] It is easy to understand the unwillingness of Damski and other involuntary conscripts to risk their lives for the Nazis.

We should not forget either that Dieppe was only the first divisional-scale tri-service amphibious assault. In Europe and the Pacific, both the Allies and the Axis powers later fought this kind of engagement on multiple occasions and were able to build a base of knowledge and experience over time. Dieppe was not an isolated incident, and so we should not overestimate its importance to either side in the seaborne-landing 'learning curve'. In the final analysis, with the human and materiel inadequacies of the western defences, especially after 1942, it was hardly likely that the Wehrmacht could beat back any well-planned and well-executed seaborne landing, however much had been learned from Jubilee or any other operation of its kind.

Ever since that day in August 1942, the German participation in the Dieppe story has evaded the inquisitive eyes of historians. This book has shone a light on places where our knowledge has been murky at best. While the Allied point of view has been thoroughly trawled and investigated, the same cannot be said for the German. Historical imbalance of this kind is dangerous. An overwhelming focus on the Anglo-Canadian perspective has led us to the false conclusion that this is the only viewpoint that matters. Furthermore, the dearth of German sources in the literature on Dieppe has created the assumption that only the Allies enjoyed any kind of agency in learning from the day's fighting. This is self-evidently wrong – any enemy can and will adapt, and this was certainly true of the Wehrmacht. If we use an inadequate and erroneous record of military events to educate students of military history, be they servicemen and women or civilians, we may well end up misleading them. In the Dieppe case, even after such a complete victory, the Wehrmacht did not stand still in evaluating its own performance, as historians seem to have simply presumed for more than seventy years. It is a great disservice to military history that the German side of Dieppe has been deprived of the proper study it deserves. No historical narrative should be one-sided. Crucially, the Germans also had a voice in how Dieppe was used as a learning experience for the future. More fundamentally, one should always remember that there are two sides to any confrontation – to disregard this idea is reckless in the extreme. The enemy always has a vote.

Notes

This book's sources are a scattered collection of published and unpublished accounts, archival material, secondary literature, memoirs and manuscripts. Most of these were accessed in person, but some were digital copies of published works or digitized archive material. Many surviving German military documents were captured by the Western Allies at the war's end and microfilmed in Britain and the US. They were later returned to West Germany. Consequently, multiple examples of some of the documents cited in this book exist – I have referenced the copy that I have accessed. References to the Canadian AHQ and CMHQ reports' appendices are to the page within the relevant appendix. Where a single source is cited consecutively, these citations are collected together in one reference.

To reduce the bulk of these notes, abbreviations and shortened alternative have been used to refer to archives, publishers and titles of collected sources whose material has been regularly cited:

ADAP – Akten zur deutschen auswärtigen Politik 1918 –1945 (Imprimerie nationale, 1950–1995)
Air Fleet 3 report – 'British Large–Scale Landing Operation at Dieppe', 28 August – 8 September 1942, in (Royal Air Force) Air Historical Branch Translation VII/109
AHQ – (Canadian) Army Headquarters report
BArch – Bundesarchiv (German Federal Archives)
Bewährung collection– *Dieppe: Die Bewährung des Küstenwestwalles*, ed. by Hans Wamper (E. S. Mittler & Sohn, 1943)
CMHQ – Canadian Military Headquarters report
EzG – Editionen zur Geschichte archive, Cologne
Führer Naval Conferences – Fuehrer Conferences on Matters Dealing with the German Navy, 1942, ed. by the Office of National Intelligence (US Navy Department, 1947).
Führer Directives – Fuehrer Directives and other Top-Level Directives of the German Armed Forces, ed. by ONI (US Navy Department, 1948)
IWM – Imperial War Museum, London
OKW War Diary – Kriegstagebuch des OKW 1942, Teilband 2, ed. by Andreas Hilgruber (Bernard & Graefe, 1963)
SD Public Opinion Reports – Meldungen aus dem Reich Band 11, ed. by Heinz Boberach (Pawlak, 1984)
MPT – Museumsstiftung Post und Telekommunikation archive, Berlin
NARA – (US) National Archives and Records Administration
Goebbels Diaries– Die Tagebücher von Joseph Goebbels: Teil II Diktate 1941–1945, Band 5, ed. by Elke Fröhlich and Angela Stüber (K. G. Saur, 1995)

TNA – The National Archives of the United Kingdom, Kew
German Naval Staff War Diary – War Diary, German Naval Staff Operations Division: Part A (US Navy Department, 1948)

Introduction
1. Brian Loring Villa, *Unauthorized Action: Mountbatten and the Dieppe Raid*, 2nd edn (Oxford University Press, 1994), p. 1.
2. Winston Churchill, *The Second World War Volume IV: The Hinge of Fate* (Cassell, 1951), p. 459.
3. Dennis Richards and Hilary St George Saunders, *The Royal Air Force 1939–1945 Volume II: The Fight Avails* (HMSO, 1954), p. 145.
4. Ken Ford, *Dieppe 1942: Prelude to D-Day* (Osprey, 2004), p. 92.
5. Ronald Atkin, *Dieppe 1942: The Jubilee Disaster* (Macmillan, 1980), inset.
6. Hugh G. Henry, *Dieppe Through the Lens of the German War Photographer* (Battle of Britain, 1993), p. 63.
7. Canadian Broadcasting Corporation broadcast, 14 October 1966.
8. Tim Saunders, *The Dieppe Raid: 2nd Canadian Division* (Pen & Sword, 2005), ch. 9.
9. George Metcalf Archival Collection (Canadian War Museum), 19800244–006, Emil Kilgast to John Mellor, 18.5.1977.
10. Reinhard Stumpf, 'Was ist Militärgeschichte?', <https://mhak.de/?page_id=138>.

Part I: The Raid in its German Context

Chapter 1: 1942 – War in West and East
1. Stalin to Churchill, 3 September 1941, quoted in Villa, *Unauthorized Action*, p. 70.
2. Quoted in Villa, *Unauthorized Action*, p. 172.
3. Charles Messenger, *The Last Prussian: A Biography of Field Marshal Gerd von Rundstedt* (Pen & Sword Military, 2012), pp. 1–2, ch. 9.
4. B. H. Liddell Hart, *The Other Side of the Hill: Germany's Generals, Their Rise and Fall, with Their Own Account of Military Events 1939–1945* (Cassell,1948), pp. 79, 243.
5. Richard Brett-Smith, *Hitler's Generals* (Presidio, 1977), p. 41.
6. Liddell Hart, *Other Side of the Hill*, pp. 237–8.
7. Günther Blumentritt, *Von Rundstedt: The Soldier and the Man*, trans. by Cuthbert Reavely (Odhams, 1952), p. 41.
8. US Army Foreign Military Study B-672, part 16.
9. Führer Directive 40, in *Hitler's War Directives, 1939–1945*, ed. by Hugh Trevor-Roper (Pan, 1966), p. 171.
10. *German Naval Staff War Diary*, vol. 34, pp. 106–7.
11. BArch, RM 6/76.
12. Führer Naval Conferences, pp. 48, 52.
13. BArch, RH 2/544

Chapter 2: The Dieppe Division: 302nd Infantry Division
1. MPT, Item 3.2002.0211, Albring to Eugen Altrogge.
2. MPT, Item 3.2013.2829, Oehus to family.
3. Atkin, *Dieppe 1942*, p. 60.

4. BArch, PERS 6/595.
5. US Army Foreign Military Study B-596, p. 10.
6. BArch, RH 26–302/16.
7. Canadian Broadcasting Corporation broadcast, 17 August 1967.
8. NARA, Microfilm T315 R2018.
9. NARA, Microfilm T315 R2019.

Chapter 3: Anticipation
1. BArch, ZSG 102/52+53, Summary of address by Otto Dietrich to journalists.
2. Quoted in Michael Burleigh, *The Third Reich: A New History* (Pan, 2001), p. 209.
3. BArch, ZSG 109/34.
4. Horst Boog and others, *Germany and the Second World War, Volume VII: The Global War*, trans. by Ewald Osers and others (Oxford University Press, 2001), pp. 958–62.
5. Führer order sent by telegram, in *Führer Directives*, vol. 2, p. 34.
6. *German Naval Staff War Diary*, vol. 32, p. 91.
7. NARA, Microfilm T321 R173.
8. 302nd ID divisional order 74, quoted in AHQ report 36, p. 24.
9. *New York Times*, 9 June 1942, p. 1.
10. BArch, RM 6/76.
11. *German Naval Staff War Diary*, vol. 35, pp. 145, 197.
12. NARA, Microfilm T315 R2019.
13. BArch, RH 2/544.
14. TNA, DEFE 2/324.
15. NARA, Microfilm T78 R317.
16. Response to Directive 40, in *Führer Directives*, vol. 2, p. 15
17. BArch, RH 2/3275.
18. Steiger, AHQ report 36, p. 11.
19. Air Ministry, *The Rise and Fall of the German Air Force (1933 to 1945)* (Air Ministry, 1947), pp. 412–13.
20. Erich Raeder, *My Life*, trans. by Henry W. Drexel (United States Naval Institute, 1969), p. 246.
21. Gordon A. Harrison, *Cross–Channel Attack* (USGPO, 1951; 1993 reprint), p. 135.
22. Raeder report to Hitler, 16 March 1942, *Führer Naval Conferences*, pp. 37–8.
23. BArch, NS 15/28.
24. Eric Brown, *Wings on my Sleeve* (Phoenix, 2007), p. 59.

Chapter 4: A New Siegfried Line?: The Myth of the Wehrmacht's 'Steely Rear'
1. Hitler to Mussolini, *ADAP*, vol. E.3, pp. 265–6.
2. *ADAP*, vol. E.3, p. 128.
3. Quoted in Martin Gilbert, *Winston S. Churchill Volume VII: Road to Victory 1941–1945* (Houghton Mifflin, 1986), pp. 176–82.
4. BArch, ZSG 109/36.
5. IWM Sound Archive, Hans Detlef Teske interview, rolls 1–2. Sadly for Teske, when he returned to Brécy many years after the war, his beloved little café had closed.
6. NARA, Microfilm T78 R317.
7. IWM Sound Archive, Hans-Paul Liebschner interview, roll 4.

8. BArch, RM 7/43, Naval Staff War Diary Part A, vol. 38, entry for 31 October 1942.
9. Canadian Broadcasting Corporation broadcast, 17 August 1967.

Chapter 5: Facing Up Across the Channel
1. Appendix C to 'Report by the Air Force Commander', in Trafford Leigh-Mallory, 'Air Operations at Dieppe: An After-Action Report', *Canadian Military History*, 12:4, p. 60.
2. Thorsten Heber, 'Der Atlantikwall 1940 – 1945: Die Befestigung der Küsten West- und Nordeuropas im Spannungsfeld nationalsozialistischer Kriegführung und Ideologie' (Doctoral thesis, Heinrich-Heine-Universität Düsseldorf, 2003), p. 241.
3. Steiger, AHQ report 36, pp. 11, 17.
4. Hugh G. Henry, 'The Planning, Intelligence, Execution and Aftermath of the Dieppe Raid, 19.8.42' (Doctoral thesis, University of Cambridge, 1996), p. 262.
5. *Rückblick auf die Geschichte der 302. Infanterie-Division*, ed. by Emil Kilgast (Self-published, 1976), p. 26.
6. TNA, DEFE 2/330.
7. Hitler to Mussolini, *ADAP*, vol. E.3, p. 266.
8. Herbert Schröder interview, United States Holocaust Museum, 1999.A.0310.14, part 1.
9. 'British Large-Scale Landing Operation at Dieppe', AHBT VII/109, p. 3.
10. Alfred Price, *The Luftwaffe Data Book* (Greenhill, 1997), pp. 62–4.

Chapter 6: Eve of Battle – 18 August
1. James Leasor, *Green Beach* (William Morrow, 1975), p. 146.
2. 'Report on the British Attack on Both Sides of Dieppe', in Appendix B to C. P. Stacey, AHQ report 10, p. 53.
3. TNA, DEFE 2/324.
4. Donald Caldwell, *JG 26 Luftwaffe Fighter Wing War Diary Volume One: 1939–42* (Stackpole. 2012), p. 269.
5. *Rückblick*, pp. 32–4.
6. Georges Guibon, *Vers la libération: A Dieppe le 19 août, 1942* (1945), p. 2.
7. TNA, DEFE 2/330.

Part II: 19 August, Day of Decision

Chapter 7: Confusion: 0430–0700 hrs
1. NARA, Microfilm T1022 R2364.
2. BArch, RM 7/1760.
3. BArch, RM 7/1757.
4. John P. Campbell, *Dieppe Revisited: A Documentary Investigation* (Frank Cass, 1993), pp. 141–2.
5. Henry, 'Planning, Intelligence, Execution and Aftermath', p. 192.
6. NARA, Microfilm T1022 R1710.
7. *Rückblick*, p. 26.
8. *Bewährung* collection, p. 31.
9. BArch, RM 7/1760.
10. TNA, DEFE 3/188, UJ 1411 signal.

11. BArch, RM 7/96.
12. TNA, DEFE 2/324.
13. Brian T. Begbie, 'Naval Gunfire Support for the Dieppe Raid', Master's thesis (University of Ottawa, 1999), pp. 57–61.
14. Capt G. A. Browne quoted in C. P. Stacey, *Official History of the Canadian Army in the Second World War Volume I: Six Years of War* (Queen's Printer, 1955), p. 365.
15. NARA, Microfilm T1022 R2364.
16. 'Artillery Lessons from the British Attack', in Appendix C to AHQ report 10, p. 3.
17. Terence Robinson, *The Shame and the Glory: Dieppe* (McClelland & Stewart, 1962), p. 241.
18. BArch, RM 7/1757.
19. *Rückblick*, pp. 34–6.
20. L'Association Jubilee Dieppe, Madame Mallet interview.
21. Stacey, *Official History*, p. 369.
22. J. R. Robinson, 'Radar Intelligence and the Dieppe Raid', *Canadian Defence Quarterly*, 20:5, pp. 39–40.
23. *Alpenländische Rundschau*, 29 August 1942, p. 2.
24. TNA, AIR 16/1044.
25. *Bewährung* collection, pp. 31–2.
26. *Alpenländische Rundschau*, 29 August 1942, p. 2.
27. L'Association Jubilee Dieppe, Georges Dauzou testimony.
28. 'Battle Report of the Commander-in-Chief West', in Appendix A to AHQ report 10, p. 4.
29. TNA, DEFE 2/324, Lt Kaltcis to Lt Wessel.
30. US Army Foreign Military Study P-038, pp. 49–51.
31. IWM, Item LBY K. 03/254.
32. 'Combat Report and Experiences Gained', in Appendix B to C. P. Stacey, CMHQ report 116, p. 15.

Chapter 8: Action and Reaction: 0700–1000 hrs

1. L'Association Jubilee Dieppe, Jacques – André Lambert testimony.
2. 'Report on the British Attack', AHQ report 10, pp. 24–25.
3. LXXXI Corps war diary, quoted in AHQ report 10, p. 17.
4. 'Report by Military Force Commander', Annex 6 to the Combined Report on the Dieppe Raid, p. 143.
5. Guibon, *Vers la libération*, p. 5.
6. W. J. A. Wood, 'Combat Over Dieppe: Victory or Defeat?', *Royal Air Force Yearbook* (1977), p. 44.
7. *Bewährung* collection, p. 42.
8. NARA, Microfilm T1022 R2364.
9. Begbie, 'Naval Gunfire', pp. 74–5.
10. NARA, Microfilm T1022 R2364.
11. Atkin, *Dieppe 1942*, p. 178.
12. Allen Mawer, *Diary of a Spitfire Pilot: Over the English Channel and Over Darwin* (Rosenberg, 2011), p. 112.
13. 'Combat Report', CMHQ report 116, p. 13.
14. TNA, DEFE 2/328.
15. 'Report on the British Attack', AHQ report 10, p. 16.

Chapter 9: Cruel Attrition: 1000–1230 hrs
1. NARA, Microfilm T312 R504.
2. 'Battle Report', AHQ report 10, pp. 7, 17.
3. *Rückblick*, pp. 38–39.
4. Norman Franks, *The Greatest Air Battle: Dieppe, 19th August, 1942* (Grub Street, 1997), p. 100.
5. *Bewährung* collection, p. 37.
6. Caldwell, *JG 26*, p. 273.
7. 'Battle Report', AHQ report 10, p. 8.
8. EzG, Anton Roos to his wife Elizabeth, c. a. end of Aug 1942.
9. 'Battle Report', AHQ report 10, p. 9.
10. *Bewährung* collection, pp. 23–4.
11. NARA, Microfilm T1022 R2364.
12. 'Artillery Lessons', AHQ report 10, p. 4.
13. *Bewährung* collection, p. 32.
14. 'Report on the British Attack', AHQ report 10, p. 20.
15. Franz W. Seidler and Dieter Zeigert, *Hitler's Secret Headquarters: The Führer's Wartime Bases*, trans. by Geoffrey Brooks (Greenhill, 2004), pp. 105, 114.
16. *TJG*, pp. 348–9.
17. US Army Foreign Military Study C-065a, p. 23.
18. 'Battle Report', AHQ report 10, pp. 9–10.
19. 'Combat Report', CMHQ report 116, p. 16.
20. *ADAP*, vol. E.3, p. 347.
21. BArch, RM 7/1757.
22. L'Association Jubilee Dieppe, Georges Dauzou interview.
23. BArch, RM 7/96.
24. *Goebbels Diaries*, p. 349.
25. BArch, RM 7/1757.
26. 'Battle Report', AHQ report 10, p. 15.
27. Jean-Louis Steinberg interview, <https://entretiens.ina.fr/memoires-de-la-shoah/Steinberg/jean-louis-steinberg>.
28. *Daily Express*, 20 August 1942, p. 4.
29. 'Battle Report', AHQ report 10, p. 10.
30. *Rückblick*, pp. 39–40.
31. Guibon, *Vers la libération*, p. 7.
32. Ross Wayne Mahoney, 'The Royal Air Force, Combined Operations Doctrine and the Raid on Dieppe, 19.8.42' (Master's thesis, University of Birmingham, 2009), pp. 115 and chart 3.4.
33. Air Fleet 3 report, pp. 5–6, 10.
34. *Bewährung* collection, pp. 33–4.

Chapter 10: Pursuit: 1230–1400 hrs
1. 'Battle Report', AHQ report 10, p. 6.
2. *Bewährung* collection, p. 26.
3. British Library Sound Archive, Item 1CD0363659.
4. 'Battle Report', AHQ report 10, p. 11.
5. *Rückblick*, pp. 40–1.

  6. J. Hughes-Hallett, despatch to Commander-in-Chief Portsmouth, in 'The Dieppe Raid', *London Gazette*, 12 August 1947, p. 3827.
  7. *Bewährung* collection, p. 60.
  8. RHLI testimony archive, Jack Kimberly interview, <http://www.rhli.ca/archives/dieppe/dieppekimberly.html>.
  9. BArch, RL 20/167.
 10. British Library Sound Archive, Item 1CD0363659.
 11. Mahoney claims in his work that this bomb came from a Do 217. Donald Caldwell, however, seems to have primary source evidence that JG 26's FW 190s delivered them, and it is this account that has been used: Caldwell, *JG 26*, p. 274.
 12. Mawer, *Diary of a Spitfire Pilot*, p. 112.
 13. *Rückblick*, p. 41.
 14. Lt Otto Stammberger quoted in Caldwell, *JG 26*, p. 275.
 15. John Mellor, '"Tat der Menschlichkeit" bei Dieppe', trans. by Marianne Kilgast, *Alte Kameraden*, January 1978, pp. 24–5.
 16. *Bewährung* collection, p. 40.
 17. British Library Sound Archive, Item 1CD0363659.

Part III: After the Battle

Chapter 11: An Ignominious Defeat
  1. 'Report on the British Attack', AHQ report 10, p. 46.
  2. NARA, Microfilm T315 R2019.
  3. Robinson, *Shame and the Glory*, p. 383.
  4. *Bewährung* collection, pp. 57–8.
  5. A. Robert Prouse, *Ticket to Hell via Dieppe: From a Prisoner's Wartime Log 1942–1945* (Webb & Bower, 1982), pp. 23–4.
  6. 'Battle Report', AHQ report 10, p. 14.
  7. Leon Goldensohn, *The Nuremberg Interviews: Conversations with the Defendants and Witnesses*, ed. by Robert Gellately (Pimlico, 2007), p. 114.
  8. *Goebbels Diaries*, pp. 352–4.
  9. BArch, RL 20/105.
 10. BArch, RM 7/1757.
 11. *Goebbels Diaries*, pp. 366–7.
 12. *Die Wehrmachtberichte 1939–1945: Band 2* (Gesellschaft für Literatur und Bildung, 1989), pp. 254–5.
 13. *Goebbels Diaries*, p. 373.
 14. *Rückblick*, pp. 29–30.
 15. 'Battle Report', AHQ report 10, p. 17.
 16. NARA, Microfilm T1022 R2364.
 17. NARA, Microfilm T312 R504.
 18. 'Battle Report', AHQ report 10, pp. 16–17.
 19. BArch, ZSG 102/39.
 20. Reuters report quoted in *The Times*, 20 August 1942, p. 4.
 21. *Daily Express*, 20 August 1942, p. 4.
 22. IWM, W.T.J. Beardmore papers.
 23. Robert Waddy, 'Horror Beyond Dieppe', *Legion* magazine, 1 September 2002.

Chapter 12: 'A Picture Like Dunkirk': The Day After
1. L'Association Jubilee Dieppe, Philippe Plantrou testimony.
2. Prouse, *Ticket to Hell*, pp. 24–5.
3. NARA, Microfilm T315 R2018.
4. 'Battle Report', AHQ report 10, pp. 18–19.
5. Schmidt's report quoted in David Irving, *Hitler's War and the War Path* (Focal Point, 2001), p. 510.
6. Paul Schmidt, *Hitler's Interpreter* (Fonthill, 2016), pp. 267–9.
7. NARA, Microfilm T315 R2019.
8. Hans J. Peterson, 'The Dieppe Raid in Contemporary German View', *American Review of Canadian Studies*, 13:1, note 34.
9. TNA, DEFE 2/324.
10. Guibon, *Vers la libération*, p. 18.
11. Quoted in Walter Warlimont, *Inside Hitler's Headquarters 1939–45*, trans. by R. H. Barry (Presidio, 1990), pp. 251–2, 259.
12. Wilhelm Keitel, *The Memoirs of Field Marshal Wilhelm Keitel, Chief of the German High Command 1938–1945*, ed. by Walter Görlitz, transl. by David Irving (Cooper Square, 2000), p. 184
13. Halder, *War Journal*, p. 397.
14. Quoted in Geoffrey P. Megargee, *Inside Hitler's High Command* (University Press of Kansas, 2000), pp. 183–84.
15. US Army Foreign Military Study B–466, p. 7.
16. Warlimont, *Inside Hitler's Headquarters 1939–45*, p. 259.
17. *SD Public Opinion Reports*, p. 4121.
18. *Meldungen aus Norwegen 1940–1945: Die geheimen Lageberichte des Befehlshabers der Sicherheitspolizei und des SD in Norwegen*, ed. by Stein Ugelvik Larsen, Beatrice Sandberg and Volker Dahm (De Gruyter, 2012), pp. 803–4.
19. NARA, Microfilm T312 R504.
20. Air Fleet 3 report, pp. 2–3.
21. *Wehrmachtberichte 1939–1945*, pp. 255–6.
22. BArch, ZSG 109/36.
23. BArch, ZSG 102/39.

Chapter 13: The Ignoble Trudge into Captivity
1. TNA, DEFE 2/330.
2. BArch, R 59/412.
3. Charles G. Roland, 'On the Beach and in the Bag: The Fate of Dieppe Casualties Left Behind', *Canadian Military History*, 9:4, pp. 16–17.
4. TNA, DEFE 2/324.
5. Prouse, *Ticket to Hell*, pp. 25–6, 35.

Chapter 14: 'Your Success is Our Success': The Occupier and the Occupied
1. BArch, ZSG 102/39.
2. Telegram from Ambassador Abetz to Foreign Office, *ADAP*, vol. E.3, p. 373. During his post-war treason trial, Pétain denied that this letter was authentic, yet all historical evidence indicates otherwise. See Richard Griffiths, *Marshal Pétain* (Constable, 1970), p. 306.
3. NARA, Microfilm T315 R570.

  4. *ADAP*, vol. E.3, p. 348.
  5. Bormann to Lammers, in *Akten der Reichskanzlei, Regierung Hitler 1933–1945: Band IX 1942*, ed. by Michael Hollmann (De Gruyter, 2018), pp. 865–6.
  6. *Le Matin*, 25 August 1942, p. 2.
  7. NARA, Microfilm T315 R2019.
  8. Jean Bellocq, 'Le retour des prisonniers dieppois (1942–1943)', *Annales de Normandie*, 29:2, pp. 236–8.
  9. BArch, ZSG 102/39.
 10. *Goebbels Diaries*, p. 397.
 11. ADAP, vol. E.8, p. 47.

Part IV: War Beyond the Beaches

Chapter 15: A Triumph for OB West
  1. 'Battle Report', AHQ report 10, p. 20.
  2. NARA, Microfilm T315 R2018.
  3. NARA, Microfilm T315 R2019.
  4. *Rückblick*, p. 31.
  5. BArch, RM 7/96.
  6. BArch, RM 7/1757.
  7. Michael Salewski, *Die deutsche Seekriegsleitung*, vol. 2 (Bernard & Graefe, 1975), p. 146.
  8. 'Intelligence Report on Landing at Dieppe', in Appendix A to CMHQ report 116, p. 1.
  9. BArch, RM 7/1757.
 10. *German Naval Staff War Diary*, vol. 36, p. 243.
 11. Appendix A to C. P. Stacey, CMHQ report 142, p. 6.

Chapter 16: 'Next Time He Will Do Things Differently': Dissecting Victory and Defeat
  1. 'Battle Report', AHQ report 10, pp. 16–17.
  2. BArch, RH 26-302/18.
  3. 'Combat Report', CMHQ report 116, p. 12.
  4. BArch, RH 26–302/16.
  5. 'Battle Report', AHQ report 10, p. 16.
  6. Stacey, *Official History*, p. 392.
  7. BArch, RH 24-81/79.
  8. 'Report on the British Attack', AHQ report 10, pp. 44–5.
  9. 'Intelligence Report', CMHQ report 116, p. 4.
 10. 'Combat Report', CMHQ report 116, p. 12.
 11. S. W. Roskill, *The War at Sea, 1939–1945 Volume 2: The Period of Balance* (HMSO, 1956), p. 241.
 12. 'Combat Report', CMHQ report 116, p. 11.
 13. BArch, RH 24-81/79.
 14. Stacey, *Official History*, p.342.
 15. *Hitler's Table Talk, 1941–44: His Private Conversations*, ed. by Hugh Trevor-Roper, trans. by Norman Cameron and R. H. Stevens (Enigma, 2000), p. 663.
 16. BArch, RL 20/167.

17. BArch, RM 7/1757.
18. BArch, RL 20/167.
19. 'Additions made by the LXXXIV Corps', in Appendix C to CMHQ report 116, p. 1.
20. BArch, RM 7/1757.
21. BArch, RL 20/167.
22. BArch, RM 7/96.
23. BArch, RL 20/167.
24. Air Fleet 3 report, pp. 9, 11.
25. 'Battle Report', AHQ report 10, p. 21.
26. BArch, RH 24-81/79.
27. Air Fleet 3 report, pp. 6–7.
28. *Tactical and Technical Trends Number 35*, ed. by Military Intelligence Service (War Department, 1943), p. 34.
29. D. Karajiev, 'Desantina pri Diepu', *Morski Sgovor*, 19:7, pp. 132–3. The author's thanks are due to Philip Petkov for his assistance in translating this article.
30. Theodore L. Gatchel, *At the Water's Edge: Defending against the Modern Amphibious Assault* (Naval Institute Press, 1996), p. 151.

Chapter 17: A War of Words, not Bullets and Bombs
1. BArch, ZSG 109/36.
2. MPT, Item 3.2002.7595, Parents to Schneiss.
3. *Goebbels Diaries*, pp. 387–8, 399.
4. *SD Public Opinion Reports*, p. 4192.
5. TNA, DEFE 2/329.
6. *SD Public Opinion Reports*, p. 4121.
7. EzG, Gustav Roos to Anton.
8. TNA, DEFE 2/324, Lt Kaltcis to Lt Wessel.
9. *Goebbels Diaries*, pp. 407–8.
10. Ernst Kris and Hans Speier, *German Radio Propaganda: Report on Home Broadcasts During the War* (Oxford University Press, 1944), p. 76.
11. BArch, RM 6/387.
12. BArch, ZSG 109/36.
13. *Hitler's Table Talk*, ed. by Trevor-Roper, p. 663.
14. *SD Public Opinion Reports*, p. 4121.
15. BArch, ZSG 102/52+53, Dietrich address.
16. *SD Public Opinion Reports*, p. 4135.
17. BArch, MSG 235/382, German air-dropped leaflet.
18. Biblioteka Jagiellońska, No. 399873 III, Item 21.
19. Hitler's Sportpalast speech, in *Hitler: Reden und Proklamationen 1932–1945*, vol. 4, ed. by Max Domarus (Pamminger & Partner, 1988), p. 1914.
20. Toni Winkelnkemper, *Der Großangriff auf Köln: Ein Beispiel* (Franz Eher, 1942), pp. 27–8.
21. EzG, Richter to Kreutzer.

Chapter 18: Dieppe Through a Strategic Lens
1. Hitler speech as quoted in Irving, *Hitler's War*, p. 510
2. NARA, Microfilm T315 R2020.

3. Martin Moll, *Führer–Erlasse 1939–1945* (F. Steiner, 1997), pp. 279–80.
4. Ike Skelton Combined Arms Research Library, N-14171, 'Enemy Capabilities for Chemical Warfare', p. 3.
5. Roskill, *The War at Sea*, p. 251.
6. Mountbatten's address in Earl Mountbatten, 'Operation Jubilee: The Place of the Dieppe Raid in History', *RUSI Journal*, 119:1, p. 30.
7. BArch, RL 20/167.
8. Völkischer Beobachter quoted in David Ian Hall, 'The German View of the Dieppe Raid August 1942', *Canadian Military History*, 21:4, p. 8.
9. Quoted in Stacey, *Official History*, p. 405.
10. BArch, RH 2/471b.
11. 'Combat Report', CMHQ report 116, p. 16.
12. BArch, RL 20/105.
13. BArch, RL 20/167.
14. BArch, RL 20/105.
15. *OKW War Diary*, pp. 1298–9.
16. Horst Boog, Gerhard Krebs and Detlef Vogel, *Germany and the Second World War, Volume VII: The Strategic Air in Europe and the War in the West and East Asia, 1943–1944/5*, trans. by Derry Cook-Radmore and others (Oxford University Press, 2006), p. 474.
17. 'O.B. West Basic Order No. 14', AHQ report 36, p. 1.
18. NARA, Microfilm T78 R317.
19. Moll, *Führer-Erlasse*, p. 282.

Chapter 19: The Enemy Within: Inter-Service Rivalry and the Response to Dieppe

1. 'Report on the British Attack', AHQ report 10, pp. 50–1.
2. BArch, RW 4/610.
3. Air Ministry, *Rise and Fall*, p. 413.
4. BArch, RW 4/610.
5. NARA, Microfilm T78 R317.
6. BArch, RW 4/609.
7. *OKW War Diary*, p. 1067.
8. OKW circular telegram, in *Führer Directives*, vol. 2, p. 55.
9. BArch, RM 7/43, Naval Staff War Diary Part A, vol. 40, p. 121.
10. Harvard Law School Library Nuremberg Trials Project, 'Record of a Fuehrer Conference', Item 3369, p. 5.
11. BArch, RM 7/43, Naval Staff War Diary Part A, vol. 40, p. 365.

Chapter 20: Dieppe in Review

1. *Rückblick*, p. iv.
2. BArch, PERS 6/595.
3. NARA, Microfilm T315 R2018.
4. *Deutschlands Generale und Admirale Teil IV, Band 5: Die Generale des Heeres 1921–1945*, ed. by Dermot Bradley, Karl Friedrich Hildebrand and Markus Brockmann (Biblio, 1999), pp. 17–18.
5. Karl W. Deutsch, *The Nerves of Government: Models of Political Communication and Control* (Free Press, 1963), p. 111.
6. NARA, Microfilm T315 R2018.

7. *Hitler and his Generals: Military Conferences 1942–1945*, ed. by Helmut Heiber and David M. Glantz, transl. by Roland Winter, Krista Smith and Mary Beth Friedrich (Greenhill, 2002), p. 314 and note 852.

8. Hitler's address, in *The Rommel Papers*, ed, by B. H. Liddell Hart, trans. by Paul Findlay (Collins, 1953), pp. 465–6.

9. *SD Public Opinion Reports*, p. 4122.

10. NARA, Microfilm T1022 R2364.

11. Williamson Murray, *Strategy for Defeat: The Luftwaffe, 1933–1945* (Air University Press, 1983), pp. 280, 283.

12. 'Combat Report', CMHQ report 116, p. 13.

13. Salmuth to Jodl, in Appendix A to A. G. Steiger, AHQ report 40, p. 1.

14. Führer Naval Conferences, 1944 volume, p. 76

15. Joel Hayward, 'Adolf Hitler and Joint Warfare', MSI working paper 2/2000, p. 41.

16. Keith Simpson, 'A Close Run Thing? D-Day, 6 June 1944: The German Perspective', *RUSI Journal*, 139:3, p. 63.

17. Russell Miller, *Nothing Less than Victory: The Oral History of D-Day* (Penguin, 1994), pp. 96–7.

Index